ESSAYS ON THE EVOLUTIONARY-SYNTHETIC THEORY OF LANGUAGE

ACADEMIC
STUDIES
PRESS

ALEXEY KOSHELEV

ESSAYS ON THE EVOLUTIONARY-SYNTHETIC THEORY OF LANGUAGE

On the Crisis in Theoretical Linguistics
Basic Meaning and the Language of Thought
The Unity of Lexical and Grammatical Polysemy

Translated by
Alexander Kravchenko
in collaboration with
Jillian Smith

Moscow & Boston
2019

Library of Congress Cataloging-in-Publication Data:

Names: Koshelev, A. D. (Alekseæi Dmitrievich), author. | Kravchenko, A. V.
(Aleksandr Vladimirovich), translator. | Smith, Jillian, translator.
Title: Essays on the evolutionary-synthetic theory of language / Alexey
Koshelev ; translated by Alexander Kravchenko with Jillian Smith.
Other titles: Ocherki çevolëiìuëtìsionno-sinteticheskoæi teorii ëiìazyka.
English
Description: Boston : Academic Studies Press, [2019] | Includes
bibliographical references and index. | Translated from Russian.
Identifiers: LCCN 2018057558 (print) | LCCN 2018058089 (ebook) | ISBN
9781644690031 (ebook) | ISBN 9781644690024 (hardcover)
Subjects: LCSH: Language and languages--Philosophy. | Language and
languages--Origin. | Cognitive grammar.
Classification: LCC P107 (ebook) | LCC P107 .K72613 2019 (print) | DDC
401--dc23
LC record available at https://lccn.loc.gov/2018057558

ISBN 978-1-64469-002-4 (hardback)
ISBN 978-1-64469-003-1 (electronic)

Typeset by LRC Publishing House
Russia, Moscow, Bolshaya Lubyanka, 13/16
http://www.lrc-press.ru/?lang=en

Published by Academic Studies Press in 2019
28 Montfern Avenue
Brighton, MA 02135, USA
press@academicstudiespress.com
www.academicstudiespress.com

Contents

Acknowledgements

This book represents the result of many years of research. Throughout that period I have benefited from the support, advice, recommendations, and critical feedback of a large number of people, from close friends and colleagues to anonymous readers. Unfortunately, in all of my researches I have not been able to find one like-minded associate who shared the fundamental principles of the theory of language presented here. Only recently, when in the final stages of writing this book, I at last found such a like-minded individual. I am very glad that this person proved to be so well-known and authoritative a linguist as Liudmila Zubkova. Her support, advice, and critical comments were extremely important to me, and it is to her that I give my first words of thanks.

I would also like to express my most sincere gratitude to my family, friends, and colleagues, who have helped me throughout the whole of this work through their discussions, comments on sections of the manuscript, and more. These are: Grigorii Bondarenko, Sergei Zhigalkin, Viacheslav Ivanov, Aleksei Kas'ian, Andrei Kibrik, Mikhail Kozlov, Sergei Krylov, Leonid Krysin, Iulia Mazurova, Igor' Mel'čuk, Nikolai Pertsov, Tat'iana Samarina, Tat'iana Skrebtsova, Georgii Starostin, Iakov Testelets and Ekaterina Iakovleva. I would also like to thank the many anonymous reviewers for their comments.

I am very grateful to the translators Alexander Kravchenko and Jillian Smith, who helped me to correct a number of inaccuracies, and to the editor Vera Stoliarova, for her tireless work on the text throughout its journey to the press.

Preface

1. The place of the evolutionary-synthetic theory of language among the ranks of linguistic theories

1.1. Why a new theory of language is needed. When reading the title of this book the reader may with reason have asked, why is yet another theory of language needed? Is it possible that the author is unsatisfied with the scores of theories that already exist? Does he intend to add yet another, thereby coming close to repeating the situation during the first third of the 19th century when, according to A. Meillet (see p. 4 below), there were as many versions of general linguistics as there were linguists?[1] (Here and throughout we point to the pages of this publication with more detailed facts and references.)

To answer these questions it is necessary to begin by outlining the current condition of theoretical linguistics. The analysis in chapter one will show that the distinctive characteristic of the current period of theoretical linguistics appears to be the existence in simultaneity of a great number of incompatible theories of language. While in the mid-1900s it was still possible to speak about the unity of the various linguistic theories then existing (R. Jakobson, p. 4), by the end of the 20th century such unity had already disappeared without a trace (p. 5). This is due to the fact that the common core of linguistic knowledge shared by differing schools of thought has dwindled to an absolute minimum.

The current situation is disastrous, not only for linguistics but also for interdisciplinary research. Representatives of other human sciences related to linguistics (psychology, biology, anthropology, etc.) make reference for the bases of their positions to different and at times contradictory theories of language, leading to growing confusion (pp. 17–18).

---

[1] "Chaque auteur procède à sa manière et il y a, semble-t-il, autant de linguistiques générales que de linguistes."

1.2. Causes of the current crisis and ways to overcome it. Regarding the original cause of this theoretical dead-end (pp. 22–26), it is necessary to point out two fundamental flaws inherent (separately or in combination) to modern linguistic theories. Firstly, the **synchronic** approach, which still predominates, ignores the processes of macro- and microevolution of language, its genealogy, and development. Secondly, when describing the mechanisms of language functions, these theories do not take into account the **complex** contribution of the related subsystems of thought, knowledge representations, memory, etc.

Overcoming these two flaws is the aim of the Evolutionary-Synthetic Theory of Language, a preliminary version of which is presented in this book.

1.3. General principles underlying the Evolutionary-Synthetic Theory of Language. The theory here set forth harkens back to antiquity, to Aristotle's conceptualization of the divide between reality, thought, and language, and the role of language as an instrument for describing the mental representations humans have of the world. According to this idea, language does not function in isolation but in close interaction with other subsystems. This principle is implemented within the framework of the synthetic component of this theory by means of a systematic merger of the basic concept of language with the knowledge and findings of certain other theories closely related to linguistics. These are theories of: (a) basic concepts (Rosch et al. 1976; Lakoff 1986 and 1987; Mervis and Rosch 1981; Mervis 1987, *inter alia*), (b) thought (Sechenov 1978), (c) motor control (Bernstein 1967: 223, 227–228), (d) visual perception and event recognition (Johansson 1973 and 1976; Bingham et al. 1995; Runeson 1977, *inter alia*), (e) neurobiological theory of memory (Tsien 2008). Selected results from research in other disciplines have also been drawn upon in the formation of the present theory.

The second principle—the study of language in macro- and microdiachrony—is implemented through a very broad use of general development theory (pp. 31–33). This theory is involved in the analysis of a wide range of language issues, from lexical representation and grammatical meaning to explanations of glottogony and the overall structure and evolution of language.

The evolutionary-synthetic theory of language is conceived as an alternative to the many incompatible theories now existing. Naturally, the question arises: is it possible to develop alternatives to these theories? Our answer is: yes, it is possible. But since such alternatives are also bound to be complex theories, there cannot be more than one or two of them. This situation, however, is characteristic of normally developing sciences.

2. Peer reviews of the evolutionary-synthetic theory

When a new theory emerges, the first peer reviews from specialists are of particular interest. In Zubkova's (2017, Moscow) monograph, *Language Theory in its Development*, chapter 15 contains an analytical review of the theory of language presented in the Russian edition of the A. D. Koshelev's (2017, Moscow) monograph, *Essays on the Evolutionary-Synthetic Theory of Language*.

I provide one excerpt below:

> The relationship between the world of external events and the inner world of man, between reality, thought, and language, occupies the central place in this theory of language. However, the fact is that the actual mechanisms connecting these two worlds remained undiscovered until the end of the 20th century.
>
> The elucidation of these mechanisms became possible through A. D. Koshelev's development of a cognitive theory of semantics which combines a referential approach to language with a concept-based approach.
>
> The inspiration for this approach, it appears, is the contrast distinguished in antiquity between two worlds: the "visible domain" (the perceptible world) on the one hand, and the "intelligible domain" (the world of ideas) on the other (Zubkova 2017: 534) [translation J. Smith].

In the preface, while analyzing the contribution of various linguistic concepts in the development of a general theory of language, Zubkova writes:

> A. D. Koshelev takes the next crucial step, toward a synthesis of cognitive and linguistic abilities in their interrelated development, toward a systematic unity of universal and specific, abstract and concrete in language. He begins with patterns in the cognition of objects, from the most basic and holistic representations of an object to the delineation of its distinct features and, further, to the synthesis of the accumulated knowledge of the various facets of an object into a cohesive system for its representation (Ibid.: 20) [translation J. Smith].

Another analysis of the present theory is given in chapter 9, section one, of Skrebtsova's (2018) monograph, *Cognitive Linguistics: classic theories and current approaches*.

3. About the book contents

This book is a translation of the first part of the Russian edition of *Essays on the Evolutionary-Synthetic Theory of Language* (Koshelev 2017) and includes chapters 1–4 and §§ 23–25 from chapter 5.

In chapter 1, it is argued that over the past 50 years theoretical linguistics has been in a state of crisis. It has remained a compendium of mutually contradicting theories on multiple levels: the level of general theories of language, the level of its main constituents (the lexicon, syntax, and the syntax-semantics interface that connects them), and the lower levels of specific linguistic problems (such as lexical polysemy, lexical-semantic combinability, grammatical meanings, etc.).

The Evolutionary-Synthetic Theory of Language aims to overcome this crisis. It implements an interdisciplinary approach in describing language (a) in its ontogenetic development, and (b) in its close interrelationship with other human subsystems: thought, memory, actions, etc.

The chapters that follow deal with the semantic component of the evolutionary-synthetic theory.

In chapter 2, a reference-based approach to the analysis of basic meanings of concrete nouns and action verbs (that is, object and motor basic-level concepts) is proposed. Two types of cognitive units (elements of the language of thought) for representation of these meanings are singled out—perceptual, accessible for sensory identification, and functional, reflecting human intentions—along with the relationship of interpretation that connects them. The mechanisms for lexical polysemy are also analyzed.

Chapter 3 brings to light the structural unity of artifacts and natural concepts (STUL 'CHAIR', TROPINKA 'FOOTPATH', DOROGA 'ROAD', OZERO 'LAKE', REKA 'RIVER', DEREVO 'TREE', etc.); object and motor concepts are defined in terms of the language of thought, and their representation in neurobiological memory codes is discussed.

In chapter 4, the mechanisms for grammatical polysemy are analyzed, and the structural unity of lexical and grammatical polysemy is brought to the fore.

Finally, in chapter 5, the notions of attributive and partitive concepts (that is, the systems of object properties and parts) are introduced; using concrete examples as illustrations, the hierarchic structure of basic meanings of concrete nouns is shown to arise as a result of their step-by-step development in ontogeny. It is shown that basic-level concepts belong to the first level, and attributive and partitive concepts, which develop from basic-level concepts, to the second level of the hierarchy.

All quotations from the Russian sources have been translated by Alexander Kravchenko unless otherwise indicated.

The transliteration system ISO 9 – 1995 has been employed throughout the book. The ALA-LC Romanization Tables have been used for transliterating personal names.

Chapter 1

On the contradictory nature of contemporary linguistic theories and how to change it for the better

§ 1. Introduction

Our attention will be focused on an analysis of the inherent contradictoriness of contemporary theoretical linguistics that harbors a number of mutually contradicting theories of language. More specifically, arguments will be given in support of the following claims:

1. Over the past 50 years theoretical linguistics has nearly failed to add anything new to the universally recognized facts about language as a global object of study. Throughout several decades it has remained a compendium of mutually contradicting doctrines on multiple levels: the level of general theories of language, the level of its main constituents (the lexicon, the syntax, and the syntax-lexicon interface that connects them), and the lower levels of specific linguistic problems (such as lexical polysemy, syntax-lexicon combinability, grammatical meanings, etc.).

2. This contradictoriness of contemporary linguistic theories is indicative of a deep crisis. However, it does not follow that *all* of contemporary linguistics is in a state of crisis. The main issue is that theoretical linguistics does not seem to build on direct intuitions of native speakers. As for the concrete research that takes linguistic intuitions into account, it has been growing in scope and in many different directions.

3. It is impossible to overcome this obvious crisis without working out a unified evolutionary-synthetic theory of language. This task, in turn, cannot be solved without (a) taking into account not only the synchronic, but also the diachronic regularities in linguistic functions, and (b) a comprehensive use of research data on the functional regularities of other subsystems in humans,

such as thought, knowledge representation, etc., that closely interact with the linguistic subsystem.

It should be noted that the parallel existence of mutually contradictory theories in contemporary linguistics has often been pointed out.[1] The phenomenon itself, however, receives different interpretations. According to some linguists, it is the consequence of linguistic theory sliding into a stagnation phase, the signs of which have recently become obvious (Beaugrande 1991: 2). Others attribute it to the very nature of the object of study (Bahner 1983), while some, following Kuhn (1962), consider this phenomenon as evidence that linguistics is at an early stage of its development ("pre-paradigmatic stage") and has not yet reached the level of maturity that could be expressed by a single dominant paradigm.

Finally, there is yet another point of view: that the apparent contradictoriness of many linguistic theories is not of a fundamental nature and can be overcome as these theories continue to develop and come to a point where they may be united. As an illustration of this quite common view, consider Fitch's (2010) *The Evolution of Language*. Fitch gives his view on the problem with the study of language at the very beginning of the book by reiterating an old Indian parable about the blind men and the elephant. Taking this parable, he draws an analogy between linguists and the blind men, who, by feeling the elephant with their hands, try to give a full description of it:

> The palm of one fell on the trunk. "This creature is like a water-spout," he said. The hand of another lighted on the elephant's ear. To him the beast was evidently like a fan. Another rubbed against its leg. "I found the elephant's shape is like a pillar," he said. [...] A core argument in this book is that each of the scholars has grasped some truth about language, but that none of these truths are complete in themselves. Language, I will argue, requires the convergence and integration of multiple mechanisms, each of them necessary but no one alone sufficient (Fitch 2010: 1, 3).

In what follows, an attempt will be made to show that the real situation in contemporary linguistics is better described by a different parable: the blind men are feeling not the same elephant which symbolizes language, but several different animals—an elephant, giraffe, rhinoceros, etc.—which symbolize different models of language. One touches the trunk of an elephant, another the neck of a giraffe, a third the horn of a rhino, and they all believe that

---

[1] Some recent examples in Russian are Zubkova (2015), Kasevich (2009), Koshelev (2013a and 2015b); Kravchenko (2015).

this is one and the same animal. Clearly, hopes for integrating the resultant descriptions into a single picture in such a case are vanishingly small.

Chapter 1 focuses on an examination of some modern linguistic frameworks, both general (various linguistic theories in §2, 3) and specific (evolution of language, lexical semantics, etc. in §4). In §5 the futility of attempts to reach a consensus via polemics and interdisciplinary contacts is discussed; in §6 the status of linguistics—whether it is a natural science—is analyzed; in §7 the causes of the crisis in linguistics are discussed; in §8 the principles of an evolutionary-synthetic theory of language are formulated, and §9 offers a discussion of a similar crisis observed in other cognitive sciences, first of all in psychology. It is shown that, just like linguistics, these sciences are ridden with conceptual contradictoriness that impedes further development. Possible ways out of the theoretical dead-end are then discussed.

§2. A compendium of incompatible linguistic frameworks

If we take an overview of contemporary linguistic research as a whole, the emerging picture will be somewhat paradoxical. We will not find a single, universally recognized theory of language (linguistic framework, school of thought) or at least two competing theories. What we will find will be a large number of **mutually contradictory** theories developed by Noam Chomsky, Ray Jackendoff, Igor' Mel'čuk, George Lakoff, Talmy Givón, Anna Wierzbicka, Ronald Langacker, Charles Fillmore, and others. The reason for this is that a newly developed theory does not replace an already existing one by more adequately representing and explaining reality; rather, it begins to coexist with the theories developed earlier.

Of course, many schools of linguistic thought are of interest now only from a historical perspective. It is not often that we find references to the theories developed by Hermann Paul, Karl Bühler, Leonard Bloomfield, and other linguists of the past. However, the theories that go out of use do not lose their topicality because the newly arriving doctrines have somehow proven them to be erroneous or deficient in one way or another. They are simply forgotten, pushed out to the background by the more "modern" approaches.[2]

---

[2] Remarkably, not any of the new theories of language has become a successor to the three frameworks mentioned. That is to say, each new framework begins to describe language anew by creating its own linguistic paradigm. In the course of this process, some very important achievements of the older theories are often ignored. For example, some findings of Paul (1970) and Bloomfield (1973), neglected by modern schools of thought,

Meillet (1928) was perhaps one of the first to point out this feature of 20th century linguistics:

> Mais, tandis que la linguistique historique a des méthodes précises, éprouvées par un long usage, la linguistique générale est encore mal assurée dans sa démarche; elle tient toujours un peu de la philosophie: chaque auteur procède à sa manière et il y a, semble-t-il, autant de linguistiques générales que de linguistes. Pour que la linguistique générale progresse, il faut qu'elle devienne plus objective et qu'on en fixe la technique.
>
> Pour se bien entendre, on a besoin tout d'abord d'une terminologie où les termes aient pour tout le monde le même sens. Or, il apparaît du premier coup une difficulté fondamentale qui tient à la nature du fait linguistique[3] (p. 29).

As is well known, ninety years after it was expressed, the wish of this outstanding linguist has not yet come true. There is no less philosophy in general linguistics, and its methods have not become more objective. Having struck this note, we think it appropriate to recall what Jakobson (1971) thought about it:

> At first glance, linguistic theory of our time seems to offer a stunning variety of clashing doctrines. [...] Yet a careful, unprejudiced examination of all these restricted doctrines and vehement polemics reveals an essentially monolithic whole behind the striking divergences in terms, slogans, and technical contrivances. [...] In the same way that a general topology underlies and encompasses a wide range of mathematical approaches, the manifold approaches to language reflect merely the plurality of its *mutually complementary* aspects (p. 712; emphasis added.—*A. K.*).

In Jakobson's opinion, it is "the cardinal principles of a structuralist [...] approach to language, common to all directions in this research", that make

---

are in line with a centuries-long linguistic tradition that goes back to Antiquity, and, in our opinion, continue to be of undiminished importance.

[3] "While historical linguistics has exact methods, approved by long use, general linguistics is still quite badly supported by its methodology; linguistics is still inclined to philosophy, as each author chooses a research method of their own, and there are, so it seems, as many kinds of general linguistics as there are linguists. For general linguistics to progress it needs to become more objective and its technique needs to become more permanent.

First of all, in order to understand each other better, we need to have a terminology in which all the terms have the universal meaning for all of us. At first, however, there seems to be a fundamental difficulty lying in the nature of the linguistic fact" [translation Anna Kosheleva].

a variety of doctrines into a whole. Therefore, "[t]he inquiry into language structure is the undeniable aim of contemporary linguistics in all its varieties" (Jakobson 1971). Today, however, it is hard to imagine that anyone would defend this thesis. Already not quite undisputed at the time, it later lost its appeal completely.[4]

As for late 20th century theoretical linguistics, there isn't even any semblance of unity. As observed by Kibrik (1995: 99),

> [...] having disintegrated into a variety of competing theories, general linguistics does not represent a system that has... a universally recognized core as the "dry residue" of all that has been accumulated by the theory and is not subject to revision in the near future.

Kasevich (2013/2000) expresses a similar concern:

> [...] while in mathematics or physics different schools of thought usually show the relationship of *complementarity* (each particular school explores its specific problematics more intensely and thoroughly), in linguistics or psychology more typical are schools that are, in effect, in a relationship of opposition (they explore the same problematics, but use different initial assumptions and/or different methods) (p. 22; original emphasis).

Speaking of today, it must be acknowledged that the number of mutually opposing theories of language has only grown.

Following Meillet and Jakobson, many researchers believe that theoretical linguistics, just as any natural science (or a discipline close to natural science), will sooner or later develop a single **dominant** theory of language and, accordingly, a single research paradigm. Such hopes have been voiced both by Kibrik (1995: 100)—"the tendency to specialize will be replaced by the tendency to generalize"—and Kasevich (2013/2000: 27): "reaching a consensus on the foundations of our science is a task for the future, the future one would like to believe in".

However, many linguists do not share such sentiments. For example, Serio (1993) believes that different linguistic paradigms neither replace nor refute one another; rather, one is superimposed on another, and they coexist, ignoring each other at the same time. According to Dem'iankov (2009: 31–32),

---

[4] See also Kubriakova (1995) for an overview of research on this topic, where she undertakes "to give a well-reasoned argument in support of the view that the situation in linguistics today is not only marked by a diversity of opinions... frameworks, hypotheses and theories, but also by some intrinsic unity" (p. 144).

> [...] linguistics is one of those disciplines in which a new theory or new ideas, when they appear, do not cause a collapse or radical revision of the facts established earlier... The humanities are destined to be multitheoretical [...] This means ... that theoretical linguistics cannot avoid being multiparadigmatic.

Being on Meillet's side, we believe that the multitude of coexisting and mutually contradicting linguistic theories is a temporary phenomenon which is at odds with the ontological essence of language; it is indicative of the "growing pains" of our knowledge about language and the cognitive environment in which it functions. Here a disclaimer must be made. We don't believe that language is a module, i.e., a specialized subsystem that generates phrases based exclusively on its internal qualities. To the contrary, it functions in intimate interaction with other human subsystems, first of all, with thought and knowledge representation. Therefore, in undertaking to work out a unified linguistic theory, independent qualities and functional mechanisms of such subsystems must be taken into account very seriously. This will give linguistic theory the much-needed "objectivity" and independence from the specific views of one theoretical linguist or another.

Our main goal is to explore the scale and the specifics of theoretical contradictoriness in mid-20th to early 21st century linguistics and the consequences of such contradictoriness for our understanding of language. The topical urgency of conceptual contradictions varied over different periods in the history of linguistics; in late 19th century practically all linguistic frameworks revealed a relationship of complementarity (Meillet 1928). With certain reservations the same could be said about the middle of the 20th century, when "exploration of linguistic structure" was a common feature of a variety of approaches to language; this variety reflected "merely the plurality of its *mutually complementary* aspects" (Jakobson 1971: 712; emphasis added.—*A. K.*).

As will be shown, in the last decades of the 20th century the situation became quite different. The unrestrained generation of new conceptions of language has become a distinctive feature of modern linguistics. Remarkably, the new conceptions do not begin to compete with the already established frameworks, as is the case in natural sciences; rather, they begin to coexist as if each of them described a certain aspect of language from its own perspective and not language as a whole. This has dire consequences. Firstly, the number of universally recognized "principles" of linguistic description goes down to zero and, secondly, instead of a single system of facts about language, a variety of encapsulated local systems of such facts is formed which are accumulated in mutually opposed linguistic paradigms, not unlike honeycombs in a beehive. However, the scope and scale of this process seem to escape the attention of theoretical linguists; from the point of view of an individual researcher, the current state of affairs doesn't seem so disheartening. Every researcher sees only "his own piece" of the general picture,[5] and, against the background of impressive achievements of particular linguistic research projects, any "local" contradictions are not seen as symptomatic at all.

The focus of our discussion is theoretical linguistics. An attempt will be made to show that, in theoretical linguistics, one cannot see any signs of attempts to elaborate and generalize a single established theory of language, unlike, for example, in physics, where Einstein's Special Theory of Relativity encompassed Newton's classical mechanics as a particular case of large masses moving at low speeds. Nor has an old theory been replaced by a new theory of a greater explanatory power, as, for example, in the case of Lamarck's and Darwin's theories in evolutionary biology, Ptolemy's and Copernicus' theories in astronomy, or the theory of phlogiston and Lavoisier's oxygen theory of combustion in chemistry. Finally, there is no sharp competition between adverse theories (on account of their proponents' belief that there may be only one true theory), as, for example, in modern physics with its several coexisting alternative conceptions of the general field theory. Instead, we witness an unconstrained growth of many mutually opposed theories of language—or one of its constituent parts (syntax, lexical semantics, etc.). All that being said, one can conclude that, as modern linguistics continues to develop, our scientific knowledge about language becomes both broader and ever more diverse and at the same time less and less profound and indisputable.

§ 3. Contrastive analysis of some mutually contradicting linguistic theories

1. Introduction

It would be natural to begin arguments in support of the abovegiven view by analyzing Saussure's theory as the "starting point of a new era in linguistics"

---

[5] Even this, however, is not always the case. A linguist belonging to a particular school of thought tends to view other theories as false rather than alternative (Kasevich 2009: 39–40). Moreover, the mutual opposition of different schools is not always obvious. Therefore, any new theory that is not thematically close to a particular linguist is seen by such a linguist as a theory which extends, and adds to, the common stock of linguistic facts. True, there is also an opposite tendency to make ungrounded conclusions about the incompatibility of different viewpoints—see, for example, an instructive analysis of the opposing propositions of generativism and functionalism given by Newmeyer (1999).

(Jakobson 1971: 717). We will also use this theory as base point in our analyses of the subsequent linguistic theories developed by Noam Chomsky, Ray Jackendoff, Igor' Mel'čuk, Anna Wierzbicka and George Lakoff. It should be noted from the outset that mutual contradictoriness between such broad areas of linguistic research as generativism and functionalism (along with cognitivism, which is close to functionalism) is well known and does not require any special comments (in spite of the fact that some features converge in certain approaches; see, for example, an overview in Mustaioki (2010: 107–108)). However, it will be shown that mutual opposition is also inherent in some closely related theories, for example in Chomsky's and Jackendoff's theories (generativism), Mel'čuk's and Wierzbicka's theories (semantic atomism, i.e. reduction of linguistic meaning to a set of semantic primes), etc. As will become clear, none of the above-mentioned theories is in a relationship of mutual *complementarity* to the other theories, as they are all based on different, often incompatible, initial assumptions. And this is despite the fact that Chomsky's and Jackendoff's theories represent generative linguistics while Mel'čuk's theory does not, though it is quite close in spirit and structure to the theories of Chomsky and Jackendoff. At the same time, Mel'čuk's theory and the version of it developed by the Moscow School of Semantics (Apresian 2009) use methods of semantic description of the lexicon that closely tie them to Wierzbicka's theory, while a cognitive approach to semantics brings the latter close to Lakoff's (1987) theory.

2. On the role of language in thought

The issue of the relationship between language and thought is of paramount importance to theoretical linguistics. Can the core functions of language be reduced to purely communicative tasks or do they include thought production as well? Is it in the nature of language to fully participate in the formation of thought expressed in a linguistic utterance (phrase) or does it serve only as a tool for the transfer of thought? The aforementioned theories answer this question differently. For Saussure, language is an instrument of thought and there may be no thought outside of language. For Chomsky, language is a tool for the formation of the general structure of an utterance while the meaningful content of the utterance itself belongs to the mechanisms of thought that are outside of language. And for Jackendoff and Mel'čuk, language is exclusively a means of communication seen as a translation of thought into linguistic form. However, between the latter two theories there is also a substantial difference.

Let us dwell on this issue in a little more detail. According to Saussure (1966) language is the main instrument of thought, which is totally and completely shaped by language as there is no thought without language. Indeed, Saussure's theory builds on a hypothesis of the primacy of the speaker's native tongue over the realm of concepts—units of thought—which is secondary to, and derivative from, language. To Saussure, thought abstracted from its expression in words is something amorphous and undifferentiated. Without the help of linguistic signs we would not be able to strictly distinguish one concept from another. Language, according to Saussure, is special in that it serves as a connecting link between thought and sound. Thanks to language, thought, which is chaotic by nature, is broken into parts and made more precise.

Thus, the primary categorization of the world into objects, events, and relations is determined neither genetically nor cognitively. It is the result of language acquisition, a projection of the native speaker's system of concepts on the initially perceived amorphous world. As Whorf put it, it is "a kaleidoscopic flux of impressions which has to be organized... largely by the linguistic systems in our minds" (Whorf 1940/2010: 6). Clearly, such an interpretation of the function of language dramatically diminishes the role of non-linguistic thought (as an independent process), because both the concepts that constitute thought and conceptual structures are reduced to linguistic meanings and the syntactic structures of language. This model simply has no room for cognitive concepts that are outside of language.

Let us now consider Chomsky's approach. According to his Theory of Principles and Parameters, language ("internal language", also referred to as "I-language", or grammar) is a "computational system of the mind/brain that generates an infinite array of hierarchically structured expressions" composed of abstract words of a specialized vocabulary, or "conceptual/lexical 'atoms'" (Chomsky 2010: 45, 52). Abstract "words" are "bundles" of properties of three types: phonological, syntactic, and semantic. Syntactic expressions made up of these bundles are used for "thought, understanding and organizing activity" (Ibid.: 46) through a system of "semantic-pragmatic" interface. This system converts each syntactic expression into Logical Form, a more semanticized expression of the same type in which the syntactic relations between the constituents fit the semantic relations more closely and which is suitable for semantic-pragmatic interpretations by the human systems of thought.[6] Simultaneously, at the sensorimotor interface, this expression is converted

---

[6] According to Chomsky (2010), generation of syntactic expressions is determined by intralinguistic causes and is not aimed at performing any functions. How such expressions are used is not an issue for linguistic theory; it belongs to the realm of linguistic performance.

into Phonological Form and bound to the acoustic and articulatory mechanisms. However, the interface systems that bind the generated expressions to these mechanisms are not linguistic. Therefore, according to Chomsky, language is "an internal system that links sound and meaning in a particular way, by means of generated expressions" (Chomsky 2010: 46).

Clearly, in such an approach to language its role in the system of thought, though not as all-encompassing as Saussure would have it, is still very important, as the combinatorial forms of thought (conceptual structures) are determined by abstract syntactic expressions.[7] As for the role of non-linguistic thought, it consists in making these abstract forms concrete by filling them with concrete meanings. In other words, while for Saussure thought is, on the whole, determined by language, for Chomsky it is a partial relationship: language is autonomous and is used as an instrument of thought only in combination with strictly cognitive mechanisms.

Staying within the generativist framework, Jackendoff (2010: 67) defines language similarly to Chomsky, as a system generating expressions based on the very same abstract "words" (see above). An expression formed by this system, however, comprises three levels instead of one. It is a "parallel architecture" comprising three structures: phonological, syntactic, and "semantic/conceptual", each formed by its own generative module, with the connection between them "established by the interfaces" (Jackendoff 2007: 49). As Jackendoff emphasizes, the semantic/conceptual component, being independent from the syntactic component, belongs to both language and thought. It follows that a thought (an "algebraic encoding", a "conceptual structure") is wholly and completely formed by the cognitive systems, while language fulfills only a communicative function, embodying this (already prepared) thought in a linguistic utterance: "According to the mentalist stance, the basic function of language is to convert thoughts into communicable form" (Ibid.: 69). Thus, language is assigned a purely communicative, "conversion" function: first, the cognitive system forms a non-verbal conceptual thought and only then does language come in to build a three-level (phonological, syntactic, and semantic) phrase that expresses this thought.

It should be noted that Chomsky specifically warns against a communicative interpretation of the function of language: "it is wrong to think of human use of language as characteristically informative, in fact or in intention"

---

[7] As claimed by Hauser, Chomsky and Fitch (2002: 1573), "the computational mechanism of recursion […] is uniquely human", while the recursive syntactic structure expressing the corresponding structure of the thought is characteristic of human language.

(Chomsky 1968/2006: 61). Later, this thought was reiterated in Chomsky 1980: 230.

Disagreeing with Chomsky, Jackendoff (2007) argues:

> Chomsky sets himself apart from common sense here in his oft-repeated claim that language is not "for" communication [...] For reasons unclear to me, he has always seemed to believe that language came into existence primarily as an aid to thought [...] In at least one recent work (Chomsky 2002) and in a discussion at a conference in Spring 2002, he has justified this stance on the grounds that most use of language is for inner speech. Surprisingly, then, he has fallen into the trap [...] of believing that inner speech *is* thought, rather than (as I will argue) the phonological structure corresponding to the thought (Jackendoff 2007: 70, footnote 13; original emphasis).

Jackendoff (2010: 68) sets his theory in opposition to Chomsky's again when he discusses language evolution. This issue will be briefly touched upon in § 4, section 3.

In the theoretical framework developed by Mel'čuk (2012a), language is described by the "Meaning-Text functional model". This model is based on the assumption that "language is a finite system of rules" for mapping a set of **linguistic meanings** on a set of **utterances in a given language**. In other words, language is described as the correspondence "{linguistic meanings} ↔ {utterances in a language}". This correspondence shows, on the one hand, which phrases express a given linguistic meaning (ideally, the model should be able to yield all synonymic utterances that express a given meaning), and, on the other, which linguistic meaning (or meanings, should there be more than one) is expressed by a given utterance. The Meaning ↔ Text Model is precisely the tool for describing language as such a correspondence (Ibid.: 21–22).

Mel'čuk's model differs from Chomsky's model in that it is not generative, but transformational (a "conversion" model). Chomsky's computational model does not use any informational input for the production of expressions. By contrast, the Meaning ↔ Text Model converts the linguistic meaning input from the Concept—Linguistic Meaning interface into a phrase (or a set of all synonymic phrases) that embodies this meaning. While structurally similar to Jackendoff's model, Mel'čuk's model includes a level to account for the specifics of a given language. While Jackendoff's model—through its semantic/conceptual component—is directly connected to the conceptual level, the Meaning ↔ Text Model is strictly separated from this level, as well as from the Concept—Linguistic Meaning interface. Mel'čuk believes that the essence of language lies in the production of phrases that adequately express not universal meanings (non-verbal conceptual structures), but purely linguistic, or **language-specific**, meaning (Mel'čuk 2012a: 27, 29, 39). Therefore, at the beginning (in the preliminary stage of phrase formation) the interface converts non-verbal conceptual structure (thought) into linguistic meaning that reflects the specific features of a given language, and after that language comes into play, that is, the Meaning ↔ Text Model; it is this model that converts the resulting linguistic meaning into a phrase of a given language. Let us stress again that, unlike in Chomsky's and Jackendoff's models, the output of the Meaning ↔ Text Model is not an abstract linguistic expression but a concrete phrase (or a set of synonymic phrases) of a given language. Thus, Mel'čuk's model stands even farther from cognitive mechanisms than Jackendoff's model.

As can be seen, all three linguistic frameworks are in opposition to Saussure's conception and to one another in their understanding of the role of language in the system of thought. These models are based on different principles, work in substantially different ways, and have outputs that are typologically different linguistic "expressions". Chomsky's model produces abstract syntactic expressions devoid of concrete meanings. In Jackendoff's model, expressions are filled with concrete but at the same time universal meanings (conceptual structures). In Mel'čuk's model, abstract expressions are replaced by phrases in a given language along with their language-specific meanings.

Note that the abovementioned linguistic frameworks are, in turn, opposed by functional frameworks such as construction grammar, for example Fillmore et al. (1988), Goldberg (1995 and 2006). The basic element of construction grammar is a linguistic construction viewed as an integral unit whose formal and substantive properties are not reduced to the properties of its constituents (e.g. conditional, comparative, adversative, and other types of constructions).

3. Is language an autonomous module ("cognitive organ")?

This question divides linguistic theories into two opposing camps. It is answered in the positive by the generative theories, as well as by Mel'čuk's theory. It receives a negative answer from the functional theories (Givón, A. Kibrik, Fillmore, Goldberg, and many others), which are based on an assumption that the fundamental properties of language are determined by its functions (mental, communicative, etc.), and from the cognitive theories based on an assumption that language uses conceptual knowledge shared by the system of thought and other cognitive systems, i.e. basic concepts, universal conceptual primes, etc.

Lakoff (1987), contrasting his cognitive approach with the linguistic theories that treat language as a "modular" system, wrote:

> One of the principal claims of this book is that language makes use of our general cognitive apparatus [i.e. that which performs non-linguistic functions as well.—*A. K.*]. [...] In fact, the most widely accepted views of language within both linguistics and the philosophy of language are based on the opposite assumption: that language is a separate "modular" system *independent* of the rest of cognition. The independence of grammar from the rest of cognition is perhaps the most fundamental assumption on which Noam Chomsky's theory of language rests (Lakoff 1987; original emphasis).

As a matter of fact, opponents of the modular view of language (in which language is viewed as a mental organ) are many and include representatives from various fields of research (cf. Bates 1994). Some other oppositions between the "basic assumptions" of cognitive linguistics (the frameworks developed by George Lakoff, Ronald Langacker, and Ray Jackendoff) and traditional reificatory semantics are discussed by Chenki (1996).

4. Other opposing assumptions in the theories under discussion

There are substantial contradictions between these theories regarding other important issues. Mel'čuk's Meaning ↔ Text Model, while subscribing to the idea of language modularity as part of Chomsky's generative model, radically differs from the latter on some fundamental solutions. In describing the syntax of a phrase, Chomsky makes use of the constituent structure while Mel'čuk uses the dependency structure; according to Mel'čuk, this is a decisive difference (cf. Mel'čuk 2012a: 128; 2012b). It should be noted, however, that this contradiction loses its edge in later versions of generative theory that make use of the concept of government. Moreover, in contrast with Chomsky's syntax-centered model, the central place in the Meaning ↔ Text Model is given to the lexicon, and the semantic description of concrete lexemes plays a very important role.

Wierzbicka's (1996) semantic theory (interpretation of linguistic meanings with the help of a "semantic metalanguage": a list of semantic primes and a set of simple syntactic constructions) is fairly close to Mel'čuk's approach to semantic definitions. Although in the course of its development Wierzbicka's theory was closely related to an earlier version of the theory developed by

Mel'čuk and his colleagues, it nevertheless does not succeed or complement the latter. Thus, while the semantic metalanguage used by Mel'čuk to define linguistic meanings is language-specific, i.e. different for every natural language, Wierzbicka's "Natural Semantic Metalanguage" (NSM) is, by contrast, universal. According to Wierzbicka, NSM semantic primes are "embodiments" (lexicalizations) of fundamental human concepts in every language, elementary innate ideas all people have regardless of their ethnic or cultural identity, while NSM syntactic structures are templates for natural combinations of such concepts (Wierzbicka 1999: 16–17, 25). Therefore, definitions of linguistic meanings in the NSM are universal expressions, not language-specific expressions as in Mel'čuk's approach. This difference, along with some other differences (for example, Wierzbicka uses her NSM to define the semantics of parts of speech while Mel'čuk does not believe that parts of speech have any semantics), makes these linguistic frameworks incompatible.

A fundamental opposition is also found between the semantic theories of Mel'čuk and Wierzbicka, on the one hand, and the semantic theory of Lakoff, on the other. Firstly, Lakoff rejects an "atomistic" approach to the definition of lexical meanings:

> Thought has *gestalt properties* and is thus not atomistic; concepts have an overall structure that goes beyond merely putting together conceptual "building blocks" by general rules (Lakoff 1987: xiv; original emphasis).

In his opinion, what this means is that there may be no "natural semantic metalanguage" (NSM).

Secondly, following Rosch et al. (1976) and other cognitive psychologists, Lakoff holds that the real world categories set by notional words such as *bird*, *bachelor*, *mother*, *game*, *healthy*, etc. are prototypical by nature as they are underlaid with "embodied" basic concepts (Gallese and Lakoff 2005: 456); therefore, both these categories and the linguistic meanings that define them are inherently fuzzy (Lakoff 1987: Chap. 2). Counter to this proposition, Wierzbicka (1996: 149, 154–155) offers a semantic analysis of the abovementioned words to show that interpretations, according to which the lexical meanings of such words define **prototypical** classes of referents, are erroneous and may be easily replaced by strict definitions.

As a concluding remark, note that our exposition of the opposing views, given above, is by no means complete. From the list of known contradictions only the most fundamental have been mentioned. And, of course, the list itself is certainly incomplete; there are many more fundamental contradictions that separate contemporary linguistic theories.

§ 4. Contradictory descriptions of particular linguistic problems

1. The incompatibility of theories of lexical polysemy

There is a tradition in lexicography to divide all the meanings of a notional word into the "basic" (literal) meaning, which describes a "fragment of the world" (and is given first in the dictionaries), and its metaphoric, metonymic, and other correlates (in an elementary case)[8] engendered by the basic meaning by means of the semantic mechanisms of the same name. These are the "derived" meanings of the word. Such an approach allows for a clear explanation of the system of meanings of a polysemous word and the origins of these meanings (for more details, see Koshelev 2011a; 2012)

In the approach used by Apresian and the Moscow Semantic School (MSS), which Apresian leads, basic meaning is defined quite differently; not qualitatively (as concrete), but statistically (as the most "actual and developed in a given language"):

> In most Russian explanatory dictionaries, the word CEL' has, as its first meaning, "target that a person intends to hit using a weapon" [basic meaning.—*A. K.*], while the second meaning is "that which a person intends to achieve" [figurative meaning.—*A. K.*]. However, [...] in modern Russian the second meaning has an indisputable advantage over the first [it is more "topical".—*A. K.*], and it is this meaning that is given preference in the active dictionary (Apresian 2010b: 72).

The new approach thus radically changes the tradition in describing lexical polysemy. All meanings are viewed as uniform and genetically indistinguishable. Metaphoric and metonymic relationships are ignored because they go against the proposed classification of word meanings. It becomes obvious that the traditional approach and the MSS framework are **incompatible**. A better understanding of this framework comes from an analysis of Apresian's definitions given in chap. 2, § 1 and § 5 (section 4) it is shown that the approaches to lexical polysemy proposed by Apresian, Lakoff, and Evans are incompatible.

---

[8] This classification of lexical meanings can be traced back to Aristotle and was studied in the Middle Ages (Anselm of Canterbury, John Locke and others), by Shishkov (1803/2010) in his linguistic research, by the Young Grammarians (Paul 1970) and and Bloomfield (1973). Starting from the mid-1930s, a similar classification of word meanings was developed by Kuryłowicz (1935 and 1955) and Jakobson (1936), and in the 1950s, by Vinogradov (1977). Later, this lexicographic framework was used in the works published, among others, by Shmelëv (1977), Leshchëva (2014), and Kustova (2004). Our interpretation of this framework has been given in Koshelev (2011b, 2012 and 2015b) and, partly, in the analysis of some examples in chap. 2.

2. Contradictory descriptions of the syntax-lexicon interface

It is a well-known fact that different syntactic theories are often opposed to one another and we are not going to dwell on that. Of a much greater interest is the division of semantic-syntactic information between the lexicon and the grammar. And the picture here does not seem to be different, as a variety of incompatible theories continue to coexist.

As noted in a review of two volumes published in the series *Oxford Studies in Theoretical Linguistics* (Erteschik-Shir and Rapoport 2005; Alexiadou et al. 2004), the "division of responsibilities" between grammar and the lexicon is made by different researchers in quite different ways (Arkad'ev 2008). Commenting on the articles included in the first volume, Arkad'ev observes:

> [T]he authors do not seem to have a consensus on a number of very important issues; in particular, the syntactic procedures for describing the non-accusative forms given in various articles seem to be quite convincing in the framework of a given article, but on comparison across the various articles they appear to be hardly reconcilable, at least, if not mutually contradicting (Arkad'ev 2008: 124).

A similar conclusion is made about the other volume, which includes the "studies carried out within different theoretical frameworks which sometimes quite obviously contradict one another" (Ibid.: 132)

3. Theories of language origin and evolution

The huge gap between animal systems of communication and human language gives rise to wild fantasies. Speaking about the multifarious theories of language origin and evolution, Bickerton (2007: 524) stresses *"the striking lack of consensus and the incompatibility* of different approaches [...] in the field of language evolution" (emphasis added.—*A. K.*; see also Hewes 1977; Fitch 2010: 401–507). Here we will only touch upon the issue of gradual vs. abrupt language development.

Humboldt (1820) and Müller (1885) believed that the abovementioned gap could be overcome "instantaneously", in one leap. This conviction is also shared by Chomsky (2010), who argues that the recursive syntactic structure characteristic of human language could not have evolved in several steps; therefore, the theory of natural selection is not applicable to the process of formation of this "cognitive organ". As will be shown, others (e.g. Bickerton 2009 and 2010; Jackendoff 2010) believe that, on the contrary, such a gap could be overcome only in stages by means of protolanguage—a symbolic communicative system that spanned the gap between animal signaling systems and human language.

A pioneer in the study of the problem of protolanguage, Bickerton (1990 and 2009) argues that human language evolved in two stages. The first stage was marked by an emergence of asyntactic "lexical" protolanguage; its "words" were "put together like beads on a string, A + B + C" (Bickerton 2009: 187) without forming a syntactic structure, and later this protolanguage transformed into full human language in which words form a hierarchical, tree-like structure.

Jackendoff (2010), arguing for a three-level structure of language, suggests that one could imagine "various scenarios in which the language capacity evolves in stages, each adding an increment to the system's communicative efficiency and flexibility" (p. 71). Indeed, since all three levels of phrase structure (phonology, syntax, and semantics) are independent, it is quite possible to hypothesize that initially only two of them emerged: the phonological and the semantic/conceptual levels. Then the scenario suggested by Bickerton (2009) becomes plausible: at first, asyntactic protolanguage emerges which later acquires syntax and transforms into full human language. Moreover, because these initial levels might gradually become more complex, the resultant picture of language evolution does not contradict Darwin's theory.

As may be seen, the antagonism of theoretical linguistic frameworks leads to incompatibility of the theories of language evolution that stem from these frameworks: while for Chomsky it was an abrupt emergence, Bickerton posits a two-step development via asyntactic protolanguage, and Jackendoff argues for a gradual evolution of the initial protolanguage.

§5. The futility of attempts to reach a consensus

1. Unproductiveness of scholarly polemics

It must be admitted that the polemics often entered by the representatives of different schools of linguistic thought turn out to be unproductive. Often linguists do not seem to understand one another—and sometimes they are simply unwilling to understand, holding other theories to be false. However, this is only one of the reasons why linguists from different schools are unable to overcome the observed contradictions or at least help draw the different schools nearer. Another and more important reason is a lack of universally recognized criteria for establishing the validity of a linguistic thesis.

The futility of linguistic disputes may be illustrated by the well-known discussion of Evans and Levinson's (2009) target article in *Behavioral and Brain Sciences*, in which a focused attempt was made to show that practically all language universals posited by generative grammar, Greenberg's typological school, etc., are illusory (unverifiable or trivial). The discussion included over twenty commentaries by representatives of various schools and traditions as well as the authors' responses; however, it didn't seem to draw the opposing sides any nearer.

A similar example is provided by another famous discussion started by Hauser, Chomsky and Fitch (2002), which attracted a lot of attention (cf. Jackendoff and Pinker 2005; Pinker and Jackendoff 2005; Bickerton 2007, 2009 and 2010, *inter alia*) and was followed by another article by the same authors (Fitch et al. 2005). No common ground seems to have been found in this discussion, either. As far as one can judge, a similar outcome marked the discussion started at the time by Newmeyer (1999).

2. Inefficiency of interdisciplinary approaches

Some linguists have great hopes for an interdisciplinary approach. Alas, such hopes also remain unrealized because, as will be shown later, psychology and other disciplines are not free from contradictoriness between different theoretical frameworks.

It should be borne in mind, however, that researchers looking for solutions to particular problems may be unaware of the hidden dangers of interdisciplinarity. Thus, at a recent conference in Moscow (*Prospects for Cognitive Research: Interdisciplinarity and Integrationism*, 3 December, 2014, Moscow), the author witnessed the following exchange when a well-known cognitive linguist called for an interdisciplinary dialogue with psychologists. When he was asked, "How do you imagine a dialogue between linguistics and psychology in view of the fact that theoretical linguistics today is a compendium of ten mutually contradicting theories, while psychology—just in the same fashion—is not a unified science, but a multitude of independent 'psychologies'?", the answer was: "It's very simple. Developing my own approach to language, I turn to psychology and borrow from it what is needed." Obviously, this linguist sees contemporary psychology as a large (and continuously growing) stock of consistent facts that can be used as needed; this may result in borrowing some facts from one branch of psychology and then some facts from another branch which is in opposition to the first one.

§ 6. Is linguistics a natural science?

Can one hope that in its future development theoretical linguistics will meet the expectations of Meillet and other linguists and become a unified theory, or does the nature of language as an object of study leave no room for such hopes? Or, in other words, is the current situation caused by the very nature of language or is it rooted in the specific knowledge about language that we possess at this stage? This question is closely connected with another question: is linguistics a natural science? If the answer is "yes", then a unified theory of language will be worked out sooner or later. If the answer is "no", the status of linguistics remains an open issue, because to ascribe it exclusively to the humanities would be, in our view, an erroneous decision.

The idea that linguistics could be justifiably recognized as a natural science or, at least, an exact science has been expressed long ago: "In the final analysis, at the turn of the centuries modern linguistics was able to proudly show a number of achievements that confirmed its right to be called a natural science" (Shor 1926: 33). As has been previously mentioned, linguists have not always been inclined to treat linguistics as a natural science, which prompted the following remark from Baudouin de Courtenay (Boduen de Kurtene 1963: 76, footnote 48): "Perhaps, in a short time I will have an opportunity to examine [...] the prejudice of scholars that the science of language is a natural science (in the sense of botany and zoology), that it is completely different from philology..." However, the focus of our attention will not be on the arguments given by the proponents of the view that linguistics is a natural science. It will be on the arguments that bear on (a) the nature of our object of study (just as in the case of objects of other sciences, language is a physical object), and (b) the method of research (it is the methodology of physical sciences that is used in the study of language).

Among the arguments of the first kind, the most convincing seem to be those given by Müller (1885) in his *Lectures on the Science of Language*, delivered at the Royal Institution of Great Britain in 1861 (10 years prior to de Courtenay's article). The first lecture was entitled "The Science of Language One of the Physical Science". First of all, one should note Müller's definition of the dichotomy "natural sciences" vs. "mental sciences" and "historical sciences". As he put it, the object of study of a natural science is a natural object, or "the works of God" (the physical world for physics, nature for biology, etc.), while the "historical" sciences (or, in modern terminology, the humanities) deal with "the works of man" (Ibid.: 22). Secondly, his arguments for viewing human language as a natural object seem quite convincing: according to Müller, linguistic change is of a purely endogenous nature and neither an individual nor a collective can change it, arbitrarily or by convention:

> Although there is a continuous change in language, it is not in the power of man either to produce or to prevent it. [...] [But if that] change takes place, it will not be by the *will of any individual*, nor by the *mutual agreement* of any large number of men [...] the first impulse to a new formation in language, though given by an individual, is mostly, if not always, given without premeditation, nay, unconsciously. [...] and the results apparently produced by him depend on laws beyond his control... (Müller 1885: 38–41; original emphasis).

It is significant that Müller's idea about the unpremeditated and unconscious character of linguistic change is shared by various linguistic schools (Saussure 1966; Paul 1970, etc.), while his dichotomy of natural sciences vs. the humanities has been accepted by many linguists. Cf.:

> Researchers in the humanities are interested not in what is natural, physical in humans, but in the artificial; [...] how to consider [...] language: is it a phenomenon of the natural or artificial order? [...] in linguistics the borderline between the natural-scientific and humanistic knowledge coincides, to some extent, with the borderline between language and speech (Shapir 2005: 45).

> Language is a natural phenomenon. Can you create language? (Plungian 2009: 5).

Arguments of the second kind—the use of natural-scientific methodology—were analyzed by Chomsky (1995), who came to the following conclusion: any science that successfully uses a natural-scientific methodology is a natural science and there is no other criterion to distinguish the natural from the non-natural.

A similar view of linguistics as a science has been expressed by Kasevich (2013/2000) in his examination of the stance taken by Lazard (1999). Elaborating on the philosophical ideas of Granger (Granger 1960 and 1979), Lazard claims that theoretical linguistics, abundant in various theories of language, in its current state belongs to the proto-sciences as it lacks a "categorical definition" of its object, explicit definitions of key concepts, elaborate formalizations, etc. Taking up this thought, Kasevich observes:

> Slightly editing and reformulating such claims, one could say that in a "true science" a researcher replaces his object of study with its formalized abstract analogue (model) with which he then continues to work, comparing

the results he gets with the results of observation and experimentation (Kasevich 2013/2000: 20).

However, Granger (1979) and Lazard (1999) believe that further development must make linguistics a "true" science with a unified research paradigm.

Two comments seem to be in order here.

1. Sharing the conviction that the use of natural-scientific methodology in the study of language is important, we would like to stress that what is crucial here is that the abstract model of language used in such a methodological framework be **adequate** to the object modeled. Take, for example, Chomsky's approach to such modeling: "*Under familiar and appropriate idealizations*, a person's language is a system of the mind/brain that generates an infinite array of hierarchically structured expressions" (Chomsky 2010: 45; emphasis added.—*A. K.*). The question is, should the linguistic community accept such an idealization? Or would it irreplaceably reduce the real object of study? Mel'čuk, who strictly separates purely linguistic meaning (which is formed by a separate model lying outside of language) from the Meaning ↔ Text Model (i.e. from the model of language which receives this meaning as input and works with it), emphasizes that "such an interpretation does not pretend [...] to correspond to the psychological reality" (Mel'čuk 1974/1999: 24). It is important here to understand to what extent such an interpretation "does not correspond" to reality, how strongly such modularity of the model distorts the object modeled.

At the same time, the abovementioned properties of language—resistance to arbitrary changes and regularity of linguistic behavior of its speakers—give serious reasons to believe in the possibility of an adequate model of language.

2. The level of formalization in modern linguistics is quite high. There are a great number of theories that use an abstract (or close to an abstract) model of language and natural-scientific methodology (the frameworks developed by Chomsky, Jackendoff, Mel'čuk, and others). Therefore, to treat modern linguistics as a proto-science would be at least questionable. Yet, despite the fact that formal models and natural-scientific methodology exist, new linguistic theories continue to appear. However, this circumstance does not seem to characterize linguistics as a proto-science either. As has already been mentioned, in modern physics there exist several alternative theories of field, including the gravitational, electromagnetic, and nuclear (weak and strong) fields. It would, therefore, be reasonable to assume that coexistence of mutually opposed theories is a sign of a particular stage in the development of knowledge (in regard to both science and proto-science) when a certain **novel aspect** of the object of study comes into focus.

The specificity of the situation in modern theoretical linguistics is defined not by the existence of various theories of language but by the fact that these theories are, essentially, subjective views of language. That is why they don't compete for the right to become a single true theory—and such a state of affairs may be acceptable neither to a representative of a natural science nor to linguists, such as Meillet, Jakobson, and many others.

§7. The crisis and its causes

1. Is "multiparadigmality" typical of linguistics?

As has been shown, modern theories of language, just as the theories of its components, tend to be one-sided and mutually contradictory. We have also seen that in some cases these theories reject, rather than develop further, traditional frameworks, taking their place as representatives of a "modern" and more adequate view of language. It should be noted, however, that this situation is not typical of linguistics as a whole; it marks only the recent stage of its evolution over the past 50 years or so.

Summing up all the arguments given above, it may be concluded that the crisis in theoretical linguistics, witnessed in the second half of the 20th century after the influence of structuralism had been weakened, has reached its culmination by the early 21st century: there is no sense in either continuing along the numerous paths of alternative directions or producing new alternatives. The time has come to start urgently looking for a way out of this "vicious circle".[9] Let us take a brief look at the current situation.

2. The status of linguistics as a science

When discussing the status of linguistics as a science, it should be borne in mind that the object of study—language—possesses three specific properties that distinguish it from the object of study of a natural science. To begin with, as an object of study it is not quite independent—unlike, say, the physical world as the object of study in physics, or the world of the living studied in biology. While in the study of a living organism we can, for some time, ab-

---

[9] This conclusion is remarkably consonant to R. Shor's (1926) assessment of the situation in theoretical linguistics of late 19th—early 20th century: "Thus, the magnificent development of language science in the second half of the 19th century, with its claims about its exclusively scientific character, stops in a theoretical dead-end" (p. 39). Of course, at that time it was a substantially different "theoretical dead-end".

stract the organism from its environment, we cannot do that even for a minute in the study of language. As has already been said, language is not an autonomous module. Therefore, in the study of language it would be an inexcusable simplification to ignore other aspects of human activity such as thought, mental representation of the world, actions, emotions, etc., because they perpetually and directly participate in the production of linguistic expressions. In this respect only cognitive science as a whole, which embraces the entire array of humanistic disciplines, could, perhaps, be considered a natural science. Man as the object of its study is, first of all, "the work of God" and not "the work of man" and, second of all, it is a separate biological species distinguished from other closely related animal species on a strict basis.

Another distinctive property that human language possesses is its complete dependence on a particular language acquired by infants, the input of speech infants hear from their caregivers. There is not, probably, another human property that is so strongly affected by the environment. For example, infants cannot learn to walk by themselves, yet this type of human locomotion depends very little on the social environment. Similarly, hardly anything will change in the communicative behavior (or other type of behavior) of a baby chimpanzee taken away from its mother and placed in another group of chimpanzees. However, an infant taken away from its native African village and brought up in a neighboring village living the same life-style but speaking a substantially different language will acquire this language and not the native language of its tribe.

Finally, the third distinctive feature of human language—or, rather, human languages as a variety of its particular versions—is the continuous and rapid change characteristic of any particular language. On the syntax–semantics and stylistic parameters the speech of children differs from the speech of their parents and even more so from their grandparents. Over greater time intervals changes in grammar may be observed. If we take biology, there is a great variety of animal species but the changes in species are slow and, therefore, the "diachronic" aspect is not of such importance in the study of their structure and function.

In view of what has been said above, it may be concluded that, as one of the most formalizable human sciences, linguistics occupies a special place within the opposition "natural sciences vs. the humanities". As a bio-social phenomenon, language is just one of a number of human abilities; the formation and function of linguistic ability are very closely connected with other conjoint abilities: perception, knowledge representation, memory, emotions, attention, thought, locomotion and interaction, social interaction, etc. This is to say that theoretical linguistics cannot develop in separation from other cognitive disciplines that study the aforementioned abilities.

> **Note.** The arguments given above, along with the cognitive analysis of lexical semantics in chap. 2 and 3, give grounds to considerably extend the narrow list of disciplines conventionally covered by the term "cognitive science". Originally, "cognitive science" (or "cognitivism") included psychology, anthropology, philosophy, neuroscience, linguistics, and artificial intelligence (cf. Gardner 1985). We believe the scope of cognitive science should be wider and include the entire range of human sciences, such as perception, knowledge representation, thought, sociology (especially those aspects that deal with language and reflexive thought), studies of attention, emotions, memory, biodynamics, etc.

3. The root of trouble

Naturally, one is tempted to ask, "Why did such an explosive growth of 'multiparadigm' linguistics occur precisely in the second half of the 20th century?" In answering this question we will lean on a well-known interpretation of how linguistics developed in the past century: "[…] after Saussure, in the focus of attention of linguistics was the question 'What is the structure of language?' […] while Chomsky shifted this focus to the question 'What is the function of language?'" (Alpatov 1999: 21). In other words, in the first half of the 20th century the focus was on the study of language structure (Jakobson 1971), while in the second half the focus was on language models. Clearly, the specific properties of language mentioned above (functional interaction with other human subsystems and continuous changes in the process of such interaction) hardly have any effect on the study of linguistic structures, particularly when synchronicity is the dominant approach; therefore, in spite of all their apparent diversity, linguistic theories of the first half of the 20th century preserved some intrinsic unity.

As soon as the focus of attention of theoretical linguistics shifted to the language function, the role of these specific properties increased dramatically. Still, in modern linguistic theories these properties continue to be underestimated. As before, the synchronic approach dominates the field. In contemporary functional models of language there is still no room for conjoint subsystems of thought, knowledge representation, etc. Moreover, the role of input in the formation of particular word-class meanings and grammatical meanings (the mechanisms of its influence and its extent, which is on a par with the universal laws of child cognitive development) has not been sufficiently studied. It is understandable that, under such circumstances, linguists allow themselves a much greater "creative" freedom in modeling language than in describing its structure.

In fact, any linguist can offer his own model[10] which reflects his own understanding of (a) the purpose of language, (b) its specific functions (generative/transformational etc. mechanism), (c) the types of produced expressions, (d) the interpretation technique, (e) the typology of structured data used by language (purely linguistic, general-cognitive, etc.) and so on. And this is what is actually happening.

Let us summarise the specific features of the five approaches to describing language mentioned above.

Chomsky's model generates (produces without the support of input) abstract syntactic expressions which don't have a direct purpose but are used by the non-linguistic cognitive mechanisms for thought and communication.

Jackendoff's model also generates abstract expressions, but these, firstly, contain additional phonological and semantic components and, secondly, have a direct purpose: to embody the speaker's thought (conceptual structure), i.e. to perform a communicative function.

Mel'čuk's model is not generative but transformational. It also performs a communicative function—but understood in a narrower sense—by mapping a given linguistic (and not universal, as in Jackendoff's model) meaning as the model input on a concrete phrase that expresses this meaning.

Lakoff has not developed a general linguistic model, although he postulated its essential properties: it must be non-modular, strictly separate from other cognitive structures of humans, its semantic constituent must be supported by complex cognitive structures (ideal cognitive models, image schemas, etc.), and so on.

---

[10] In particular, Mel'čuk wrote about this situation:

There is a fundamental difference between functional models in physics and other nature-based hard sciences, on the one hand, and functional models in linguistics, on the other: Physical sciences are buttressed by a fundamental physical theory of the universe, so that any model proposed by a physicist must "fit" into this theory; this drastically reduces the set of possible models and makes them more reliable. The science of language does not have anything similar: there is no fundamental theory of the human brain, or at least of mental behavior, that could be a solid framework for linguistic models. As a result, today's linguistic models are still far from the level of reliability achieved by physical models (Mel'čuk 2012a: 19).

Other approaches display their own requirements for a universal linguistic model. Thus, Wierzbicka's framework is based on the central concept of "natural semantic metalanguage" (a set of universal conceptual primes and simple conceptual structures); "construction grammar" proposes that simple whole linguistic constructions be used as the basic units, and so on.

§ 8. Principles of an evolutionary-synthetic theory of language

There seems to be only one way out of the current situation: to work out a new theory of language, not just another theory as an alternative to the already existing theories, but an all-encompassing evolutionary-synthetic theory. The goal of such a theory should be a **comprehensive** study of language that would, as far as possible, take into account **all the multiple aspects** of its properties, thus ensuring, by "probative force", a long-awaited consensus among theoretical linguists.[11]

Along with many other linguists we believe that sooner or later such a theory will be developed in linguistics (if not a single universally recognized theory, then at least a **dominating** theory, similar, for example, to Darwin's theory in evolutionary biology). In the spirit of the synchronic-diachronic approach, it must be a unity of two constitutive parts: synthetic and evolution-ary.[12] The synthetic constituent should account for both intra-systemic, purely linguistic properties of language and its functions in synchrony and inter-sys-temic requirements posed by other subsystems, such as thought, knowledge representation, emotions, memory, etc., which intimately interact with the subsystem of language. The evolutionary constituent should serve as a basis on which language evolution and its ontogeny are explained.

Let us stress again: an evolutionary-synthetic (or simply synthetic) theory cannot be purely linguistic. Along with the linguistic component, it will com-prise systemically conjoint cognitive, mental, social and other components. In fact, a new theory of language should develop within the framework of a new cognitive paradigm which could also be called synthetic as it will unite, in a

---

[11] Clearly, if such a theory is worked out, all contemporary linguistic theories—except, perhaps, one—will lose their relevance, becoming part of the history of linguistics (two or three mutually contradicting theories cannot serve as a basis for a single theory).

[12] Dobzhansky's (1964: 449) popular thesis "nothing makes sense in biology if it is not viewed in light of evolution" could be paraphrased, with regard to linguistics, as follows: a study of language and its constitutive parts—lexicon, syntax, and syntax-lexicon inter-face—makes sense only if it is evolutionary and ontogenetic.

systemic way, the paradigms of separate cognitive disciplines—linguistics, psychology, neurobiology, etc.

§ 9. Crisis in the cognitive sciences

1. Contradictory frameworks in cognitive sciences

To better understand the real magnitude of the problem, it should be kept in mind that linguistics, like a drop of water, reflects the critical situation in other cognitive disciplines as well. There is no sign of a unified paradigm that would direct research in linguistics, psychology, and other closely related disciplines along the same channel. Each particular discipline develops independently according to its specific perception of its object of study—one or another set of facts about humans and human activity. Undeclared *de jure* but established *de facto*, such "independence" of particular cognitive disciplines cannot but tell on their development in a most destructive manner. Just as linguistics, practically each of these disciplines features a great variety of mutually contradicting research paradigms (schools of thought, conceptual frameworks). While studying one and the same object, researchers working in different frameworks get different results that cannot be reconciled. At the same time, each school of thought insists that its theoretical framework is thoroughly grounded while the theoretical frameworks of competing schools are untenable.

Regrettably, such theoretical plurality does not bear any fruit; it shows that "progress" in this area of knowledge has reached a dead-end, turning into a "vicious circle" from which it cannot escape relying only on its own resources. Consider the following four examples, showing that theoretical contradictoriness characterizes cognitive research on all levels, from general theories to quite specific interpretations.

1.1. Theoretical contradictoriness in general psychology. Psychology, which is very closely connected with linguistics, has suffered the same fate: today it has been fragmented into a variety of independent "psychologies". Addressing this issue, Schultz and Schultz (2012: 17–18) quote some contemporary researchers:

> Noted historian Ludy Benjamin wrote, "A common lament among psychologists today... is that the field of psychology is far along a path of fragmentation or disintegration [with] a multitude of independent psychologies that soon will be or already are incapable of communicating with

one another" (Benjamin 2001: 735). Another contemporary psychologist described the field "not as a unified discipline but as a collection of psychological sciences" (Dewsbury 2009: 284).

A similar situation is found even within independent psychological disciplines, for example, in the theory of implicit learning (Ivanchei 2014) and the psychology of understanding.

1.2. Contradictory frameworks in psychology of attention. The same tendency—growing numbers of contradictory frameworks—may be observed in psychology of attention as well. Falikman (2010) observes:

> With the development of psychology of attention new problems keep arising, while the old problems don't disappear... While some psychologists have given up the idea of viewing attention as a selection mechanism in information processing... others continue their attempts to resolve the issue of the role of selection and get new interesting experimental data. While some authors have become convinced that visual attention is directed at holistic objects, others continue to look for and describe some simple features which allow to automatically single out an object among other objects and draw attention to it [...]. If some daring theoreticians do not come around and ...attempt to conceptualize the essence of attention as a holistic phenomenon, psychology of attention faces the danger of becoming a dismantled mosaic, a multitude of colored pieces of glass never to be put together as a complete picture (pp. 425–426).

1.3. Contradictory descriptions of honeybee communication. The contradictoriness we have been discussing goes deeper, to the level of study of very concrete problems. This is how Panov (2012) sums up the opposition in describing honeybee communication in ethology:

> So, there are three schools with three views on communication among honeybees. K. von Frisch represents classic ethology. To him, the essence of communication among honeybees lies in the mechanisms of paired interactions or interactions among a small number of individual bees which use an innate signaling code. N. G. Lopatina is an adept of the conditioned reflexes doctrine. In her interpretation, a bee-dance is conditioned reflex activity that requires learning and is ineffective without it. Communication takes place on a dialogical model. A. M. Wenner adopts a population ecology approach... Here, communication is a complex stochastically determined system of relationships that unite, at any given moment, a great

number of individual bees from a given population. Population density is an important parameter; its change affects both the type and the efficiency of communication.

What is of peculiar interest in the entire situation is that the hypotheses themselves are not at all speculative; from the point of view of their proponents, each theory is validated by numerous experiments, or, as we usually put it, is supported by rich empirical data. However, what is seen as an indisputable fact by a proponent of one theory is not a convincing fact to its opponents (p. 84).

Obviously, with numerous theoretical paradigms available it is more likely for a researcher to select only those experimental data which support his theory (the danger Karl Popper warned against). In such conditions, the often used and seemingly irrefutable argument "according to the data corroborated by numerous experiments" becomes a relative statement. In isolated synchronic cognitive research this argument cannot serve as a basis for theorizing. Thus, Gentner (2003), discussing some researchers' appeal to "an innate language of thought" with which humans are born, gives a witty comment on the reverential attitude to experiments common among psychologists: "Oh, go away—can't you see we're busy doing experiments?" (p. 225).

1.4. Discrepancies in the study of the biomechanics of human motions. The discrepancy of various approaches becomes especially obvious in the study of problems that are the focus of interdisciplinary cognitive science and which draw the attention of a whole array of disciplines (on the broad interpretation of the concept of cognitive science see § 7, section 2). Among such problems is the biomechanics of human motions, first of all walking and running. This problem has been topical in lexicography (definitions of motion verbs), cognitive linguistics (Talmy 1975 and 1985, *inter alia*), cognitive psychology (Gentner 2006; Pruden et al. 2008), recognition of biological motion (Johansson 1973 and 1976; Shipley 2003; Troje 2002), physiology (Bernshtein 1947/2008), mirror neurons theory (Rizzolatti and Fabbri-Destro 2008), human dynamics (Alexander 1992; Bingham and Wickelgren 2008), robotics (Raibert 1986; Collins et al. 2009; Manoonpong and Woergoetter 2009) and other disciplines. The overall picture here is rather peculiar. Firstly, research in different disciplines is uncoordinated and often quite contradictory. Secondly, the results of research in various disciplines are disconnected and cannot be joined together in any way. And thirdly, Bernstein's (Bernstein 1967 and 1947/2008) outstanding theory of human biological motion, which could become a common ground for research in various disciplines and help join together the results of such research, is practically forgotten and is hardly used at all.

To illustrate what has been said above, let us consider the issue of the perception of biological motion. According to one trend in research, perceived motion is identified by its shape (kinematics), i.e. by the directly observed visual characteristics of motion, such as, for example, loss of **contact between the feet and the surface** (running event) or no loss of contact (walking event). According to another trend, perceived motion is identified by its dynamics, i.e. by implicit (inaccessible to direct perception) force-dynamic characteristics manifested by the form: whether there is loss of surface **support for the feet** (running event) or no such loss (walking event).

Within the first trend, three alternative approaches have developed: recognition by holistic form, by separate features, and by combination of both (for a review, see: Blake and Shiffrar 2007; Troje 2008). The dynamics trend also displays several approaches (see reviews in Runeson and Frykholm 1983; Bingham and Wickelgren 2008). As for the mirror neurons theory (Rizzolatti and Fabbri-Destro 2008), developed at the very end of the 20th century, it explains the perception of biological motion quite differently. As already mentioned, none of these frameworks uses Bernstein's theory of biomechanical motion—although his research, also published in English (Bernstein 1967), used to be well-known in academic circles. Bernstein started to develop a systemic kinematic-dynamic study of biological motion in the 1920s; it was exhaustively presented in a recapitulating monograph (Bernshtein 1947/2008: 40–46, 144–147, 249–317). The monograph also contained a physiologically and neuro-biologically substantiated classification of various types (levels) of human actions.

However, there are some rare exceptions when Bernstein's theory is applied in actual research. Thus, Manoonpong and Woergoetter (2009) describe a walking robot, *Runbot*, that uses bipedal locomotion. It moves like a human, keeping a steady balance. In this robot the mechanism for the bipedal walk that was originally described by Bernstein in the 1930s, has been reproduced.

Characteristically, many contemporary doctrines are oblivious of the classic scientific theories of the past. Analyzing the contradictoriness permeating theories of animal behavior and communication that have become popular over the past 40 years, Panov (2013: 668) observes: "[…] the scientific framework, well-established in this area of research by the 1970s on the basis of a wide scope of empirical facts, was practically rejected later as unneeded". Summing up our review, let us stress again that conceptual frameworks in contemporary cognitive science are characterized by one-sidedness, contradictoriness, and "contemporaneity" (i.e. loss of continuity and ties with the classic theories of the past and an aspiration to create new theories rather than develop the already existing ones). As we have seen, the same is true of contemporary linguistic frameworks.

2. The cause of the crisis

As a matter of fact, that various approaches to the solution of a given problem should be contradictory and in opposition to one another is typical rather than extraordinary. Quite expectedly, this phenomenon has been under close scrutiny; it will suffice to mention the seminal work by Kuhn (1962). Kuhn's analysis left aside for the present purpose, it should be noted that the contradictoriness in cognitive disciplines has its own characteristic features caused by the specific features of their object of study. Namely, in contrast with natural sciences (physics, chemistry, etc.) and their independent objects of study, the object of study of a given cognitive discipline (psychology, linguistics, evolutionary biology, etc.) represents only one out of many aspects of all that is known about humans and their activities; therefore, it cannot be quite independent and strictly separate from the objects of study in other cognitive disciplines.

This genetic unity of cognitive disciplines is one of the reasons for the striking fact that they all experience an inter- and intradisciplinary crisis almost simultaneously. In explaining this phenomenon, we will lean on the general theory, or orthogenetic principle, of development (Werner 2004; Chuprikova 2007). According to this theory, development essentially consists in the transformation of a globality into a system of its components. The process is usually represented as consisting of two consecutive stages: differentiation and integration. Initially, a homogeneous globality grows and is differentiated into parts—separate "particular" globalities. These parts are then integrated into a system, the function of which corresponds to the function of the initial globality. This two-stage process may be called an elementary development cycle and represented in the form of the following schema:

Homogeneous globality
↓
Totality of independent parts (differentiation stage)
↓
System of independent parts (integration stage)

We will use a more detailed schema for the elementary cycle suggested by Koshelev (2011a). In this schema there is one more stage: an incompletely differentiated globality, where parts are already isolated within a globality but are not yet separate independent units (a state of structured globality). Now, the elementary development cycle may be represented by a more exact schema as shown in Figure 1.

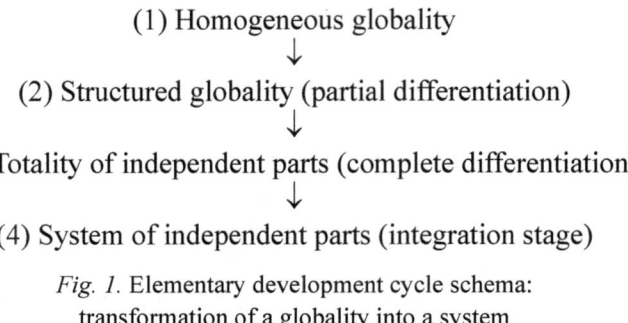

(1) Homogeneous globality
↓
(2) Structured globality (partial differentiation)
↓
(3) Totality of independent parts (complete differentiation)
↓
(4) System of independent parts (integration stage)

Fig. 1. Elementary development cycle schema:
transformation of a globality into a system

Following this schema, cognition as a process is a sequence of elementary cycles of the same kind: through accumulation and growth, global syncretic knowledge becomes a structured globality, which is then differentiated into independent components—more specialized kinds of knowledge. These already independent kinds of knowledge are further integrated into a system (level (4) in Fig. 1); then the same cycle involves the separate kinds of knowledge—components of the established system, and so on. In short, and as a first approximation, cognition as a process may be defined by these five words: accumulation and systemogenesis of knowledge.

Let us consider the development of initially global scientific knowledge about humans, the kind of knowledge that in the old times (before the 19th century) used to be accumulated by philosophy. Starting from antiquity, for over two millennia what are today independent sciences were developed within philosophy, becoming more and more isolated from one another (this is level (2) in Fig. 1—philosophy as a structured globality). Later, in the 19th century, these areas of knowledge began to branch off from philosophy, becoming independent scientific disciplines: first, it was linguistics (first quarter of the 19th century), then formal logic (mid-19th century), followed by psychology (last quarter of the 19th century). Each had its own object of study, goals, and research methods. Since then, over the next century and a half (up to present day) these sciences have existed as independent, practically unconnected areas of knowledge (level (3) in Fig. 1—a totality of independent parts of the old philosophy). Each science, in the course of its internal development, accumulated knowledge and differentiated into more specific, usually independent, disciplines; these fell into ever more specific themes of research, and so on.

However, at none of these stages was there any integration of structured parts that would make them into a system—a process that concludes every elementary cycle (level (4) in Fig. 1—a system of independent parts). As a result, what used to be a global area of scientific knowledge about humans disintegrated into a variety of more or less independent "isles" of knowledge. It makes sense today to speak of the utmost differentiation of the various spheres of knowledge about humans. It was precisely this differentiation that caused a general crisis in the cognitive sciences.[13] However, if this is the case, then, in accordance with the general law of development, integration of some of these differentiated cognitive "isles" should begin soon. Clearly, only "isles"of true knowledge should be integrated into systems (since there also exists a great amount of false knowledge). To energetically facilitate such systemogenesis of knowledge must be a priority to cognitive scientists. The key issue, therefore, is finding a **way to glean the grains of true knowledge** from a huge mass of disparate "isles" of knowledge and integrate them into systems.

3. Towards a unified cognitive paradigm

The arguments given above, supported by a more detailed analysis of the state of affairs in cognitive science given by Koshelev (2013b), allow us to come to the following conclusion: the only way to overcome the growing crisis in contemporary cognitive science is to develop an integrated cognitive paradigm. None of the concrete cognitive disciplines can struggle out of the crisis on its own because their objects of study are closely connected. In this respect, only **cognitive science** that unites the main areas of human studies (see Note in § 7 section 2) may be considered a **natural science**, as the object of its study—man—is, firstly, an independent biological species strictly separate from other closely related animal species and, secondly, a natural physical object—a "work of God", not a "work of man", in Müller's words (see § 6). There are, therefore, reasons to believe that it is quite possible to develop an integrated cognitive paradigm.

---

[13] This apparently paradoxical situation has an explanation. As has been repeatedly stressed by Lewin (1952) and other researchers, development as a process is not permanently progressive and may contain points of local regress.

Such a paradigm may be seen as a diachronic-synchronic model of man that represents a sequence of ontogenetic stages (synchronic levels) from early childhood to adulthood, and phylogenetic processes (diachronic transitions) that support transformation from the previous to the next level. The model must include all the main directions of human development—language, thought, world view, emotions, memory, attention, actions, etc.—and account for the relationships between them.

Naturally, the question arises of how to build such a model. One possible way would be as follows. First, the core part of the model is built, representing three consecutive levels in child development—the ages of 12, 18, and 24 months—along the main lines of knowledge representation, thought, language, etc. Then, if this core model is accepted by the learned community as adequate, researchers in concrete cognitive disciplines begin to "grow" it "in height and breadth", "interweaving" it with new lines of development (coordinating them with the already existing lines) and completing the preceding and subsequent levels, at the same time coordinating them with the already existing levels. If, however, the proposed model is rejected, another alternative model, both diachronic-synchronic and synthetic, is taken instead, one that would **include a number of main stages and lines in child development**. The process itself would not be infinite, as **hardly more than two or three such synthetic core models can be built**.

The suggested path opens the possibility to use an interdisciplinary approach **correctly**: the core model, already built and accepted by the learned community, will constrain (content-wise and systemically) contributions made by individual researchers, preventing them from going on "a wild goose chase". Thus we get what we want: **a way to select and integrate the grains of true knowledge**.

Chapter 2

A reference-based approach to describing notional words

Chapter 2 offers an exposition of a reference-based approach to describing basic meanings of sensory lexical items, that is, nouns and verbs that denote "visible" referents (things and physical actions). The central goal of the reference-based approach is to give a rigorous definition of the basic meaning of a word and, accordingly, of the category of its direct referents.

§ 1. A reference-based approach to lexical semantics

1. The dual structure of lexical meaning

1.1. The problem with reference (designation). A native speaker uses words—with much ease and without giving it a second thought—to name various fragments of the world around him such as things, actions, states, qualities, situations, etc. And he does it, as a rule, in full accordance with other native speakers. For example, seeing coffee beginning to froth in a coffee pot, a native speaker of Russian will exclaim, *Kofe bežit!*, lit. 'The coffee is running!' ('The coffee is overflowing!'), and we will understand him clearly, experiencing no difficulty in understanding the referent of this utterance. In a similar fashion and to the same effect, the speaker may say, *Moloko bežit!* lit. 'The milk is running!' However, if it is water, rather than milk, beginning to boil and overflow, he will not say, **Voda bežit!* 'The water is running!' because, just like any other native speaker of Russian, he knows that you can't say that about water. This naturally begs the question, "Why?", as outwardly the referential situations in these cases are practically indistinguishable. One might argue that in the former case the liquid froths while in the latter it does

not. However, soup also froths when beginning to boil, yet an utterance such as
?*Sup bežit!* 'Soup is running!', though admissible, nevertheless sounds odd.

Explanatory dictionaries don't help here either, as may be seen from a definition offered in Aktivnyj Slovar' (2014, 1: 183):

bežat' **4.4** ['(be) run(ning)'], rare or obs. *Kofe bežit.* ['The coffee is running']
　　MEANING. *A1 bežit* 'Liquid substance, A1, is flowing over the edge of the vessel, A2, which contains it, because it is boiling' [usually about a currently observed process].

This definition does not impose any constraints on the utterance **Voda bežit* ('Water is flowing over the edge of the vessel because it is boiling').[1]

It is worth noting that neither explanatory dictionaries nor lexicographic research provide strict definitions of lexical meanings that would explain in which case an observed phenomenon may be designated by a given word, in which case such designation would appear less acceptable, and in which case it would be simply impossible. This is true not only for derivative meanings of the type **bežat' 4.4**, but also for the basic meanings of words—not just referentially versatile words like *igra* 'game', but even very simple words such as *stul* 'chair', *kreslo* 'armchair', *idti* 'go/walk', *bežat'* 'run', *staryj* 'old', and the like.

The traditional account of a word's basic meaning. Let us touch very briefly upon the main propositions of the traditional approach, exemplified by the seminal works of John Lyons and Dmitrii Shmelëv.

We will start with a quotation from Shmelëv (1977):

> In lexicology […] words are studied, first and foremost, as units of denotation, i.e., as linguistic units that serve the purpose of naming things and phenomena in the real world, the purpose of singling them out and forming respective notions (p. 3).
>
> **The meaning of a word is the reflection in it of one or another real world phenomenon** (a thing, a quality, a relation, an action, a process). […] The meaning of every notional word is based on a particular **notion** which contains some general essential features of a particular fragment of the real world, that is, features that make it possible to group single things and phenomena into definite classes […] It is a notion that lies at the basis of a word's lexical meaning (pp. 58; 60; original emphasis).

---

[1] A more accurate explanation, showing why utterances such as *Voda/sup bežit* 'The water/soup is running' are odd or incorrect, will be given in § 4, section 1.7.

Apparently, Šmelёv followed the traditional approach to a word's meaning defined by Lyons (1968: fig. 23 on p. 404), who used the following schema of a linguistic sign:

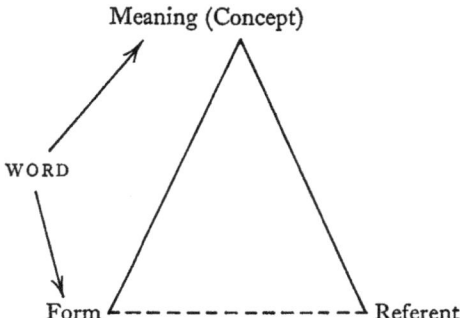

The broken line connecting the form and the referent shows that the relationship between them is not direct; the form relates to its referent by the mediating meaning associated with each of them independently.

The sign schema given above sets a **relationship of reference**: a word denotes a thing by means of meaning (notion). If we omit the dotted line (since there is no direct relationship between the form of a word and its referent), and substitute the class of all possible referents for a particular referent, we will obtain the following (linear) version of a word's semantic schema:

(1) *Word*—Meaning (notion)—Class of referents

where the dash stands for an associative relationship.

The meaning-notion shown in (1) is usually called the **basic meaning** of a word; it is the most concrete and obvious of all the word's meanings. It describes a class of similar fragments of the real world, cf.: "By designating a phenomenon or a thing, the word [in its basic meaning] [...] reflects our understanding of a 'piece of the world' and its relationships to other parts of the same world" (Vinogradov 1977: 163).

It should be kept in mind that the traditional approach has not been universally accepted; as argued, for example, by Krongauz (2001: 72), "most of the criticisms [...] have been caused by the very notion of 'notion'. It may not be observed and is but a scientific construct".

One of the central problems of the traditional approach is giving an explicit description of basic meaning. As a rule, an explanation of a word, which should play the role of such a description, fails to solve any of the tasks indicated by Vinogradov (1977). Firstly, rather than providing a complete description of a class of direct referents, it characterizes only a subclass of a word's typical referents. Secondly, it does not aim at a description of the relationships of a word's referents to "other parts of the same world".

Let us take, as an example, the word *banan* 'banana'. A contemporary explanatory dictionary (BTS: 58) offers the following explanation (abridged here for space considerations):

***Banan* 1** = An oblong yellow sweet mealy fruit of a banana tree (= a tall tropical plant with huge leaves…).

A scientific explanation, offered by Apresian, differs only in providing more details:

***Banan* 1.1.** MEANING. 'A southern fruit of an elongated and slightly curved form, usually a little longer than a human hand, with a thick smooth yellow skin and very tender and slightly mealy sweet flesh without seeds inside, which grows on a herbacious plant and is usually eaten raw'…

COMBINABILITY. *Zelënye <spelye> banany* 'Green <ripe> bananas'; *gnilye <isporčennye> banany* 'rotten <bad> bananas'… (Aktivnyj Slovar' 2014, I: 148).

Clearly, such explanations characterize only a subclass of **typical** banana referents. Outside of this subclass, one can find quite a few less typical but still accepted referents, such as a green unripe banana, a brown overripe banana, or, simply, a banana that has gone bad. It is also easy to see that such explanations cannot elucidate the semantic combinability of the word *banana* with other words. For example, the phrase *zelënyj banan* 'a green banana' is quite correct and has a lot of referents. However, if a dictionary explanation insists that a banana is yellow, it follows that *zelënyj banan* is inadmissible. The same holds for the phrase *gor'kij banan* 'a bitter banana', which is absolutely correct and may have a real referent; yet, if we are guided by the feature 'sweet' as part of the given explanations, we cannot but admit that it is incorrect. True, the scientific definition includes some of the possible combinations such as *zelënye banany* 'green bananas', *gnilye banany* 'rotten bananas' etc.; however, they contradict the definition which asserts that a banana is yellow and sweet. And this contradiction may not be resolved in any way.

The problems just mentioned will be the focus of the following analysis.

Chapter Layout. In what follows, we are going to examine only sensory lexical items such as concrete nouns and verbs, the referents of which (things and actions) may be discerned visually (or perceptually, in more general terms). We hope to demonstrate the following:

(1) The basic meaning of a sensory word (either a noun or a verb) has a dual structure "Prototype—Function", where "Prototype" reflects the features

(primarily visual) of a word's typical referents, while "Function" is a characteristic feature of all its referents, both typical and non-typical.

(2) Dictionary and scientific definitions of sensory words focus on describing only the prototypical component of the basic meaning of a word; i.e., they capture only the typical features of its referents. Dictionaries lack definitions of the functional component of a word's meaning.

(3) These two propositions will be illustrated by an analysis of the nouns *stul* 'chair', *kreslo* 'armchair', *taburet* 'stool', and the verbs *idti* 'walk', *bežat'* '(be) run(ning)', and *udarit'* 'hit'.

(4) For the words *stul, kreslo, taburet,* and *udarit'* explicit descriptions of their basic meanings will be given based on the schema 'Prototype—Function'

(5) For sensory lexicon will be considered the structure of polysemy (§ 5).

1.2. Definitions for the nouns *stul* 'chair' and *kreslo* 'armchair'. As an illustration for Proposition (1), let us consider different definitions of basic meanings of the words *stul* and *kreslo* found in traditional explanatory dictionaries and published research. Both dictionary and scientific definitions are similar in that they describe only prototypical referents.

Explanatory dictionaries:

(1a) ***stul* 1.** A kind of furniture used for sitting on that has a back (for one person) (Ushakov, IV: col. 571).
(2a) ***kreslo* 1.** A kind of chair with supports for elbows (Ibid., I: col. 1510).
(1b) ***chair* 1.** A piece of furniture for one person to sit on, which has a back, seat and four legs: *a kitchen chair* (Longman 2009: 262).
(2b) ***armchair* 1.** A comfortable chair with sides that you can rest your arms on (Ibid.: 77).

Scientific definitions:

(1c) ***stul* 1.** 'An object that has a seat and a support for the back and, usually, four legs, used for sitting on by one person' [a kind of furniture].
(2c) ***kreslo* 1.** 'An object that has a seat, a support for the back and two supports for the arms, used for sitting on by one person' [a kind of furniture]. (Sannikov 2010: 668, 670).

As may be easily seen, **none** of these definitions gives a precise description of a corresponding "piece of the world". What they all do is describe **typical** chairs and armchairs. In other words, they define **prototypical** chairs and armchairs.

The prototype of a referent is, indeed, an important characteristic of a word's meaning. For example, if a foreigner learning Russian comes across the words *stul* and *kreslo* in a text and turns to their definitions of the kind given above, he will **understand** their meanings at once because he will know (a) what objects are referred to by these words and (b) how these objects differ: a chair doesn't have arm-rests, while an armchair does. Thus, a definition of a word that describes the prototypical component of its meaning (characteristic features of its typical referents), serves an important semantic task: it facilitates **understanding** the word a person hears or reads.

However, it should be clear that a prototype is only a part (a component) of a word's meaning. Obviously, "prototypical" definitions (1a)–(2c) do not help in serving another task, conversely related to the first one: to help the very same foreigner decide which word would be the correct name for visually perceived articles of furniture designed for sitting. The outward distinctive feature used in such definitions (presence or absence of armrests) is not a characteristic feature of the classes of referents 'chairs' and 'armchairs'. Indeed, on the one hand, articles of furniture with armrests but a low back are called chairs rather than armchairs (the first three chairs on the left in Figure 1). On the other hand, armchairs sometimes come without armrests (the three objects on the right in Figure 1). Therefore, knowledge of what a prototypical chair or armchair is may not help our foreigner perform the reverse operation of naming real-life chairs and armchairs correctly[2].

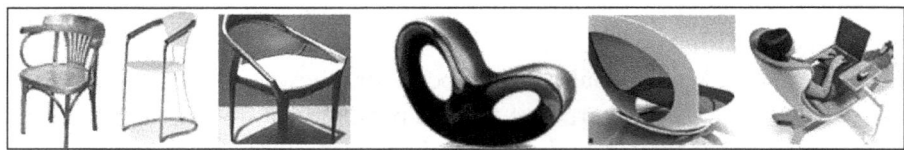

Fig. 1. The feature "presence/absence of armrests" is not a distinctive feature for the categories 'chairs' and 'armchairs'; compare the three chairs with armrests on the left and the three armchairs without armrests on the right

Undoubtedly, to a native speaker of Russian the categories 'chairs' and 'armchairs' are somehow separated. Indeed, it would be hard to design an article of furniture that could qualify (or not qualify) equally well as a chair or an armchair. This can be easily tested by turning to any search engine on the Internet and typing in the word *stul* 'chair'. Clicking on the "Find" button will bring a great number of different pictures of chairs (both with arm-rests and without), but

---

[2] These two operations—**understanding** a word and its **reference** (designating objects in the world)—perform two basic semantic functions of a word in speech. Therefore, knowledge, on which these operations are based, belongs to the linguistic meaning of the word and, more broadly, to linguistic knowledge—the information "a foreigner needs to speak correct Russian" (Mel'čuk's words, personal communication).

there won't be among them a single borderline item one might call an armchair-chair; each and every one of them can be unambiguously identified as a chair or an armchair. If you type in the word *kreslo* 'armchair', you'll get a similar result.

1.3. On the structure of the meaning of noun. Thus, the central issue is this: what feature does a native speaker use to **identify** a chair or an armchair? Let us agree to call this feature the **function**. It will be only natural to assume that it is the second and **principal** component of the basic meaning of a word, because the basic meaning of a notional word defines the category of its direct referents, while the first component, the prototype, does not.

Thus, it seems plausible to assume that the basic meaning of a concrete noun possesses a dual structure of the following type:

(3) Basic meaning of a noun = Prototype → Function,

where "Prototype" reflects **typical features** of a noun's referents (mainly visual), and "Function" reflects **a feature characteristic of all direct referents of the word**, both typical and non-typical—'the common work they do'. More specifically, the Function is "invisible" **work** (static or dynamic) **attributed** to the referent on the basis of its **shape** (the structure of its parts): the shape of a chair allows for sitting on it in a specific posture, the shape of a path for walking or running on it, and the shape of the banana (which contains the edible flesh protected by the skin) for consuming it in a specific manner, experiencing an accompanying sensation, and so forth. The connecting arrow shows that there is a relationship of interpretation between the components: the prototype (the shape of a typical referent) predetermines the function attributed to it.

We will give a description of prototypes and functions for the words *chair* and *armchair* later, in section 2; and now, let us consider some more examples.

1.4. Definitions of the verbs *idti* 'walk' and *bežat'* 'run'. A very similar situation is found in the case of verbs of action, motion, and spatial orientation (so-called posture verbs). Here, again, both dictionary and scientific definitions describe only prototypical actions-referents.[3] As an illustration, consider definitions for the verbs *idti* and *bežat'* from traditional explanatory dictionaries and lexicographic research.

Explanatory dictionaries:

(4a) *idti* **1.** Move by walking, making steps (about humans and animals) (MAS, I: 631).

---

[3] Justification for treating concrete actions denoted by the verb as its referents, is given in section 3.1 of this paragraph.

(4b) *bežat'* **1.** By intensely speeded motion, and quickly shifting one's feet up and down, to move in some direction (MAS, I: 68).

(5a) *walk* **1.** to move forward by putting one foot in front of the other (Longman 2009: 1966).

(5b) *run* **1.** MOVE QUICKLY USING YOUR LEGS; to move very quickly, by moving your legs more quickly than when you walk: *He was running towards the door* (Ibid.: 1531).

Lexicographic research:

(6a) *idti* **1.** To move, shifting one's feet up and down, at a normal speed;
     bežat' **1.** To move fast, shifting one's feet up and down (Gak 1977: 28).

(6b) *Čelovek X idët iz Y-a v Z* [lit., 'A man, X, is walking from Y to Z'] ≈ 'A person, X, moves over a surface from Y to Z, shifting one's feet up and down and never completely losing contact with the surface crossed' (compare, by contrast, with *bežat'*—'periodically losing contact with the surface') (Apresian 1974/1995: 108).

It is not hard to see that all such definitions describe **prototypes** for the human walk and run and their distinctions: greater or lesser speed of motion and preserving or losing contact with the surface. Again, these definitions may help a foreigner understand the meanings of the verbs *idti* and *bežat'* in speech; however, it is far from being the case that they can always be used correctly to denote different kinds of human bipedal locomotion with the help of the phrases *Čelovek idët/bežit* 'A person is walking/running'.

For example, counter to definition (6b), a native speaker will, without giving it a second thought, describe the mincing shuffling run of an elderly person whose feet don't lose contact with the ground with the phrase *Čelovek bežit* 'A person is running' (in its basic meaning). And a reference such as *Čelovek idët* 'A person is walking' would be considered incorrect. The sliding run of a ballerina, whose feet don't lose contact with the floor of the stage, would not qualify as a walk, either.

Obviously, the speed of motion cannot serve as a reliable criterion for distinguishing between a walk and a run; one and the same person can walk fast and run slowly (at a lesser speed as when walking). As can be seen, the problem that arises here is of the same nature as in the case of reference of the words *chair* and *armchair*. A native speaker knows whether he sees a person walking or running. In his mind the categories (classes of locomotion) "The man is walking" and "The man is running" are strictly separated: there are no in-between hybrid cases, when bipedal locomotion could be simultaneously referred to as either walking or running. Yet lexical definitions lack information about how this is done (this issue is treated in more detail in § 4, p. 100).

1.5. The dual structure of basic meaning. All of the above allows us to hypothesize that the basic meaning of an action verb has a dual structure analogous to that of a noun, as in (3). As will be illustrated by further examples, the basic meaning of a sensory word may be approximated as follows:

(7) Basic meaning of a word = Prototype → Function

"Prototype", here, is the visual feature (shape) of the typical referents (objects and actions), and "Function" the "invisible" work **attributed** to all direct referents on the basis of their shape. For example, the visible shape of a running person ('periodically **losing** foot **contact** with the surface') is attributed an invisible function, 'periodically **pushes off** with his feet from the ground with **the goal of moving** to the target place'. The arrow, "→", sets a relationship of interpretation, indicating that the prototype (shape) of a typical referent predetermines its function.[4] As an illustration (7), consider the following two examples:

chair 1 (basic meaning)[5]

Prototypical chair   →   Function

→   designed for sitting on by a single person in a **half-steady (semi-relaxed)** posture

tree 1 (basic meaning)

Prototypical tree   →   Function (= 'the original work that it does')

→   grows from the ground by itself, blossoms, and bears fruit

---

[4] We may assume that "Prototype" and "Function" are independent cognitive units of different natures stored in separate cells of the lexicon—the domain of long-term memory which contains the lexical data of a language. It is also a storage place for the relationship of interpretation which connects them and is effected as a stable associative tie between them. For neurophysiological data in support of this hypothesis see section 2.3.

[5] The definitions of meanings that we give are not explanatory interpretations since they often use words and pictures as terms designating cognitive concepts; that is why the quote-unquote marks are not used.

1.6. Basic meaning of the verb *udarit'* 'hit'. As another illustration of the dual structure, (7), let us take a brief look at the meaning of the verb *udarit'* 'hit'. We'll begin by analyzing the following well-known definition:

A udarjaet Y-a X-om ~ 'A hits Y with X' ≈ 'A forcefully and briefly brings a compact object X into contact with object Y' (Apresian 1974/1995: 108).

The basic meaning of an English correlate is explained in a very similar way:

hit 1. TOUCH SB/STH HARD; to touch someone or something quickly and hard with your hand, stick etc: *He raised the hammer and hit the bell* (Longman 2009: 832).

Obviously, both of these explanations are essentially imprecise. They describe only a visual prototype of the action "X hit Y", namely, "X came into contact with Y", while the function, as its second and primary component characterizing the **aftereffect** of X's contact with Y, is missing: 'Y **experienced a momentary hard push**'. Also missing is the **causal relationship** (THEREFORE) which connects the prototype with the function. Here is a short version of a more precise description of the basic meaning of the verb *udarit'* 'hit', found in such uses as *noga udarila po mjaču* 'the foot kicked the ball', *palka udarila po zaboru* 'the stick hit the fence':

Object X hit Y (basic meaning) =
   Prototype: Compact object X forcefully and briefly came into contact with
       object Y →
   Function: THEREFORE Y experienced a momentary hard push and got
       into a state of shock (and pain, if Y is a living being).

This meaning is described in detail in § 2, p. 65.

1.7. The role of 'prototype' in describing a word's meaning. One might be puzzled by the fact that such an experienced lexicographer as Iurii Apresian, who offered a scientific explanation, and such an authoritative dictionary as Longman, where a commonly used definition is provided, describe only the outward feature (prototype) of a hit, leaving aside its substantive characteristic: 'a push, a shock to Y'. Yet, as has been shown above in the analyses of the nouns *chair* and *armchair*, and the verbs *walk* and *run*, this is a typical situation. As will be shown later in § 2, section 3, explanatory interpretations of the verbs *padat'* 'fall', *fall* etc. are no exception.

The paradox may be explained as follows. As has already been mentioned, in a native speaker's memory the prototypical component of a meaning is closely (by association) related to its functional component (explanatory interpretation). That is why perceiving or imagining a description of the prototype, the native speaker unconsciously "recalls" the function that is associated with it. Because of this, the speaker receives the impression that **the prototype represents the whole meaning**. Only a focused referential analysis allows us to detect the deficiency of prototype-based definitions.

1.8. Pictures of prototypes in dictionary entries. The above reasoning explains the common lexicographic practice of illustrating some definitions by pictures of typical referents—things and actions. A picture is the most direct way to illustrate the meaning of a word (first to its prototype, and then to the function).

As an example, consider the definition of the word *banana* given in the Longman dictionary (Longman 2009: 114), accompanied by the image of a half-peeled yellow banana (Ibid.: 705):

banana **1.** a long curved tropical fruit with a yellow skin, see picture…

In the definitions given by Apresian and in the Comprehensive Dictionary (BTS, cf. section 1.1), a verbal description of a typical banana is used instead of a picture. However, it would be much more informative to replace such verbal description by three pictures showing: (1) a tropical plant with a bunch of ripe bananas, (2) the process of peeling a banana, when it is held in one hand and peeled with the other, (3) a man nibbling on the peeled part while holding the banana at the unpeeled part. Of course, to make the description complete, a purely functional feature would have to be added: 'the flesh of a ripe banana has a pleasant sweetish taste'.

Another illustration of the promoted thesis is provided by the following fragment of a "pictorial" dictionary of English action verbs (Fig. 2). Here, each **action** is represented by a **single**, most typical **frame**; this appears to be enough for a quick and reliable identification of the action which the frame symbolizes. It should be stressed that we are able to identify not only the action's kinematics (we know how it is going to develop), but its dynamics as well (which efforts on the part of an individual give rise to the action's kinematics). In other words, using a typical frame of an action, we reconstruct its prototype (its kinematics), and with the help of the prototype, the function (the dynamics, or supporting force) of the action. Thus, a definition (a verbal description of the word illustrated by the picture) is here completely unnecessary. This accounts for the **universality** of the given dictionary fragment—its ability to be comprehended by anybody, of any ethnic background.

Fig. 2. Pictures of prototypes of human actions that help us instantly identify these actions.[6] There is no need for any additional definitions to explain the meanings of the words which name these pictures

In dictionaries, such pictures are often used as visual supports for definitions, when subtle distinctions between look-alike referents, such as animal species, similar actions, etc., need to be explained.

The important role of pictures in describing concrete lexical items has been stressed by Apresian (2010a: 22):

> The dictionary [Longman] contains hundreds of color pictures, drawings, schemas, and photographs of various material objects supplied with the names of their parts, components, and types. In other words, the principle of ostensive definition of lexical items has been realized here. Moreover, many physical actions are also defined ostensively, because it is easier to show subtle distinctions between them with the help of a clear picture, rather than with a verbal description. Examples of such pictures are the pictures showing *a jump, a hop, a leap* and *a skip.*

---

[6] Adapted from the dictionary English Verbs of Motion (URL: http://www.fluentland.com/groups/learn-english/forum/topic/english-verbs-of-body-movement/. Accessed on 24.03.2018)

Fig. 3. The English taxonomy of jumps—*hop, jump, skip, bounce, leap* (adapted from Longman 2009: 949)—essentially differs from the Russian one: *pryžok, skačok, podskok, podpryg, poskok*. However, guided by these prototypical images, a native speaker of Russian can, in most cases, comprehend such an unusual taxonomy of jumps

The pictures in Fig. 3 are a good illustration of the human ability to identify, using static images, outwardly similar but nevertheless different actions—kinds of jumps. These pictures are clear because they show **different** kinds of jumps, that is, **different functional features** (different functions) characteristic of the jumps shown. Otherwise, it would be more natural to conclude that all these pictures show variations in jumping as a single action with a single function: 'a hard push by the foot/feet on the ground resulting in temporary loss of ground support'.

The fact that, using pictures, a native speaker of Russian gets a fair understanding of the meaning of the English words *jump, leap, bounce* and *skip* allows for the following inference: in his cognitive taxonomy of human jumps, these kinds of jumps are also represented by separate functional (causal) functions. The Russian people simply prefer to include names for other kinds of jumps in such classification, i.e., other functional features. Of course, this is just a hypothesis based on introspective observations, and its verification would require a series of thorough psycholinguistic experiments.

1.9. Analytical definitions. More than once throughout this book attempts will be made to show that "analytical definitions", which use a "special semantic metalanguage—a simplified and standardized sublanguage of the natural language described" (Apresian 2005: 13)—are incapable of providing adequate definitions of basic meanings of notional words **in principle**. First of all, it is impossible to differentiate, with the help of such metalanguage, between two meaning components that are essentially different—the prototype and the function—because each of these components requires a metalanguage of its own. Definition of a prototype relies on perceptual cognitive units, and definition of a function relies on functional, or causal, cognitive units.

At the same time, a simple dictionary definition fulfils, and quite efficiently, its task of ensuring that the lexical meaning is understood. Granted, it cannot fully represent even the prototypical component of the basic meaning (that is, the typical visual image of the referent), which provides the understanding of the word. However, a definition, **regardless of how exhaustive it may be**, plays the role of a verbal indicator to the prototype quite successfully. The main requirement is that it describe the most salient features of the prototype. Why are imprecise definitions of the words *chair* and *armchair* (see § 1, section 1.2) so widely used and, moreover, perceived as quite adequate? Because we know these objects and their functions well without their definitions. We have all used chairs and armchairs, and called them what they are, many times; therefore, the basic meanings of the words *chair* and *armchair* are retained in our memory. Consequently, such definitions are comprehensible to any representative of any culture in which chairs and armchairs are widely used because, to activate in memory the meanings of these words, it is enough to describe their prototypes. Moreover, verbal definitions may be replaced by images of a typical chair or armchair, as in Figures 2 and 3.

However, neither a Pirahã from Amazonia nor an Australian aborigine, who have never used a chair or armchair, would find such definitions or pictures sufficient. Likewise, in our endeavors to understand the names of different kinds of boomerangs used by the aboriginal people of Australia, we would not be satisfied with typical images of these boomerangs.

It should be emphasized that a brief definition that includes only the most characteristic features of a visual prototype would, in most cases, effectively perform its function of pointing to the prototype stored in a native speaker's mental lexicon and, via this prototype, to the function. Therefore, it **would be in greater harmony with the native speaker's intuitions than a detailed scientific definition**. Moreover, both circularity and tautology are admissible in a definition if they facilitate understanding of the prototypical meaning.

In his objection to such definitions, Blaise Pascal wrote:

> There are those who are absurd enough to explain a word by the word itself. I know some who have defined light in this wise: *Light is a luminary movement of luminous bodies*, as though we could understand the words *luminary* and *luminous* without the word light (Pascal 2007: 432).

Pascal's reproach is undoubtedly just if referring to a rigorous definition of the word *light* as a physical term, or as a description of its function which sets a closed category of its referents. But a dictionary definition is far from being one or the other, and it is not a rare thing for it to display tautology or circularity.

Let us go back to Pascal's quote in an attempt to show that one cannot, in principle, avoid circularity in defining the word *light*, because what must be described is a specific visual percept. If one has direct experience (has perceived light and darkness), any definition describing this perception—or, rather, pointing at it—will be comprehensible to him. If, however, such experience is lacking (due to congenital blindness, for example), any possible definition would be incomprehensible. Consider, as an illustration, different definitions of the word *light*:

(1) "Luminous energy, perceived by the eye and making the surrounding world accessible to sight, visible" (Ushakov, IV: col. 81)

(2) "Electromagnetic emanation, perceived by the eye and making the surrounding world visible" (MAS, IV: 44).

The first—and the clearest—definition features a disguised circularity, as the meaning of the word *luminous* cannot be separated from the meaning of the word *light* that is being explained. In the second definition, the word *luminous* is replaced by the physical term *electromagnetic*; thus, circularity is avoided, but the definition loses its explanatory power. By way of comparison, consider the following two excellent definitions dating back to the 19th c., which are obviously circular:

(3) "The shining or beams coming from a celestial body" (Shishkov 1803/2010: 30).

(4) "Light—a state opposite to dark, darkness, gloom, dusk that makes seeing possible; some take light to be the shaking of the minutest corpuscles of matter, others—a special finest substance, spilled far and wide by the sun and fire" (Dal', IV: 156).

Incidentally, even the definition quoted above from Pascal ("Light is a luminary movement of luminous bodies"), is not devoid of meaning and still explains something, namely, that light is a moving multitude (flow) of minuscule luminous particles.

Note. It is claimed in Vol. I of *Aktivnyj slovar' russkogo jazyka* ['Active Dictionary of the Russian Language'], in the section "General Scientific Requirements to Definitions", that "definitions […] must be complete (the Condition of Necessity), non-redundant (the Condition of Sufficiency) and non-tautological" (Apresian 2014: 14). However, a reservation that follows the claim effectively cancels these requirements: "Of course, one should not expect from definitions of lexical meanings the same degree of rigor as from definitions of scientific notions". The aforementioned requirements for definitions give a formula for "a certain ideal to be pursued, with an understanding that it cannot be achieved even in 'laboratory' conditions, not to say anything about a real dictionary". Such a contradictory position, unimaginable for a physicist, for example—for, indeed, if requirements are known to be unrealizable, why strive for their fulfillment?—may be explained as follows. On the one hand, the entire lexicographic program of the Moscow Semantic School (MSS) is aimed at formulating precisely such (rigorous scientific) definitions. On the other hand, the vast experience of the MSS' Head as a lexicographer seems to attest to the impossibility of making explanatory interpretations into strict definitions.

The results of a referential analysis of basic lexical meanings allow us to claim that **the scientific goal set by the MSS may not be reached via interpretations as** purely **verbal definitions**. Paradoxically, such a referential analysis is attainable only outside language itself, by using strictly cognitive units such as visual image, prototype, functional (causal) feature, interpretation relationship, etc.

2. Basic meanings of the words *chair* and *armchair*

2.1. Categorical distinction between chairs and armchairs. Let us go back to the problem of distinction between the categories "chairs" and "armchairs". As a thorough analysis of various referents of these words has shown, non-arbitrary differentiation between the categories "chairs" and "armchairs" by their outward differences (presence of armrests, incline of the back, low seat, etc.) may not be made. Their categorical distinctions may be formulated only on the level of **functional** features.

Thus, a chair allows one to sit only in a **semi-relaxed, half-steady posture,** remaining mobile and **capable of carrying out activities that require the use of one's hands**—as a rule, at a table or a desk: eating, reading and writing, playing games (cards, chess, etc.), using a sewing machine, etc. That is why a chair usually features a straight back that allows the sitting person to, on the one hand, lean on it and relax the muscles of the back, and, on the other hand, quickly lean forward in order to do something, turn to his company at the table, etc. At the same time, the sitting person must keep his balance and have **control over the vertical position of his body**. Therefore, his feet are usually on the floor so that they can be used in sustaining the body's balance or changing its posture.

By contrast, in an armchair one may **rest while sitting, in a quite steady posture (and, consequently, in relaxation)**; there is only moderate control over the lateral balance of the body because of the support for arms provided by the armrests. Thus, the body is in a much steadier posture when a person is sitting in an armchair rather than on a chair. In particular, one can doze or even sleep in an armchair without the risk of falling to the floor; the body may simply slump to one side if the arm slides off the armrest. That is why the back of an armchair is usually more slanted than that of a chair, while the seat is lower. This allows one to take a more horizontal, reclining posture, leaning on the back and stretching one's legs (they are not used to support the body).

Of course, the question that begs to be asked is, "How can descriptions containing such loose criteria—'half-steady' vs. 'quite steady' posture of the sitting person—delineate rigid distinct categories 'Chairs' and 'Armchairs'?" A brief answer appears to be this: there are two kinds of human activity in a sedentary position which are intrinsically distinct, (a) doing something with one's hands, alternately bending over a table and leaning back, and (b) relaxing, resting one's feet during a break from motion. For each of these activities one posture is appropriate while the other is not; therefore, these postures are essentially different, even though outwardly and in regard to support of the body they seem to be alike.

It should be stressed that an armchair is typically used for a brief, sedentary rest as a forced break in a person's activity, such as on board a plane, in the lobby of a hotel, etc. A person may sit in an armchair at home while entertaining guests, watching TV at night, or reading something before going to bed, but he can at once become active again—for example, to meet or see off guests etc. This is a rest "in public", in the sense that one sits in an armchair with the outer clothes on. Sometimes a person can work, sitting in an armchair, when the body must be in a state of sustained balance (see the note below on *kreslo voditelja* 'driver's seat', lit. 'driver's armchair').

Figure 1 illustrates the adequacy of the suggested functional differentiation of chairs and armchairs. Armchairs (on the right), even without armrests, provide for a quite steady posture of the sitting person, while chairs with armrests (on the left) do not, but rather allow for greater mobility.

Now, we can formulate the definitions of basic meanings of the words *chair* and *armchair*. Let us begin with *chair*. In contrast to definitions (1a)–(3a), in which the visual and functional features of a chair are syncretized, we will set them strictly apart: the Prototype shall represent exclusively the outward appearance of a chair, and the Function—exclusively its anthropocentric (functional) features.

(8a) **chair 1** (basic meaning) =

Prototypical chair → Function

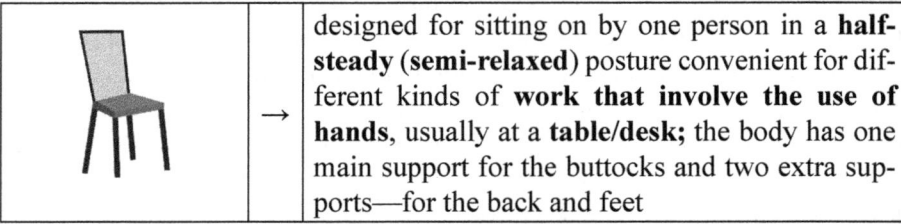

| | designed for sitting on by one person in a **half-steady (semi-relaxed)** posture convenient for different kinds of **work that involve the use of hands**, usually at a **table/desk;** the body has one main support for the buttocks and two extra supports—for the back and feet |

Presented in this way, basic meaning (8a) sets the category "chairs" on two planes: the Prototype sets it as a fuzzy category (degree of similarity to Prototype), and the Function—as a strict Aristotelian category.

Now, let us turn to armchairs:

(8b) **armchair 1** (basic meaning) =

Prototypical armchair: "image" →

Function: designed for sitting on in **a quite steady, secure (almost relaxed)** posture **comfortable for a brief rest**, usually in public (with the outer clothes on); the body has one main support for the buttocks and two extra supports—for the back and the arms.

A bed, in contrast to an armchair, allows one to take **a fully recumbent posture** providing for full relaxation of the body, which has supports for all of its main parts: the head, the back, the buttocks, and the legs. A bed is meant for a prolonged night rest without outer clothes, on bed sheets with a blanket.

> **Note.** In light of what has been said above, let us analyze the uses of the word such as in *kreslo voditelja* 'driver's seat' (lit. 'driver's armchair'). In our view, a driver's seat possesses most of the features characteristic of an armchair. Indeed, the driver must sit, slightly leaning on the back of the seat, in a sufficiently steady posture; his feet and hands must be free from the function of supporting and keeping balance, available for work: stepping on the clutch, accelerator, and brake pedals for the feet, and steering the wheel and working the stick-shift (in the case of a mechanical transmission) for the hands. A driver's seat often has armrests (for enhanced stability).

At the same time, a driver's seat must provide for sufficient body mobility, so the driver could, when necessary, turn left or right or look back—the degrees of freedom allowed by a chair. As can be seen, in sum, the features of an armchair prevail in a driver's seat.

Let us remember our foreigner now. Having at his disposal the functions from (8a) and (8b), he will be able to use correct designations *chair* and *armchair* for perceived objects designed for sitting on. Therefore, these definitions explain (a) how the listener understands these words in discourse or a text, and (b) how the speaker chooses a suitable word to designate an object for sitting.

The arguments given above allow for the following hypothesis: a native speaker of Russian, before naming a perceived article of furniture with a seat for one person either a chair or an armchair, first decides, judging by its outward appearance, what its corresponding Function is, i.e., what posture will be taken by a sitting person: half-steady (for work) or almost steady (for a rest or a friendly conversation). And in order to decide, one must mentally "sit" on this object. Depending on the result of such a virtual experiment, the perceived object will be named either a chair or an armchair.

It follows that the visual features (presence of armrests, incline of the back, height of the seat, etc.) are used not to directly identify the perceived object (i.e. to decide whether it is closer to the prototype of a chair or an armchair), but to evaluate its functional potential from the point of view of a sitting person. Consequently, the category "chairs" includes not only typical chairs but also non-typical "designer" chairs (Fig. 4) which are nevertheless capable of functioning more or less as typical chairs.

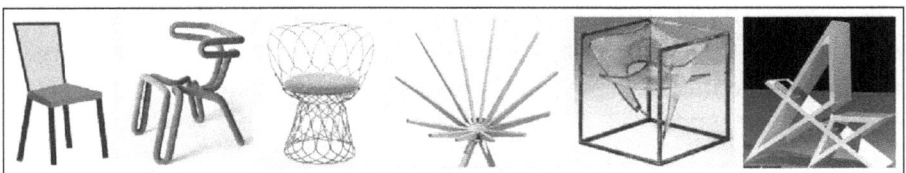

Fig. 4. A prototypical chair (left) and non-typical (designer) chairs (right).
The unusual shapes of designer chairs do not prevent their inclusion
in the category "chairs", designating them as *chairs*

2.2. What makes chairs, armchairs, and stools distinct? Now, let us take a look at a stool. It allows one to sit on it in an unsteady posture, demanding full control over the body's vertical alignment. As a result, the sitting person's body acquires a higher degree of mobility: his back not leaning on anything, it is easier for him to stand up, turn his body to the left or to the right, etc. And here certain problems with reference may also arise, because there are articles of furniture with legs, a seat, and a very low back (e.g., American barstools). The height of the back, as a criterion in including such an object into the class of chairs, is also assessed functionally by its ability to serve as a full-fledged support for the back of the sitting person.[7]

As a result, this is what we come to:

(8c) **stool 1** (basic meaning) =
      Prototype: "image" →
      Function: designed for sitting on **in an unsteady (non-relaxed)** posture that provides for maximum body **mobility** (such as standing up, turning around, etc.)

Summing up the arguments given above, the following important conclusion may be drawn: the **discreetness** of the categories 'kresla' (armchairs), 'stul'ja' (chairs) and 'taburety' (stools) is caused by the **differentiation** of the three postures (states) of a human body when sitting, and by the three kinds of human sedentary activity characteristic of these states. Based on this assertion, it seems reasonable to believe that the suggested functional (causal) differentiation of armchairs, chairs, and stools is **cross-cultural** by nature; it is characteristic of those nations in which these kinds of sedentary activity are very common and, therefore, clearly distinct. In particular, it is true about the Russian and English lingua-cultures, which is circumstantially attested by the prototypical chair given in Longman (2009: 263): it does not feature armrests and fully coincides with the Russian prototype given in (8a). It means that the categories set by the Russian words *kreslo* and *stul* and their English correlates *armchair* and *chair*, are strictly separate, despite the fact that in the Russian and English definitions, (2a) and (2b), an armchair is defined as a subclass of chairs.

---

[7] The aforementioned functional differences characteristic of stools, chairs, and armchairs, account for the localization of their "habitats" in the sphere of human activity connected with sedentary position. A stool is used to sit on for a brief period of time, with an option to quickly stand up, turn around, sit down again to face the person sitting next to you, etc. (that is why there is no use for armrests or a back in this case)—in bistros, bars, an eye doctor's office, where you must sit straight while your eyesight is being tested, etc. A chair is for a more prolonged sitting, with a possibility to do some work using one's hands (that is why armrests are not needed)—at a desk or a table, etc.; and an armchair is for rest, allowing for a relaxed posture—e.g., in hotels, on trains, on board of airplanes and the like.

2.3. Strict segregation of Prototype and Function. There are several important reasons to represent the basic meaning of a word in the form of a pair "Prototype → Function", where the visual and the functional features of the referents are not mingled (syncretized) but strictly segregated. We will note just two of them.

(1) Prototype and Function often take separate parts in generating meanings derived from the basic meaning via metaphor. Consider, as an example, the mammoth stone chair in Rene Magritte's painting (Fig. 5): metaphorically, it may well be designated by the word *chair*, although it resembles a chair solely by its outward appearance and its function is quite different.

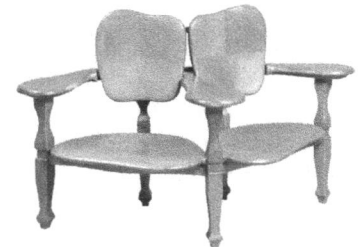

Fig. 5. The Legend of the Centuries, by Rene Magritte (c. 1950)

Fig. 6. Electric chair

Fig. 7. Double Bench, by Antoni Gaudi (c. 1907)

Another example is an electric chair (Fig. 6), which looks like a typical chair. However, its functional (causal) characteristic is totally different and, judged by this component, it does not satisfy the function of meaning in (8a), cf.: the arms of the man sitting in it are strapped to the arm-rests, and he cannot (nor is expected to) engage in any activity. The metaphorical expression *electric chair* is motivated solely by its outward resemblance with a prototypical chair.

Finally, one more example—a piece of furniture made by Antonio Gaudi (Fig. 7). This object may be metaphorically called either a chair (cf. its Russian name *Stul dlja dvoix* 'Chair for two'), or an armchair.[8] Since it is an object of art and it wasn't Gaudi's intention to make it comfortable for sitting, it combines, in equal measure, the features of both a chair and an armchair (low seat, but straight back etc.).

---

[8] Its name in Spanish, "Banco Doble Casa Batlló" (Barcelona, Gaudi, 1907) translates as 'Bench for two from Batlló's Estate'. Note that the word *banco* translates as 'bench' or 'seat', not as 'chair' or 'armchair'.

Now let us imagine a stack of bricks set by a tree in such a way that, while sitting on them, one can lean on the trunk of the tree. It is quite possible to say about such a construction, metaphorically: *This is my chair.* By the look of it, it does not resemble a prototypical chair, but in its function it is similar to the function of the prototypical chair (and this is what motivates the metaphor).

(2) There is neurophysiological data that seems to prove segregated localization of the visual prototype and function in human long-term memory:

> Connecting Wernicke's area and Broca's area is a tract of fibers known as the arcuate fasciculus (Carlson 1998). Damage to this pathway produces a condition known as conduction aphasia. People with conduction aphasia are unable to repeat nonsense words. However, if they are given a known word such as "horse", "cow", "house", etc., they will often be able to repeat the word. However, they are likely to produce some very uncharacteristic forms of error. For example, when the word "wolf" is given as a stimulus, they are very likely to reply "dog". If the stimulus word is "porpoise" they are likely to respond with "dolphin". [...] When the person with conduction aphasia hears [...] a familiar word, the sound of that word, after it is converted into a certain pattern of neural impulses, stimulates the memories associated with that pattern in Wernicke's area. Thus, when they hear the word "wolf" it calls up a visual image of a wolf, which is indiscernible from the visual image produced from the word "dog". Consequently, the patient produces that word instead of the target word (Palmer and Palmer 2002: 94–95).

2.4. Bloom's approach to object taxonomy. There is a vast literature on object categorization and lexical taxonomy (cf. Carey 2009; Murphy 2002; Lakoff 1987). We are going to touch upon just a few points of Bloom's (2000) approach. Discussing the issue of the basic feature of an artifact category, and taking the categories of 'chairs' and 'clocks' as an example, Bloom decides in favor of intended function:

> Chairs and clocks come in a range of shapes and sizes: there are beanbag chairs, basket chairs, deck chairs, chairs for dolls, chairs shaped like hands, and chairs suspended from ceilings on chains; there are grandfather clocks, digital clocks, clocks shaped like coke bottles, and clocks for the blind that tell the time at the press of a button. [...] What makes these things chairs and clocks plainly does not reduce to facts about their appearance.

What about function? Perhaps chairs are things we sit on; clocks are things that tell time. But this is also a nonstarter. One can sit on the floor, but this doesn't make it a chair. And a fragile chair that would break if you tried to sit on it is nonetheless still a chair. I can tell the time by looking at the shadow of a tree, but a shadow is not a clock, and if Big Ben stopped working—if it could no longer fulfill the function of telling time—it would not cease being a clock.

What about intended function? This is more promising. Perhaps a chair is something that was built with the intention that people sit on it; a clock is something that was built with the intention that it tell time. This is a better cue to artifact-kind membership than current function; in studies in which intended function and current function are pitted against each other, intended function wins out [...]. A theory based on intended function also accounts for our intuitions that the floor isn't a chair and a shadow isn't a clock, but a broken chair and broken clock remain a chair and a clock (Bloom 2000: 161).

A brief commentary is in place here. In keeping with our approach, a perceived object may be designated by the word *chair* if the speaker sees (knows) that its functional features satisfy the Function from (8a); it is designed to allow a single person to sit on it in a semi-relaxed posture at a certain level above the floor and work conveniently using his hands (perhaps, at a table), resting his feet on the floor (in order to be able to lean forward easily, turn around, and keep bodily balance). Thus, surfaces such as the floor, a step in a flight of stairs, and many others on which one could sit, must be deliberately excluded. The aforementioned function allows for great diversity in chair shapes, but a chair of any shape must provide for (a) the ability to sit above the surface of the floor, (b) support for the back, and (c) the ability to move the chair of this shape in space without forsaking the first two functions (and this is ensured by the chair's legs). For example, one could imagine a chair made of two pieces of plastic (a seat and a back) held in their positions by invisible magnetic fields; however, it is important that these pieces move synchronously to the desired place. In that case, legs (vertical pieces as props) would be superficial.

As for the current or intended function of an artifact, these notions are not relevant with respect to categorization. Why is the shadow of a tree not a clock even though it tells the time? For the sole reason that it is not used for this function. As soon as they start doing it, the tree at once gains the right to be called a sun clock—for example, it is used in this function by country folk, though that has never been its intended function. By the same token, a wide TV stand may well be used as a table, and if there are books on it and a chair by the side any native speaker will call it a table. Another drawback to Bloom's argument is that it does not apparently extend to natural (generic) categories, such as trees, lakes and the like. Examples of extending our approach (Function) to these categories see on pp. 41, 43 and 156–161.

Now, let us consider clocks and watches. This is a typical example of an object category with several prototypes: "sun clock", "clock with a face and hands", "electronic clock with a digital display", etc. Common to all of them is one function: "they are made to tell the time" (at daytime or round the clock). In most cases, if we want to know what time it is, we simply look at a clock (or a watch). Sometimes a simple action must be performed, like opening the lid of an old hunter-case pocket watch; some electronic watches show time at the press of a button.

§2. An analysis of basic meanings of the action verbs *udarit'* 'hit-PF', *tolknut'* 'push-PF', *padat'* 'fall-IMP', *brat'* 'take-IMP' and *vzbirat'sja* 'climb-IMP'

1. Introductory remarks

1.1. Sensory words. Let us go back to the term "**sensory** words". One often comes across it in linguistic literature, cf.:

> A semantic analysis shows that at this time [when a child is about 18 months old] the source speech is dominated by sensory—visual and tactile—adjectives […] *white, yellow* […] *big, little* […] *crooked, round* […] *merry, dirty, pretty, young, clean* (Voeikova et al. 2015: 524).

We use it with reference to words for which the referents are identified by immediate perception by the senses—sight, touch, etc. Examples of sensory words are *stul* 'chair', *derevo* 'tree', *sobaka* 'dog', *bežat'* 'run, v', *kričat'* 'shout, v', while *ideja* 'idea', *blagodarnost'* 'gratitude', *rukovodit'* 'lead, v', *zamyšljat'* 'plan/scheme, v', etc. are examples of non-sensory words.

The qualitative difference between sensory and functional concepts and meanings was noticed long ago (Anselm of Canterbury, John Locke, and others). Perhaps, most detailed on the issue was Shishkov (1803/2010). Over 200 years ago he wrote:

> All things known to us are divided into visible and invisible, or, put in other words, some are grasped by our senses, and others by reason: *solnce* 'sun', *zvezda* 'star', *kamen'* 'rock', *derevo* 'tree', *trava* 'grass', etc. are visible things; *sčastie* 'happiness', *nevinnost'* 'innocence', *ščedrota* 'boun-

ty', *nenavist'* 'hatred', *lukavstvo* 'slyness', etc. are mental things, that is, they are grasped by reason (p. 35).

In this section we are going to show that the dual structure

(1) Basic Meaning = Prototype → Function,

introduced in § 1, section 1.5, applies to sensory verbs.

1.2. Basic meaning and the referents of a sensory verb. There isn't a consensus in linguistics on verbal reference. Should actions be seen as referents of the verb that designates them? In the case of sensory verbs (*pit'* 'drink', *idti* 'walk', *padat'* 'fall', *pilit'* 'saw', *govorit'* 'speak', *kričat'* 'shout', etc.) this question can be answered in the affirmative. Let us assert from now on that a sensory verb is used in its current meaning if it names an action (such as 'drink', 'walk', 'fall') that can be identified very quickly, almost instantaneously. Such **current meaning** will be called **basic meaning** for sensory verbs, and the **actions named by a verb the referents of this verb**.

Let us briefly elaborate on the notions just introduced. Consider the phrase: *Ivan p'ët vodu*, lit. 'Ivan is drinking water'. The verb *pit'* 'drink' is used here in its current (i.e. basic) meaning. Its action referent is uninterrupted and identified by the observer at once, in 1–2 seconds.

In the phrase *Ivan p'ët čaj*, lit. 'Ivan is drinking tea', the meaning of the verb *pit'* 'drink' is, however, not current but **actual**. Here the action referent 'drink' is far from being immediately observed because it is interrupted by Ivan's other current actions, for example "eating jam", "talking", etc. However, even while Ivan is stirring tea with a tea-spoon it would be quite correct to say *Ivan p'ët čaj*. Such meaning will be called "actual meaning". It describes the action 'drinking' over a longer time interval (over many).

Finally, in the phrase *Ivan vtoroj den' p'ët vino*, 'Ivan has been drinking wine for two days' (or: [...] *on p'ët odno / stakanom krasnoe vino*, lit. 'he drinks only one thing / red wine by the glass' (Pushkin), the verb *pit'* 'drink' has a **background** meaning and its referent is identified over a long period of time: hours, days, etc.

The current, actual, and background meanings are the three aspectual meanings of a verb which express an action set over a micro-, mini-, or macro-interval.

1.3. Verbal reference. We believe that, for the current meaning of a verb, visible actions named by the verb are full-fledged referents, just as things are full-fledged referents for a concrete noun. In fact, **a single shot or picture** of a running/walking/drinking person, or a person throwing a ball or a stone, is enough for instantaneous identification of the action.

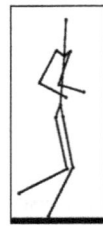

The figure on the left shows a shot of a human run, and the figure on the right shows a shot of a human walk. Each of these manners of motion is quickly identifiable from the picture despite the fact that both locomotions, as well as their pictures, are very much alike. In the same fashion, we could place a picture of an armchair on the left and a picture of a chair on the right.

2. Contact verbs: *udarit'* 'hit-PF', *kosnut'sja* 'touch-PF', *tolknut'* 'push-PF'

2.1. Prototype of the referents of the verb *udarit'* 'hit-PF'. Consider again the definitions given in section 1.6 (on p. 44):

(2) *A udarjaet Y-a X-om* ~ 'A hits Y with X' ≈ 'A forcefully and briefly brings a compact object X into contact with object Y' (Apresian 1974/1995: 108).

(3) *hit* **1.** TOUCH SB/STH HARD; to touch someone or something quickly and hard with your hand, stick etc: *He raised the hammer and hit the bell* (Longman 2009: 832).

As can easily be seen, definitions (2) and (3) specify the visual prototype of the action 'hit'. This prototype is very far from the function as not a single feature it contains is obligatory for the action it describes.

To verify this claim, the agent (A) will be excluded from the examination and the focus will be directly on the basic meaning of the verb and its action referents. Thus modified, definition (2) takes the following form:

(4) *X udarjaet Y* 'X hits Y' (*noga udarila po mjaču* 'the foot hit the ball', *palka udarila po zaboru* 'the stick hit the fence') (Prototype) =
At a certain moment *t*
1) between a moving compact object, X, and a stationary object, Y,
2) sharply and for a brief moment,
3) a contact occurs typically accompanied by a loud noise.
4) As a result, Y may move.

This definition covers most of the referents of the verb *udarit'* 'hit-PF'. However, it includes at the same time a number of "alien" referents. Consider the following situations that satisfy definition (2) but cannot be designated by the verb *udarit'*:

1) In an attempt to hit the rival, a boxer's gloved hand came short of the target and just touched the rival's face lightly

2) A football touched a post of the goal

3) A dot is made on the blackboard with a piece of chalk, or a document is stamped

4) A match is lighted

5) Shoes are polished with a brush

6) A circus actor catches a heavy ball using his shoulder

None of the contexts in these counter examples may be described as *udar* 'hitting'. As a matter of fact, neither the definition in (2) nor the counter examples above contain the main characteristic feature of a hitting event (*):

(*)   Y suffers a **sharp shock** from a moving X.

It must be stressed that this feature is, in principle, of a different nature than the features in the definition in (2). In contrast with the latter it is not visual, accessible to immediate perception. Let us go back to counter example (1). The referee sees the movement of the arm (X) of boxer A toward the face (Y) of boxer B. He also sees contact between X and Y and that Y swerves after the contact. However, the referee cannot in principle see the manner of the contact—whether it was a "sharp shock" that swerved the boxer's head or a "touch" which coincided with the boxer moving his head aside—i.e. what **caused** the boxer to swerve. The referee "computes", "attributes" this cause to Y guided by circumstantial evidence: a sound produced by the contact of X with Y, the sharpness of Y's swerve, etc. Such perceptually inaccessible features will be called causal, or interpretative, features in contrast to the visual (perceptual) features accessible to perception.

It will now be shown that the difference between (*) and (2) or (4) is radical: definition (*) is obligatory for any hitting event while all, or nearly all, of the outward features in definition (4) ("sharply", "briefly", "compact", "come in contact", etc.) are, though typical, not obligatory. Consider hitting events not covered by definition (4):

1′) The contact doesn't have to be sharp and brief, cf.: *Gružonaja kirpičom platforma medlenno pod"jexala k stojavšemu na eë puti vagonu i udarila po nemu*, lit. 'A flatcar with a load of bricks slowly approached the freight car standing in its way and hit it' (the flatcar may well be coupled, upon hitting, with the freight car).

2′) X doesn't have to be compact, cf.: *Volna udarila v bort korablja*, lit. 'A wave hit the ship broadside'; *Struja para udarila v poršen'*, lit. 'A jet of steam hit the piston'.

3′) X and Y don't have to be objects (things). In regard to X, this already follows from 2′): a jet of steam can hardly be considered an object. In regard to Y, this is illustrated by the following examples: *Ivan udaril veslom po vode / xlopuškoj (knutom) po vozduxu*, lit. 'Ivan hit the water with an oar / the air with a flapper (a whip)'.

4′) Finally, the feature 'come into contact' should also be defined more precisely. Firstly, X could be in contact with Y even before the shock, for example in the case of a hammer drill impact or a rifle recoil. Incidentally, in such a situation X isn't seen to move. Secondly, it isn't quite clear how the phrase 'come into contact' should be interpreted in the context of cracking a whip. Thirdly, X may be invisible, and we can guess that a contact took place relying only on circumstantial evidence, cf.: *Vzryvnaja volna udarila Ivana v grud', i on poterjal soznanie*, lit. 'The shockwave hit Ivan in the chest and he passed out'.

Lastly, note that the notion of "contact" is much more abstract than that of "shock" or "application of force", known to us since childhood.

2.2. Function of the verb *udarit'* 'hit-PF'. Now we have seen that all the features used in (2) or (4) are not obligatory for a hitting event, not only "sharply and briefly", "bring into contact", "compact X", but also "X and Y are things" (X may be a jet of steam, a bolt of lightning, a sea wave, while Y may be air, water, etc.), "X comes into contact with Y", and even "X moves" (in the case of a hammer drill impact X is already in contact with Y and doesn't move). Consequently, all these features should be excluded from the definition of the function because the examples these features don't satisfy are all literal (non-metaphoric) utterances.

But what features of X and Y are retained in all the examples considered above, that is, what features define a hitting event or a 'sharp shock'? Obviously, they are characteristics of the force-dynamic interaction between X and Y that emerge upon hitting and are guessed on the basis of the above given and other observable features, specifically, the consequences of a hitting event. In terms of force dynamics (let us assume, for the sake of clarity, that X moves while Y is stationary) a hitting event may be described as follows:

(**) Function *Udar X-a po Y-y (v Y-a)*, lit. 'a hit by X on Y (in Y)' = At a certain moment *t*
  1a) between a moving object X, possessing a considerable 'force of motion', and object Y, possessing a considerable 'force of steady state'
  2a) a momentary

3a) force interaction occurs: X transfers to Y all or most of its force of motion

THEREFORE

4a) Y suffers a sharp shock (= is shaken hard); X also suffers a sharp shock and is shaken hard.

Note. The notions used in (**) are simple and clear even to a child from his personal experience of playing with toys, without any knowledge of physics or, to be more precise, before any such knowledge. A child understands very well that a moving object (e.g. a ball) possesses some force of motion and that to stop it some force should be exerted to block this motion, and that when hitting (e.g. a ball), the force of motion (of a foot or a hand) is transferred to the stationary object and it starts moving (if the force is sufficient).[9] These notions belong to the initial notions that a child forms early on in his active experience of the world. Through these and other similar notions a child interprets the surrounding world (for more details on the development of such notions in children see chap. 2, § 7). Later, these initial notions add up to form basic meanings of the words of the mother tongue acquired by a child.

Let us continue the referential analysis of the verb *udarit'* 'hit-PF', taking the formula in (**) as a working definition.

First, X does not necessarily lose its force of motion (as in hitting a ball with a foot) nor Y its force of steady state (as in a stick hitting a fence). Second, the 'shock' suffered by Y must be substantial—cf. the following utterance, questionable in a typical situation: **Snežinki udarjali v lobovoe steklo mašiny* 'Snowflakes kept hitting the car's windshield'. However, the following is quite normal: *Krupnye kapli doždja udarjali v lobovoe steklo mašiny* 'Large raindrops kept hitting the car's windshield'. On the other hand, the force of Y's steady state (resistance) must also be considerable—cf. the questionability of the phrases with the past tense form *udarila* 'hit' in the following examples: **Pulja udarila v steklo* 'A bullet hit the glass', when the bullet easily

---

[9] For example, 7-months-old infants understand the action 'prjamoj tolčok' ['direct push']. Thus, if a child sees object A moving toward object B and then coming into contact with it, after which object B immediately starts moving, the child believes that the cause of B's motion is A exerting force on B by contact. It has been shown experimentally (Subbotskii 2007: 176–178) that a child doesn't establish such causal relationship in the case of B beginning to move if A stops without coming into contact with B (a space is left between A and B), or when B begins to move not immediately after the impact, but after a noticeable delay.

pierced ordinary glass leaving a little hole, and *Vzryvnaja volna udarila v stenu doma* 'A shockwave hit the wall of the house', when the house in question, along with the neighboring houses, was demolished by the shockwave.

Of course, being hit with or by X may lead to destruction of Y, cf.: *Stupka udarila po čaške i razbila eë* 'The mortar hit a cup and broke it'. What is important is that Y's resistance be commensurate with X's sufficiently strong force of motion and able to neutralize or considerably diminish it.

Lastly, the requirement that transfer of the force of motion from X to Y be instantaneous is characteristic precisely of a hitting event. In a pushing or throwing event transfer of the force of motion does not occur so quickly.

Using the definition of a hitting event in (**), we come to the following description of the function of the verb *udarit'* 'hit-PF':

(5) **X udaril po Y-u** 'X hit Y' (Function) = At a moment *t*
  (1a) between a moving object, X, possessing a considerable 'force of motion', and a stationary object, Y, possessing a considerable 'force of steady state'
  (2a) a momentary
  (3a) force interaction occurs: X transfers to Y all or most of its force of motion
  THEREFORE
  (4a) Y suffers a sharp shock, is shaken hard; if Y is a living being, it experiences a feeling of pain.

2.3. Basic meaning. Now we have all the necessary information to organize a description of the basic meaning of the verb *udarit'* as a dual structure shown in (1):

(6) **X udaril po Y-u** 'X hit Y' (basic meaning) = Prototype (4) → Function (5).

When the word *udaril* 'hit-PF Past Tense' is used in speech, each of its meaning components (the function and the prototype) performs its own semantic function. Imagine that the speaker observes a collision of a moving object, X, with a stationary or moving object, Y. The identification procedure for the perceived action allows the native speaker to instantaneously (and regardless of his own will) decide which **function** is satisfied by the action. Let us suppose that, by its causal features, this action satisfies the function in (5). In that case the verb *udarit'* is instantly foregrounded in the speaker's mind and the speaker can use it to designate the perceived action.

Let us now assume that the hearer perceives not the action itself but the phrase *Molotok udaril po gvozdju* 'The hammer hit the nail'. The interpretation procedure for the phrase instantly suggests a possible referential situation. The word *udaril* triggers foregrounding of the **prototype**, which gives a clear representation of the typical referent, and through the intermediacy of the prototype the **function** is put forward, providing a substantial interpretation of the prototype. The phrase becomes understandable.

Now it shouldn't be difficult to come up with a definition of the basic meaning of the phrase *Čelovek A udarjaet Y-a X-om* 'Person A hits Y with X'. A more general case would also require an introduction to our consideration of valency of the animate patient P, when X plays the role of instrument for A and Y plays the role of the part of P which suffers the blow (the locus). Cf.: *Sosul'ka* (X) *udarila Petra* (P) *po golove* (Y) 'An icicle hit Peter on the head', vs. *Ivan* (A) *udaril Petra* (P) *kulakom* (X) *v nos* (Y) 'Ivan hit Peter on the nose with his fist'. Here the specific purposefulness of the meaning of the verb *udarit'* should be emphasized. First, A had a purpose, to 'cause P physical pain or insult P'. This is a component of the function. Second, the position of a direct object may be taken only by an animate P, cf.: *Ivan udaril sobaku/ *stul nogoj*, lit. 'Ivan hit the dog/*chair with his foot', vs. *Ivan pnul sobaku/ stul nogoj*, lit. 'Ivan kicked the dog/chair with his foot'.

2.4. On the nature of the prototype and the function. By way of conclusion, compare, component by component, the **visual** features of the prototype in (4) and the **functional** (causal) features of the function in (5) to elucidate their differences.

X udarjaet po Y-u 'X hits Y' (basic meaning)

PROTOTYPE (visual description) Typical but not obligatory features of the action referent	FUNCTION (functional description) Obligatory features of the action referent
At a moment *t*	At a moment *t*
1) between a moving object X and a stationary object Y	1a) between an object X, the carrier of force of motion, and an object Y, the carrier of force of steady state
2) sharply and for a brief moment,	2a) a momentary
3) a contact occurs, typically accompanied by a loud noise	3a) force interaction occurs wherein all or most of X's force of motion is transferred to Y THEREFORE
4) Y may move	4a) Y suffers a sharp shock and is shaken hard; if Y is a living being, it experiences a feeling of pain

Each feature of the prototype is a typical manifestation of the corresponding functional feature of the function.

Item (1a) attributes to objects X and Y the functions (roles) that define a hitting event. Specifically, it covers cases such as a drill hammer impact and a rifle recoil, where X is practically motionless (but for Y it possesses the force of motion!), as well as counter examples such as *Voditel' iduščej szadi mašiny neožidanno uveličil skorost', dognal našu mašinu i udaril eë v zadnij bamper* 'The driver of the car behind us suddenly increased his speed, came close to our car, and hit it on the rear bumper', where Y is a moving object possessing force of steady state and X is moving at an even higher speed. Item (1) in the prototype shows the most typical, though not obligatory, realization of feature (1a) in the function (X is moving while Y is steady).

Feature (2a), in contrast to (2), covers hitting events characterized by a momentary force interaction but not by a soft and/or prolonged contact (cf. the loaded flatcar example), as well as the cases when contact is not visually detectable at all (for instance, X is a shock wave) and therefore cannot be described.

Special attention should be given to the term "contact". The visual characteristic of a contact is simple: it is the absence of any distance between X and Y. The interpretation of "contact", however, is not unambiguous and may vary from situation to situation (a hit, a touch, a push, etc.). Therefore, in a description, "contact" must always be interpreted. In our case, feature (3a) practically always provides such an interpretation ("hitting") for (3); in other words, it defines the consequences of a contact interaction between X and Y as a hitting event. Besides, this feature explains instances of hitting events when one can hardly speak of visual contact (perceived as "zero distance")— for example, where X is a flapper or a shock wave).

2.5. The verbs *kosnut'sja* 'touch-PF' and *tolknut'* 'push-PF'. The verb *kosnut'sja* conveys the information that X possessed a low force of motion and therefore, in the course of a force interaction with Y, exerted a **low pressure** on Y. This description covers, in particular, utterances such as *Lëgkoe dunovenie / ego dyxanie kosnulos' eë ščeki*, lit. 'A light breeze / his breath lightly touched her cheek'.

Determining the type of contact—a hit or a touch—often depends on how the speaker evaluates the magnitude of the applied pressure (whether it is strong or weak), cf.: *Paroxod kosnulsja pričala / udaril v pričal*, lit. 'The steamboat touched the pier / hit the pier'; *Myl'nyj puzyr' kosnulsja steny (udarilsja o stenu) i lopnul*, lit. 'The soap bubble touched the wall (hit the wall) and burst'; *Vosdušnyj šarik udaril po kartočnomu domiku i tot ruxnul*, lit. 'The balloon hit the house of cards and it collapsed'.

The verb *tolknut'* 'push-PF' describes a force interaction between X and Y similar to that described by the verb *udarit* 'hit-PF'. *Tolknut'* is distinguished from *udarit'* by the following features: 1) transfer of the force of motion from X to Y is not instantaneous but rather lasts for a brief period of time—that is, over a short time interval a considerable pressure is applied to Y by X; 2) as a consequence of this pressure, Y begins to move away from X.

3. The verb *padat'* 'fall-IMP'

Lexicographic definitions of the verb *padat'* are flawed in the same way as definitions of the verb *udarit'* 'hit-PF'; they describe only prototypical features of the "falling" process. To substantiate this claim, we turn to examples of such definitions.

padat' 'fall-IMP' 1. To tumble to the ground, pitch, plunge under the influence
    of one's own weight (Ushakov, III: col. 14).
    To tumble to the ground, plunge under the influence of one's own weight,
    losing whatever support there was (MAS, III: 9).
    To decline, tumble to the ground, downwards (Ozhegov: 478).
fall 1. MOVE DOWNWARDS—to move or drop down from a higher position
    to a lower position: *The book fell from his hands* (Longman 2009: 613).

These definitions highlight the typical visual feature of a falling event: 'move downwards'. Apart from that, MAS and Ushakov's Dictionary provide its typical causal interpretation: 'under the influence of one's own weight'.

Starting from the two definitions above, the following visual prototype of the process of falling for a person or object X may be formulated:

X padaet na zemlju 'X is falling to the ground' (Prototype) = X is rapidly
    moving fast downwards, to the ground.

Our task is to isolate the functional component of the basic meaning of the verb *padat'* following the logic of the discussion above. We begin by listing the obvious causal features of direct referents of this verb:

1. The force of gravity must be the main cause of X's motion toward the ground. A stone hurled downward or a rocket flying to the ground at great speed cannot be described as "falling".

Apart from this no other force must impede the motion of X. For example, X must not have any solid support while moving downward. Thus, a wheel rolling down a steep hill is not falling because, while moving, it is supported by the hill. A fall begins only on a sheer descent when the support practically ceases to affect the speed of the wheel. Similarly, a hewn tree falls because its support does not affect the process. Consider the following questionable utterance: ?*Pylinki medlenno padali na stol* 'Specks of dust were slowly falling on the table' (instead of *padali* 'were falling' it is better to say *opuskalis'* 'were descending'). In this example the downward motion of the specks of dust is impeded by the resistance of the air.

2. A landing may cause damage to X. Let us ask ourselves: why cannot one say about a skydiver moving rapidly toward the ground that he is falling, while it is possible to say so about a balloonist whose balloon begins to descend, slowly but uncontrollably? An answer such as "a skydiver can control his motion and the balloonist cannot" may not be accepted, because, instead of a man with a parachute, it can be a dog or even an inanimate object—for example, a tank. Moreover, one can hardly say about a person diving from a diving board or jumping to the ground from a truck that he is falling, although his motion toward the ground depends only on the force of gravity and is not impeded by any auxiliary means.

An answer to the question above may be formulated as follows: the utterance *X padajet* 'X is falling' is correct if X's downward motion ends in an **uncontrolled landing**, i.e. collision with the ground wherein X receives/may receive a very strong shock. Indeed, in a parachute descent the impact is weakened and doesn't lead to deadly consequences, as is also the case with pole vaults, jumping from a diving board or from a truck. On the contrary, when descending with an umbrella instead of a parachute, or jumping off a 10-storey building, a person is unquestionably falling because the impact with the ground is not weakened. If a person jumps from a high-rise onto a stretched canvass below, which cushions the impact, to say that *on padaet* 'he is falling' would not be quite correct.

Clearly, the observer's viewpoint, his knowledge about the perceived descent of an object, and his interpretation of the consequences of the object's contact with the ground, play an important role. For example, it is incorrect to say about a dive-bomber (and its pilot) *On padaet* 'It (he) is falling' because the pilot controls the dive and can stop it at any time. However, the utterance becomes correct if control over the bomber is lost. By the same token, this utterance can be used about a skydiver in free fall (he intentionally delays opening the parachute), but only metaphorically. At the same time, a person unfamiliar with parachutes and their use may well say about a descending skydiver: *On padaet s kakim-to gribovidnym predmetom*, lit. 'He is falling with some mushroom-like object', because the speed of the skydiver's descent is fast enough to allow for such an interpretation.

Now, a definition of the basic meaning of *padat'* 'fall' can be formulated:

(7) **X padaet na zemlju** 'X is falling to the ground'(basic meaning) =
Prototype: X is moving rapidly downward →
Function: 1) X is under the influence of its own force of gravity (the main cause of its downward motion) and no other forces are speeding up or slowing down its downward motion; and
2) (prediction) this downward motion will result in X's collision with the ground, wherein it will receive a strong impact leading to X's damage or destruction.

> **Note.** The utterances *Pizanskaja bašnja padaet*, lit. 'The Tower of Pisa is falling' (The Tower of Pisa is leaning), *Sputnik padaet na zemlju uže vtoroj god* 'The satellite has been falling on Earth for a second year' possess metaphoric meanings. The Tower of Pisa is kept from falling by the forces which hold it, and the satellite is influenced by the unusually weak (for earthly conditions) force of its weight. Such uses are also specific in that they realize not the current (referring to what is being observed) but the background meaning of the verb *padat'* related to very slow and long-lasting processes (about this meaning see p. 59). Nevertheless, both situations feature important properties which meet the definition in (7) and this is what motivates the metaphors. Indeed, the motion of the Leaning Tower of Pisa or of the satellite is such that in the future they (a) will reach the ground under the force of gravity, and (b) will be destroyed (such is our prediction).

4. The verb *brat'* 'take-IMP' / *vzjat'* 'take-PF'

4.1. Definitions. Just as in the previously discussed cases, definitions of the verb *brat'* (both dictionary and lexicographic) give a good description only of its typical action referents. In a manual on writing dictionary entries for *Aktivnyj slovar' russkogo jazyka (Active Dictionary of the Russian Language)*, Apresian (2010b) gives a definition (synopsis) of the basic meaning of the verb *brat'*: **Brat' 1.1** 'to begin to hold' (*brat' knigu v ruki* 'to take a book in one's hands') (p. 83). In an earlier work by Dobrushina and Paiar (2001) a similar definition is given: "to begin to hold Y [e.g. a book] with the fingers, or the hand, or the hands" (p. 125). V. Apresian's definition is based on the very same feature:

brat' **1.1** MEANING. A*1 berët A2* ('A1 takes A2') 'A living being, A1, begins to hold an object, A2, or a part of it, A3, with the fingers or some other part of the body, A4 (Aktivnyj Slovar' 2014, I: 341).

In explanatory dictionaries a different feature is used as the main one— 'seize with a hand, with hands':

brat' **1**. To seize with a hand, receive into one's hands (Ushakov, I: col. 183). To receive into one's hands, catch hold of with hands (teeth, etc.) (MAS, I: 113).

4.2. The problem with reference. None of the above characterizations give a more or less full description of the basic meaning, i.e. a strict definition of direct referents of the following phrase:

(8)   *Petja berët/vzjal predmet Y* 'Pete takes/took an object Y'.

For instance, these characterizations do not explain why a native speaker of Russian would easily and without any doubt point out that in the following pairs the phrases on the left are correct while those on the right are not:

Petja vzjal jabloko iz korziny	— *Petja *vzjal jabloko s dereva*
	(correct: *sorval* 'picked')
'Pete took an apple from the basket'	'Pete took an apple from the tree'
Petja vzjal šljapu so spinki kresla	— *Petja *vzjal šljapu s krjučka*
	(correct: *snjal* 'took off ')
'Pete took his hat from the back of the armchair'	'Pete took his hat off the peg'
Petja vzjal zapisku so stola	— *Petja *vzjal zapisku s pola*
'Pete took the note from the desk'	'Pete took the note from the floor'
Petja vzjal košku so stula	— *Petja *vzjal beguščuju košku*
	(correct: *pojmal* 'caught')
'Pete took the cat from the chair'	'Pete took the running cat'.

Note that in all the situations designated by incorrect phrases X 'begins to hold' Y and 'seizes it with his hand/hands'.

4.3. Presupposition and assertion. Let us examine the meaning of the phrase in (8) in more detail. It will be shown to consist of two parts: presupposition and assertion. These will be considered separately.

Presupposition. The phrase in (8) in its basic meaning may be used only in a situation when Y is (a) an independent object (not a part of an object) which is (b) in a steady and (c) unobstructed state (is not engaged with or attached to other objects). In most cases it is a situation in which Y lies or stands on a surface, which may be illustrated by the following.

1. Object in a steady state: Pete may 'begin to hold' (having caught or grabbed in his hand) a moving object Y (a ball, a butterfly, a cat, etc.) but it cannot be said about him, *Petja *vzjal Y (a ball/butterfly/cat*, etc.). Such uses as *Vratar' vzjal penal'ti*, lit. 'The goalkeeper took the penalty kick', should be considered metaphoric.

2. Object in an unobstructed state: It is quite correct to say *Petja vzjal knigu s polki* 'Pete took a book from the shelf' if the book was freely lying on the shelf. However, if it was squeezed between other books or pinned to the shelf, being at the bottom of a stack, the phrase becomes incorrect because the verb *vytaščil* 'pulled out' must be used. If Pete pulls out a book squeezed between other books only half-way, he 'holds it in his fingers'; yet he cannot be said to have taken it. The above notwithstanding, the phrase *Ivan vzjal u Petra knigu siloj*, lit. 'Ivan took the book from Peter by force', is quite correct. However, uses of this kind should be considered metaphoric, cf.: *Nalëtčiki vzjali kassu*, lit. 'The smash-and-grab gang took the cash' (they took the money by force).

Similarly, if a coat lies on the back of an armchair it is appropriate to say *Petja vzjal pal'to i nakinul sebe na pleči* 'Pete took the coat and slipped it over his shoulders'. However, if the coat is hanging on a peg this phrase in its **current meaning** loses its correctness since the coat is held not only by its weight but also by the peg. One should say *Petja snjal pal'to s krjučka*, lit. 'Pete took the coat off the peg'. Still, it is quite accurate to say that Pete 'began to hold' the coat or 'seized it with his hand'.

3. Object's independence: Similarly to the examples above, in the phrases *Pojdi v sad i sorvi jabloko / slomaj vetku sireni*, lit. 'Go to the orchard and pick an apple / break off a branch of lilacs', the verb *voz'mi* 'take-IMPER' cannot be used instead of the verbs *sorvi* 'pick-IMPER' and *slomaj* 'break-IMPER'. However, just as in the example with the coat above, one can 'begin to hold' or 'seize with a hand' a branch of a lilac tree or an apple hanging on an apple-tree. This stands to reason: neither the apple nor the branch is a fully independent object that can be moved from one place to another without breaking its physical connection with something else. It is precisely the actions of 'picking' and 'breaking' that make them independent. If the apple has already been picked or the branch has already been broken, the use of *voz'mi* becomes correct: *Pojdi na kuxnju i voz'mi iz vazy jabloko / voz'mi iz buketa vetky sireni*

'Go to the kitchen and take an apple from the vase/take a branch of lilacs from the bouquet'. For the same reason it is strange to say *Voz'mi kusoček dyni 'Take a piece of melon' in the sense 'cut yourself a piece of melon', because there isn't a piece of melon as an independent object in this situation. Similarly, one can say Vyžmi sok iz apel'sina, lit. 'Squeeze [some] juice from an orange' but not *Voz'mi sok iz apel'sina 'Take [some] juice from an orange'.

It follows from the above that before using the verb vzjat' the speaker must see or imagine an object, Y, in detail to evaluate its position in space. As a matter of fact, it is incorrect to say *Pojdi, voz'mi gde-nibud' kamen'/nožik/jabloko, lit. 'Go take somewhere a stone/knife/apple', because, as is clear from the phrase itself, the speaker doesn't know anything about Y. Here, the verb najdi 'find' or poišči 'look for' should be used. Similarly, if, for example, a boy finds a knife on the street, it isn't correct to say *Mal'čik vzjal nožik na ulice, lit. 'The boy took the knife on the street', since it is clear that the speaker doesn't know about there being a knife in this particular location. However, the phrase Petja vzjal nožik v komnate brata, lit. 'Pete took the knife in his brother's room', is quite correct because it presupposes the speaker knows about the knife.

Thus, the visual feature of the presupposition is as follows:

Presupposition (prototypical visual feature) = Y—an independent object unconnected with its surroundings (its visual image), staying in a steady state on a surface.

4. The functional feature of presupposition. An attempt will be made to understand what kind of interpretation stands behind the visual feature. Let us go back to the branch-of-lilacs example and, by way of comparison, imagine a medical apparatus for measuring the volume of the lungs. A patient exhales all the air into a tube connected to a cylinder by a long flexible hose and the gauge on the cylinder shows the volume of the exhaled air. In such a situation it is quite possible to say Pacient vzjal trubku v rot i sdelal vydox, lit. 'The patient took the tube in his mouth and exhaled', because the tube is interpreted as a functionally independent object and its connection to the cylinder does not prevent the patient from moving the tube as needed. The phrase Ivan vzjal ruku Maši v svoju, lit. 'Ivan took Masha's hand in his', is interpreted in a similar way. In the case of a branch of lilacs such an interpretation does not work as the branch has a much more rigid connection with the lilac bush.

From a consideration of such examples, the following definition may be formulated:

Presupposition (functional feature) = object Y possesses the force of steady state due to its gravity.

Resultant presupposition: At the moment of speech (over the micro-interval of a few seconds) the speaker knows (sees, remembers, or assumes) the following about Y:

(9)   Presupposition =
       Prototype (visual feature): object Y, physically complete and uncon-
       nected with its surroundings, is in a steady state on a surface →
       Function (functional feature) = object Y possesses the force of steady
       state due to its gravity.

Assertion. It may be shown that a similar formula for assertion has the following form:

(10) Assertion =
       Prototype (visual feature): X grips object Y and shifts it →
       Function (functional feature) = X, having a goal to control the move-
       ment of object Y, overcomes its force of steady state (caused exclu-
       sively by its gravity) and can begin to move it in any direction.

First of all, it should be stressed that "taking" is a purposeful action performed by X in order to have the ability to move object Y in the desired direction. Additionally, the action 'taking Y' cannot change or destroy Y—specifically, Y cannot be spent, consumed, enlarged, reduced, torn off, attached to something, taken apart, mixed with something, etc. One can say *S"eš'jabloko*, lit. 'Eat an apple', but not **Voz'mi jabloko* 'Take an apple' in the same sense. The phrase *Voz'mi stakan vody* 'Take a glass of water' cannot be interpreted in the sense 'drink a glass of water'.

Next, imagine the following situation: Pete put an old can of paint on a shelf and some time later the can became stuck to the shelf. Outwardly it still satisfies the prototype in the presupposition in (9), but not the function. In an attempt to take the can, extra effort would be required to "tear" it off the shelf and it would be incorrect to designate this action by the verb *vzjal* 'took'.

Here is another situation. If Pete clasps a glass of water and, without raising it, moves it a little toward himself, the action corresponds to the prototype but doesn't correspond to the function of the assertion in (10). Therefore, the expression **vzjal stakan* 'took a glass' cannot be used. The expression may become correct if Pete overcomes the weight of the glass. By so doing, he would become able to manipulate the glass in the fashion needed. Note also that if a book is being held by two persons, and each of them wishes to keep it, one cannot say *Oni vzjali knigu* 'They took the book'. This phrase will become correct only on condition that they are going to do something with it together.

4.4. Basic meaning of the verb *brat'* 'take-IMP' / *vzjat'* 'take-PF'. Let us continue our analysis. Rozina (2003), in the interpretation of the phrase in (8), uses the following characteristic: "Y is in X's hand, and he can do with Y anything he wants" (p. 233). This characteristic needs to be made more precise because, for example, pulling on a branch of lilacs and holding it in his hand a person can, in fact, do anything he wants with it: smell it, break it, wave with it, etc. However, as mentioned earlier, it is not correct to say **On vzjal vetku sireni* 'He took a branch of lilacs'.

Rozina points out that the verb *vzjat'* 'take-PF' "in its basic meaning belongs to the class of verbs of motion, more precisely—to the subclass of movement of an Object (examples of other verbs from this class are *sxvatit'* 'grab', *stjanut'* 'pull off/away', *ukrast'* 'steal', *utaščit'* 'drag away', *unesti* 'carry away'" (p. 231). This claim reflects a typical visual feature. However, it is not obligatory; this is proven by a later example given by Rozina: *Zaxar ostanovil na nëm krovavyj, tjažolyj vzgljad, potom, ni slova ne govorja, vzjal butyl' za gorlo* (Bunin), lit. 'Zakhar laid a heavy look of his bloodshot eyes on him, then, without saying a word, took the large bottle by the neck'. It is clear that the bottle may have been tilted, but not necessarily shifted. As for the main (functional) feature, Zakhar now has the ability to move the bottle in space.

According to Seliverstova (2004: 276–277), uses such as *Petja vzjal knigu* 'Pete took the book' are characterized by the feature "X becomes a spatial support for Y". It is the absence of this feature that explains the impossibility of changing the verb *sxvatit'* 'grab' to the verb *vzjat'* 'take-PF' in utterances such as *On sxvatil (*vzjal) eë v svoi ob"jatija*, lit. 'He grabbed her in his embrace' (here X doesn't become a support for Y). "Certain exceptions" are also mentioned for which the absence of this feature doesn't bar the use of the verb *vzjat'* 'take-PF', for example: *Ona vzjala ego za pleči i načala trjasti*, lit. 'She took him by the shoulders and started to shake him'; *On vzjal eë za ruku i potjanul za soboj*, lit. 'He took her by the hand and pulled her after him'.

The characteristic offered by Seliverstova is, on the whole, correct (and functional!), but too strong. If X clasps his fingers on the neck of a bottle and tilts it slightly, the bottle still continues to be partially supported by the surface but may be moved by X as needed. Therefore, the phrase *Ona vzjala ego za pleči i načala trjasti* 'She took him by the shoulders and started to shake him' is quite correct; compare with the similar phrase *On vzjal kadku za uški i stal trjasti*, lit. 'He took the tub by the tabs and started to shake it', which doesn't mean that the tub was lifted. The phrase *On vzjal eë za ruku i potjanul za soboj* 'He took her by the hand and pulled her after him' is a different matter. If it is about a woman following the agent of her own will and using her own energy, it is metaphorical—compare with the phrase *On vzjal lošad'pod uzdcy i povël eë*, lit. 'He took the horse by the bridle and led it after him'. If, however, the situation is such that the insensible body of a woman is pulled on its arm, then the meaning is literal—compare with the phrase *On vzjal mešok za uško i potaščil za soboj*, lit. 'He took the sack by the tab and dragged it'. Here the sack is only **partially supported** by the agent. As can be seen, Y may be a living being but only on condition that it is profiled in the situation as a physical body.

Joining the presupposition and the assertion gives the following resultant definition:

(11) ***Čelovek X berët/vzjal ob"ekt Y*** 'Person X takes/took object Y (basic meaning) = Presupposition (9) + Assertion (10).

To give this definition the heretofore accepted form "Prototype → Function", the visual and functional features will be combined separately, yielding the following:

(11a) ***Čelovek X berët/vzjal ob"ekt Y*** 'A person X takes/took an object Y (basic meaning) =

Prototype: (presupposition) object Y, physically integral and unattached to its surroundings, is in a steady state on a surface + (assertion) person X grips the object Y and shifts it →

Function: (presupposition) object Y possesses the force of steady state due to its gravity + (assertion) person X, having a goal to control the movement of Y, overcomes its force of steady state (caused exclusively by its gravity) and can begin to move it in any direction.

4.5. Explanation of incorrect uses. The definition in (11a) makes an explanation of the incorrect examples given in section 4.1 possible. In the phrase *Petja *vzjal jabloko s dereva* 'Pete took an apple from the tree' Y (the apple) is not detached from the branch and, therefore, possesses an additional force of steady state, while in the phrase *Petja *vzjal beguščuju košku* 'Pete took the running cat' Y (the cat) doesn't possess a force of steady state at all.

The two remaining phrases, *Petja *vzjal šljapu s krjučka* (correct verb: *snjal* 'took off') 'Pete took his hat off the peg' and *Petja *vzjal zapisku s pola* (correct verb: *podnjal* 'picked up') 'Pete took the note from the floor', are incorrect because the verb *vzjat'* 'take-PF' in these contexts designates not only the action of "taking", but also the actions that follow. In the first example, Pete took hold of the hat and raised it a little to get it off the peg, while in the second example he bent over, took hold of the note, and then resumed the initial posture.

Indeed, the verb *brat'* 'take-IMP'/*vzjat'* 'take-PF' in its basic, i.e. its current, meaning names only X's overcoming of Y's force of steady state, that is, the action which gives X control over Y's movement. Here is an example of the verb used in its current meaning: *Slepoj mal'čik tjanulsja za dudkoj, bral eë drožaščimi rukami i prikladyval k gubam* (Korolenko, *The Blind Musician*), lit. 'The blind boy would reach for the pipe, take it in his trembling hands and hold it to his lips'.[10] All three actions are designated separately: "reach", "take", and "hold". To the action "vzjal" ['took-PF Past Tense'] only one subsequent action may be added, namely, bringing Y nearer to X; it increases X's control over Y's movement, cf.: *Petja vzjal stakan vody i otpil dva glotka*, lit. 'Pete took a glass of water and sipped twice'. The verb *vzjal* here names two actions: "took" and "held to his mouth". Other current actions immediately preceding or following the action of taking **cannot be designated by the verb in its current meaning**.

Consider the examples of sequences of actions which cannot be correctly designated by the phrase *X berët/vzjal Y*, 'X takes/took Y'. According to Seliverstova (2004: 279), the incorrectness of the phrase *X *vzjal šljapu s gvozdja* 'X took the hat off the nail' is explained by the fact that the verb *vzjat'* is not used if X must overcome the resistance which exceeds the force of gravity of Y. In our opinion, such incorrectness is due to the fact that the verb *vzjal* 'took' designates not only the action of taking but also the subsequent and quite independent action of raising the hat. In fact, the noun phrase *s gvozdja* 'off the nail' indicates that, firstly, the verb is used in its current meaning (it designates a directly observed action) and, secondly, that the action designated is not just the action of taking but a sequence of actions: "taking the hat with one's fingers", "raising it higher than the nail", and "moving it toward oneself". And the verb *vzjat'* cannot designate this sequence as a whole. At the same time, the phrase *X vzjal šljapu so spinki kresla* 'X took his hat from the back of the armchair' is quite correct since only two actions are implied, "taking" and "moving something toward oneself".[11] Note that the phrase *On vzjal*

---

[10] The example is from Seliverstova (2004: 276).

[11] Seliverstova (2004: 278) notes that "[…] the verb *vzjat'* can inform about the shift of Y to a new position in space, when X holds Y at arm's length, in his teeth, under his armpit, etc. (*vzjat' v ruki* 'take in one's hands', *vzjat' na ruki* 'take in one's arms', *vzjat' pod myšku* 'hold [smth.] in one's armpit', *vzjat' za pojas* 'take [smb.] by the belt', *vzjat' za pazuxu* 'take [smth.] in one's bosom', *vzjat' na otlët* 'hold at arm's length', *vzjat' za plečo* 'take by the shoulder', *vzjat' k sebe na koleni* 'take in one's lap')". In all such cases Y, shifting to a "new position in space", comes nearer to X; cf. incorrectness of the phrases *Otec *vzjal*

šljapu 'He took his hat' is correct even in a situation when the hat was taken off the nail, because in this case the verb is already used **not in its current, but in its actual** meaning

The incorrectness of the phrase *Ona *vzjala zapisku s pola* 'She took the note from the floor' (correct: *podnjala* 'picked up'), as contrasted to the correctness of the phrase *Ona vzjala zapisku so stola* 'She took the note from the desk', is explained by Seliverstova differently: "the verb *vzjat'* implies that the position from which Y is moved is at the level of X's torso" (Seliverstova 2004: 279). However, according to our analysis the incorrectness is here due to the fact that the verb *vzjat'* is used to refer to a sequence of actions: "bending over", "taking the note", and "picking it up". Indeed, if we assume that X is lying on the floor next to the note, the phrase *Ona vzjala zapisku s pola* becomes correct. A similar explanation applies to other examples given by Seliverstova: "one cannot say: *Ona vzjala iz sumki den'gi i protjanula ix prodavcu* [lit. 'She took the money from her purse and offered it to the salesperson'] [...] *Ona vzjala iz kuxni korzinu s jablokami i vysypala v mešok* [lit. 'She took the basket with apples from the kitchen and emptied it in a sack']" (Ibid.: 280). Here, the verb *vzjala* 'took' in its current meaning is used to refer to a whole sequence of actions.

4.6. The prototype and the function compared. To conclude, compare, by component, the **visual** and **functional** features of the meaning of (11a).

X berët/vzjal Y (basic meaning)

PROTOTYPE (visual description) Typical but not obligatory features of the action referent	FUNCTION (functional description) Obligatory features of the action referent
(Presupposition) object Y, physically complete and unattached to its surroundings, is in a steady state on a surface + (Assertion) person X grips object Y and shifts it	(Presupposition) object Y possesses the force of steady state due to its gravity + (Assertion) person X, having a goal to control the movement of object Y, overcomes its force of steady state (caused exclusively by its gravity) and can begin to move it in any direction

syna na koleni materi, lit. 'The father took the son in his mother's lap', and *Petja *vzjal knigu v škaf*, lit. 'Pete took the book into the bookcase'.

Each feature of the prototype is the typical manifestation of the corresponding feature of the function.

4.7. Extended meanings of the verb *vzjat'* 'take-PF'. It is not our aim to analyze the extended—and these are mainly metaphoric—meanings of this verb. They are quite diverse. Only a brief list of some types of such uses will be given to strictly separate them from the basic uses that are defined in (11a).

In most cases, metaphoric uses of the verb *vzjat'* do not refer to current actions (actions lasting only for a few seconds); they refer to actual and background actions unfolding over a much longer time interval. Moreover, in extended uses Y is often not a thing but a place, height, weight, time interval, etc., cf.: *vzjat' knigu v biblioteke* 'borrow a book from the library' / *vzjat' knigu s soboj v komandirovku* 'take a book with oneself on a business trip' / *vzjat' škaf v mebel'nom magazine* 'buy a wardrobe at a furniture store' / *vzjat' kupejnoe mesto* 'book a seat in a compartment car' / *vzjat' vorota sopernikov* 'to win the rival's goal' / *vzjat' vysotu 2 metra 10 sm* 'take the height of 2 meters and 10 cm [in high jump]' / *vzjat' štangu v 200 kg* 'lift a 200 kg barbell' / *vzjat' pervoe mesto* 'take the first place [in a contest]' / *vzjat' otpusk* 'take a leave' / *vzjat' učenika* 'take a student', etc.

5. The verb *vzbirat'sja* 'climb'

This section will focus on the verb *vzbirat'sja* 'climb'. An analysis of its English correlate *climb* in the 1980s became the focal point of the opposition between two semantic approaches to describing lexical items. According to one approach (Fillmore 1982; Jackendoff 1985; Lakoff 1986, *inter alia*), the class of referents of a notional word is fundamentally fuzzy, because it is set by a prototype. A. Wierzbicka holds the opposite view (see below) that this class of referents is rigorous and therefore it has an invariant—a set of necessary and sufficient features satisfied by all and only referents of a word. These approaches and their outcomes will be discussed in as much detail as possible.

5.1. Analysis of interpretations of the verb *climb*. Discussing the above-mentioned opposition, Wierzbicka (1996) writes:

> Alongside *bachelor* the verb *climb* has played an important role in semantic theory as a key example of a word which—allegedly—cannot be defined in terms of any necessary and sufficient components and which can only be analysed in terms of a prototype (p. 165).

Analyzing prototypical interpretations suggested by Fillmore and Jackendoff (the latter made Fillmore's interpretation more precise), Wierzbicka concludes:

> ... this analysis is unsatisfactory, too, because it fails to predict, for example, that if a train went quickly up a hill it couldn't be described as 'climbing'.
> I would propose the following [...]:
> X climbed . . . [a mountain, a tree] =
> sometimes in some places
> if people want to move upwards
> they have to move both their legs and their arms
> X moved like people move at those times in such places (p. 166ff).

As before, the meaning of the verb *vzbirat'sja* will be described as a dual structure "Prototype → Function". A crucial **distinction between the Function and the Invariant** must be emphasized. The Function does not describe a complete set of meanings (uses) of a word; it describes only the **basic meaning**, and therefore **only the direct referents** of a word. Along with the basic meaning, the word *vzbirat'sja* has extended, metaphoric meanings. For example, the following uses are unquestionably metaphoric, which is why no attempt needs to be made to include them either in the Prototype or the Function: *The train climbed the mountain, The temperature climbed to 102 degrees, Bill climbed down the ladder, Traktor vzbiraetsja na goru* 'The tractor is climbing the mountain', *Ulitka vzbiraetsja po stvolu dereva* 'The snail is climbing up the tree-trunk'. Anna Wierzbicka and her opponents do undertake to include such examples in their definitions of Prototype and Functions, in fact making no distinction between the basic meaning and an extended meaning. But they offer different definitions.

Ray Jackendoff speaks of the possible suppression of now one, now another component of the prototype. Wierzbicka's invariant contains (a) a functional part which defines the prototypical motion 'a person climbing', and (b) a relationship of similarity for other "climbing" agents (trains, temperatures, etc.)—"X is moving in a way people move in such places". Thus metaphorization appears to be implicitly built in the invariant: such occasional uses are explained on the grounds of their similarity to prototypical uses.

In the Longman Dictionary (2009) some of the abovementioned uses, on the contrary, are explained separately (see below).

5.2. Basic meaning of the verb *vzbirat'sja* 'climb'. Dictionary definitions of this word usually contain both visual ("move upward") and functional ("with difficulty") features, cf.:

***vzbirat'sja* 1.** *S trudom vzlezat', podnimat 'sja vverxh na čto-nibud'* 'To climb up with difficulty, to rise to the top of something' (Ushakov, I: col. 271).

***climb* 1.** MOVE UP/DOWN—to move up, down, or across something using your feet and hands, especially when this is difficult to do: *Harry climbed the stairs.*

2. TEMPERATURE/PRICES ETC. To increase in number, amount or level (Longman 2009: 300).

***vzobrat'sja*,** *Vzobrat 'sja na gorku* 'Climb-PF up a hill'; *Malyš vzobralsja na stul* 'The kid climbed up on the chair'; *Oni vzobralis' na čerdak po derevjannoj lestnice* 'They climbed to the attic by the wooden ladder'.

MEANING. *A1 vzobralsja s A2 na A3* ['A1 climbed-PF from A2 to A3'] 'A living being, A1, usually making a big effort and using all the limbs, moved from a surface or from a place, A3, to a surface or a place, A2, higher than A3, often by using a contraption or an object, A4' (Aktivnyj Slovar' 2014, II: 106–107).

It will be assumed that the action referent of this verb in its **literal use** can be performed only **by a living being**, A, which has limbs (a human, an animal, an insect).

To begin with, consider the examples of motions of A which satisfy the component "move up using both the feet and the hands" (this component is used both by Wierzbicka and her opponents) but which are not referents of the phrase *A vzbiraetsja* 'A is climbing':

1) A diver is coming back up to the surface of the water.

2) A house-painter is going up in a bosun chair on a cable, rotating the pedals of the lifting mechanism with his hands and feet (cf. the definition component "often by using a contraption or an object, A4" from *Aktivnyj Slovar'*).

3) A young man is going up a convenient spiral staircase (or is boarding a bus), holding the handrails.

Now, let A be an animal or an insect moving, as Wierzbicka (1996) would put it, "in a way people move in such places":

4) A cat or a leopard is climbing [*lezet*] (?*vzbiraetsja*[12] is questionable) up the tree.

5) A cockroach is crawling [*polzët*] (*vzbiraetsja is incorrect) up the wall.

---

[12] The Russian verbs *lezt'* and *vzbirat 'sja* are both translated as *climb* in English, the difference being that *vzbirat 'sja* implies 'with difficulty'.—*Translator's note.*

Consider now some motion events, similar to those in (3)—(5), which allow for the reference *A vzbiraetsja* 'A is climbing':

1') An elderly person is moving with difficulty up a spiral staircase (or is boarding a bus), grasping the handrails with both his hands and pulling up his body.

2') A captive with bound feet is climbing up [*vzbiraetsja*] a rope ladder to the chopper, using only his hands.

3') A wounded leopard is climbing up a tree with difficulty; a bear is climbing up a tree.

4') A cockroach that fell in a jar with honey is slowly crawling up, leaving a trail of honey.

The motions of A in space in examples (1')–(4') differ from the motions in (3)–(5) on at least two features: first, A uses his or its limbs to seize (clutch at) a vertical surface to **substantially facilitate his or its upward motion** (pulls himself/itself up); second, in the speaker's opinion, such motion requires considerable effort on the part of A.

These initial observations allow us to formulate a preliminary definition of the basic meaning of the verb *vzbirat'sja*. (A more precise definition requires an analysis of semantically close verbs: *karabkat'sja* 'clamber', *lezt'* 'climb', *podnimat'sja* 'rise', and *vspolzat'* 'crawl up'.)

(12) *A vzbiraetsja* 'A is climbing' (basic meaning) =
    Prototype: A is moving up on a steep surface →
    Function: 1) By turns, A clutches at (clings to) a higher spot on a surface with one limb while holding on to the previous spot with another limb, and
    2) using its limbs, pulls its body up to the new spot;
    3) from the perspective of the speaker, such motion must require considerable effort on the part of A.

If A has four limbs or more, each time it can clutch at a new spot with more than one limb. As can easily be seen, the upward motions in (1)—(5) "don't belong" to the function by satisfying its conditions, while, on the contrary, the motions in (6)—(9) do "belong" because the conditions are satisfied.

Wierzbicka's (1996) example does not contradict this definition: *Watching him climb the cliff quickly and effortlessly I was filled with pride and admiration* (p. 167). The speaker's admiration is caused precisely by the fact that the motion in space ("climbing"), which normally **must** take a lot of effort, is performed quickly and with ease.

Let us now turn to the English verb *climb*. It will be examined in detail as it is a good opportunity to discuss one of the central problems of describing the basic meaning of a word (its function, to be more exact): which of its uses should be treated as basic, and which ones as extended. In this case, two solutions are possible.

First, one may be guided by the definition given in the dictionary (Longman 2009: 300): "**climb 1**. MOVE UP/DOWN". This will give us the following (the bold type highlights the changes as compared to (12)):

(12a) ***A was climbing*** (basic meaning) =
> Prototype: A is moving up **or down** on a steep surface →
> Function: 1) A, by turns, clutches at (clings to) a higher/lower spot on a surface with one limb while holding on to the previous spot with another limb, and
>> 2) **moves his/its body to the new spot with the help of his/its limbs**;
>> 3) from the perspective of the speaker, such motion must require considerable efforts from A.

Second, it may be assumed that the verbs *vzbirat'sja* and *climb* have the same basic meaning (12)—'move up'. It is just that *climb* has a much wider and more culturally specific scope of metaphoric extensions, which include A's downward motion, rising temperature, and so forth. From the point of view of the linguistic consciousness of Russians, such an interpretation seems more adequate because, to a Russian, a difficult descent with the use of the limbs is a substantially different kind of motion than a difficult ascent designated by the verb *vzbirat'sja*. An indirect evidence of that is, perhaps, the fact that the verb *karabkat'sja* 'clamber', which is close in meaning to *vzbirat'sja* 'climb', doesn't have uses such as *karabkat'sja vniz* 'clamber down' (in the case of *vzbirat'sja* such a use is blocked by the prefix *vz-* indicating upward motion).

This hypothesis is supported by a shrewd observation made by Aleksander Shishkov over 200 years ago: "[…] one and the same word from a particular language may, in different styles of speech, be expressed in another language sometimes by such, and sometimes by a different word" (Shishkov 1803/2010: 36–37). Illustrating this claim by a comparative analysis of the Russian verb *trogat'* 'touch' and the French verb *toucher*, Shishkov notes that they have both a shared part, i.e. basic meaning—for example, *trogat' rukami* 'touch with hands' and *toucher avec mains*—and distinctive parts (extended meanings). Thus, in the expression *toucher le clavecin* the verb *toucher* cannot be substituted by the verb *trogat'* 'touch', "for we do not say *trogat' klavikordy* 'touch the clavichords', but *igrat' na klavikordax* 'play the clavichords'". Likewise, in the French expression analogous to the Russian expression *trogat'sja s mesta* 'start off', instead of the verb *toucher* the verb *partir* is used (Shishkov 1803/2010: 38–40). And this happens, as Shishkov points out, because "the origin of words, or the coupling of notions, for every people happens in a unique way" (Ibid.: 36).

Thus, one and the same function for the verbs *vzbirat'sja* and *climb*, due to cultural specificity of the "coupling of notions", in the Russian language gives rise to one scope of metaphoric extensions and in the English language to another, wider scope. Therefore, metaphors such as *The train climbed the mountain* and *Poezd vzobralsja na goru* 'The train climbed the mountain' are possible in both languages, while metaphors such as *Bill climbed down the ladder*, *The temperature climbed to 102 degrees* are impossible in Russian.

From the point of view of the linguistic consciousness of the English-speakers, such human actions as '**ascending** with difficulty, catching hold with one's hands and feet', and '**descending** with difficulty, catching hold with one's hands and feet', are, perhaps, quite close. Therefore, the basic meaning of *climb* should include this latter action, i.e. it should be broader in meaning than the basic meaning of *vzbirat'sja*. We believe the issue may be resolved with the help of the following test: if the phrase *Bill climbed down the ladder* is correct only in the case when Bill descends **with difficulty**, the meaning of *climb* is broader than the meaning of *vzbirat'sja*. Otherwise, their basic meanings coincide and only the set of extended meanings turns out to be broader in English.

§3. Verbs of spatial orientation:
stojat' 'stand', *sidet'* 'sit', *ležat'* 'lie', and *viset'* 'hang'

1. The verb *viset'* 'hang'

1.1. Prototype. Let us look at four dictionary definitions of the basic meaning of the verb *viset'* 'hang':

(1a) *viset'* 1. While fastened to something, to be in a vertical position, with the bottom part not supported by the ground, floor, or solid surface (Ushakov, I: col. 298).

(1b) *viset'* 1. To be held up by something without a support at the bottom, to be fastened to something, with a possibility to move sideways (MAS, I: 177).

(2) **viset'** **1.1.** ...MEANING. *A1 hangs on A2* 'While connected by its part,
     A3, with object A2, object A1 is held by A2 so that its bottom part is not
     supported by anything' (Aktivnyj Slovar' 2014, II: 134).
(3) **hang** 1. TOP PART FASTENED—to put something in a position so that
     the top part is fixed or supported, and the bottom part is free to move and
     does not touch the ground: *Philip hung his coat on a hook behind the
     door* (Longman 2009: 795).

As one may easily notice, these definitions, just like the definitions we
considered above, are short descriptions of a typical referent. They describe
the prototype (typical appearance) of hanging objects with the help of various
characteristic features: "is in a vertical position", "is not supported by the
ground", etc. To a native speaker, all such definitions are perfectly clear and
seem to be quite adequate, as this prototype is stored in his memory (it has
crystallized as a result of using the verb *hang*) and helps him understand the
perceived word *hang* (in its basic meaning). Thus, hearing a phrase such as
Lustra visit, lit. 'The chandelier hangs' or *Zanaveska visit*, lit. 'The drape
hangs', the hearer has no difficulty in mentally reconstructing its referent
(substituting it by the prototype) and at once understands (decodes) its general
sense.

Imagine an Englishman who knows some Russian but is unfamiliar with
the verb *viset'* 'hang' coming across the phrase *Pal'to visit*, lit. 'The overcoat
hangs'. Knowing the word *pal'to* and turning to any available Russian definition of the verb, he will have no difficulty in understanding the phrase because
the definition instantly activates the analogous prototype of the referents of the
word *hang* stored in his memory.

Let us formulate the prototypical component of the basic meaning:

(4) **X visit** (Prototype) = X is
     (i) fastened to something,
     (ii) in a vertical position above the ground and can move freely,
     (iii) motionless, and its bottom part doesn't touch the ground.

1.2. Function. Let us now see if definitions (1a)—(3) can perform the role of
Function. Obviously, they can't. This is to be expected, because the prototype,
by its nature, cannot account for the native speaker's ability to correctly establish the reference of the phrase *X hangs* to non-typical, rare referents. For example, we can't say **Šarik visit*, lit. 'The balloon hangs' about a balloon filled
with a light gas and held by a piece of string which prevents it from going up.
Yet its position in space satisfies the first three (Russian) definitions: it is "fas-

tened", "in a vertical position", its "bottom part is not supported by the ground", and it "can move sideways". A similar case is presented by the phrase *Vetka visit*, lit. 'The branch hangs' used to describe a sagging branch. It isn't correct, either (unless it is broken and held just by its bark), although the position of its referent satisfies all four definitions. Indeed, a sagging branch would possess all the features given in the definition from the Longman dictionary: its "top part is fixed, and the bottom part is free to move and does not touch the ground". The same would apply to a cigar-shaped balloon filled with a light gas and attached to the ceiling by its top part (while the bottom part is vertically directed at the floor). And in this case, too, it wouldn't be quite correct to say *Šarik visit* (*pod potolkom*), lit. 'The balloon hangs (under the ceiling)', if the verb is meant to be used in its basic meaning. By contrast, a phrase such as *Zanaves visit*, lit. 'The curtain hangs', used to refer to a curtain that is slightly **touching the floor**, is quite correct, though it is unacceptable according to the first and the fourth (English) definitions.

This naturally begs the question, "What features inform a native speaker's decision about the correctness or incorrectness of the direct reference of the phrase *X hangs*?" Looking for an answer, we will maintain a strict dichotomous division of a hanging X's features into (a) **visual** features, **accessible to direct perception** ("is in a vertical position", "doesn't touch the ground", etc.), and (b) **causal or functional** features which may not be visually identified in a straightforward manner and are **attributed** to object X on the grounds of perceived visual features ('not supported (at the bottom)', 'fixed', etc.).

> **Note.** Let us illustrate the "visual vs. causal features" dichotomy by an example. 'Presence/absence of support' is a causal (functional) feature which may not be straightforwardly identified, in contrast with the immediately identifiable visual feature 'presence/absence of contact'. If, for instance, a passenger on the bus is holding on to the overhead handrail with both hands, for most of the ride his feet are supported by the floor (he **stands**). However, if the bus suddenly pulls to a stop, for a short moment the passenger **hangs** on his arms and hands (which are fixed to the handrail) while his feet lose the support of the floor, even though they may still be in contact with it. But this would be **non-supporting contact**, a kind of touching. An observer doesn't see this directly; he "computes" it, guided by the indirect perceptual data such as the bus's sudden pull up, change in the passenger's body posture etc., and attributes it to the passenger (he interprets the passenger's body posture as unsupported at the bottom). For example, if the passenger had seen an obstacle to the bus's motion and

braced himself for a sudden pull up, outwardly his body posture might have remained the same (he kept his balance with the help of his hands). However, because support at the bottom (his feet on the floor) changes to support at the top (his hands on the rail), **the very same** (visually) **body posture** should be designated by the verb *visit* 'hangs', and not *stoit* 'stands'. It follows that the relevant referential feature of the verbs *stoit* and *visit* is **not the visual** appearance of an object (vertical position, in contact with the floor, handrails, etc.), but a **causal, force-dynamic** schema of its position in space.

We will now show that, just as in the previously considered cases, the **Function is a set of strictly causal features**. We will consider them one by one.

Back to the balloon example: if the gas in it is heavier than air and the balloon is directed downward, the utterance *Šarik visit* ('The balloon hangs') becomes correct. Thus, it is important that the balloon **possess** certain **weight** pulling it down (the force of gravitation) and be **fixed at the top** to prevent it from falling down. In other words, X must be positioned (fully or mainly) **below** its **fixing point**. More precisely, it is its center of gravity that must be below the fixing point, while X itself doesn't have to be vertically oriented with respect to its longitudinal axis, cf.: *Provoda visjat*, lit. 'The [electrical] wires hang'; *Nastennaja lampa visit*, lit. 'The wall-bracket hangs' (even though its axis is aligned horizontally).

Now, let us look for an answer to the question of why phrases such as *Vetvi dereva visjat*, lit. 'The tree branches hang', or *Lampočka visit*, lit. 'The [electric] bulb hangs' (in a lamp base) are doubtful, to say the least, while it is quite correct to say *Jabloko visit na vetke*, lit. 'An apple hangs on a branch' or *Lustra visit*, lit. 'The lamp hangs'? It is bad Russian to say about a handle nailed to the door, *Ručka visit*, lit. 'The handle hangs'; however, this can be said about a handle held loose by a single nail. Similarly, the following objects can be said to hang: a slack (but not taut) string, a broken branch, a loose wall hook, and the like. Examples like these show that object X cannot be 'fastened hard to something', that is, 'fixed' and, therefore, immobile. Its top part must only have **support that prevents it from falling down** but not from moving sideways; moreover, all of X must be able to move sideways, not only the bottom part as in the case of a tree branch growing out of a trunk and held fast to it. And this is the reason the phrase *Vetka visit* ('A branch hangs') becomes correct with reference to a broken branch held only by a strip of bark. The phrase *Jabloko visit na vetke* ('The apple hangs on the branch') is quite correct for a similar reason: the stem by which the apple is attached to the branch doesn't fix it hard. And to continue in the same way, one cannot say about a handle nailed to the door that it hangs, while it is perfectly alright to say that about a handle dangling on a single nail.

It should be emphasized that X may be in contact with other objects below it; the important requirement is that it be neither supported by nor fastened to them. It is quite natural to say about a curtain touching the floor that it hangs; compare this with the bus passenger (see the note above) hanging on to the handrail while touching the floor and, possibly, the passengers next to him with his feet. This means that, in order for the phrase *X hangs* to be used referentially correctly, the position of X must be (or, rather, appear to be) unsteady in the following sense: an external force applied to X can easily move X or make it fall. By applying an external force, it would be **hard** to change the position of a taut string or a handle nailed to the door, but **easy** to do so in the case of a slack string or a dangling handle. One might raise an objection, pointing out that tree branches can be moved easily by the wind. However, it is not quite so, for it is the tips of the branches that sway, while the parts closer to the tree trunk, on the contrary, do not shift and 'hold' the branches fast. At the same time, the fixedness of an apple or even a cherry is relatively weak and does not prevent their shifting in space, compared with the strong fixedness of an electric bulb which doesn't allow for shifting.

Thus, the verb *viset'* 'hang' characterizes X's **unsteady position** in space (**its ability to move sideways or fall**), though such unsteadiness is explained by the presence of support only for the top part. The third feature, 'motionless', is also characteristic of this verb, but in a functional sense: X can slightly move relative to its support. Cf.: *Ot ètix tolčkov visjaščaja nad nami gromadnaja lustra stala raskačivat'sja*, lit. 'From these shocks the huge chandelier hanging above us started to rock'.

Let us now define the function:

(5) *A person/object, X, visit* '**hangs**' (Function) = X:
   (1a) has an **upper** support (above its center of gravity),
   (2a) is in an **unsteady** position on this support (can move sideways or break loose and fall down),
   (3a) is **functionally motionless** (motionless relative to its immediate vicinity).

Ultimately, this is what we get as a result:

(6) *X visit* '**hangs**' (basic meaning) = Prototype (4) → Function (5).

1.3. The referential mechanism. A series of referential experiments have shown that, before describing the position of X with the phrase *X visit* 'X hangs' (in its basic meaning), the speaker, guided by the outward (visual) features of X's position, "computes" its force-dynamic schema hidden from direct observation. In other words, X's outward features serve as indirect reference-points or symptoms, so to speak, which guide the speaker in automatically building in X's spatial locus a support-and-balance schema with such characteristics as: 'X possesses weight which pulls it down', 'X has a support which prevents it from falling down because of its weight', 'this support is above its center of gravity', etc. And if this schema corresponds to the Function (5), then it is correct to designate the position of X in space by the phrase *X visit* ('X hangs') regardless of the visual features which characterize its position: X may be positioned non-vertically, be in contact with other objects (slightly touching them or preventing from falling), etc.

What has been said above means, specifically, that a native speaker (whether a five-year old child, a half-literate farmer, or a professor of philology), designating the position of object X by the verb *visit* 'hangs', subconsciously computes X's center of gravity and sees that its support is above the center of gravity, thus failing to provide stability.[13] This is best illustrated by the example of the bus passenger given in the note above: first, the passenger stands (with his feet resting on the floor), and then, when the bus suddenly pulls up, he hangs for a moment, almost his entire support being moved to the hands and arms. Outwardly, a change in his posture might not be noticed at all. However, because of a sudden change in the force-dynamic schema, the initial reference (*The passenger is standing*) must be changed to *The passenger is hanging (on)*. And if the abovementioned Englishman relies on the Function (5), he will be able to produce (and substantiate) this reference.

1.4. Dictionary definitions and the function. It should be kept in mind that the Function (5), despite its precision, cannot serve as a dictionary definition of the verb *viset'* 'hang'. The expressions it contains—"support above the center of gravity", "unsteadiness"—designate causal features, are used in a **terminological sense**, and require a special explanation. Strictly speaking,

---

[13] This shouldn't be surprising even in the case of a child. As is known from experimental psychology, even during the early developmental stage (up to 18 months) the child, perceiving the surrounding objects, subconsciously furnishes them with a force-dynamic schema in which the object's estimated weight, its supports, steadiness etc. have been defined (for more details see § 7).

bringing together in one scientific definition the outward features from the Prototype (4) and the features from the Function (5) would not be correct because their nature and purpose differ in principle. The role of the Prototype is to explain the typical, routine uses of the word *viset'* 'hang', whereas the role of the Function is to give an interpretation, not only of typical, but of all direct referents of this verb (thereby ensuring that Xs, differently positioned in space, are correctly designated by this word).

In conclusion, it should be noted that out of the two components of the basic meaning, the function and the prototype, the function is the main component. Due to its recurrent use (in establishing reference), a typical aspect of the referent (X hanging), that is, its prototype, gradually crystallizes in human memory.[14]

2. The verbs *stojat'* stand', *ležat'* 'lie', and *sidet'* 'sit'

2.1. The verb *stojat'*. Consider some of the definitions of the basic meaning of the verb:

stojat' 1. Be on one's feet in a vertical position, remaining motionless (of humans and animals) (MAS, IV: 278);

Be in a vertical position, remaining motionless (Ozhegov: 761);

Be in an upright, up-ended, perpendicular, standing position, stick out; be on one's feet while in a state of rest, opposite of *ležat'* ('lie'), *sidet'* ('sit'), *padat'* ('fall') (Dal', IV: 332).

stand 1. BE ON FEET (also **be standing up**) to support yourself on your feet or be in an upright position: *She stood in the doorway* (Longman 2009: 1712).

All these definitions describe an outward look (image-prototype) of a typical referent—standing X. This prototype may be explicated as follows:

(7)   ***X stoit* 'stands'** (Prototype) = *Human* (*animal*) X

1) touches a surface with the feet,

2) is in a vertical position,

3) is visually motionless relative to the surface of contact.

---

[14] In real life, the process of formation of a word's meaning is more complicated: at first, the child forms a general prototype, then this prototype is given a meaning, that is, a general function—the so-called generalized meaning (overextension)—is formed, and later, by about the age of three, this doublet comes close to the word's meaning as it is known to adults (for more details, see Koshelev 2013b: 735–736).

Starting from this definition, let us build a description of the meaning's function. First, we take feature (1): 'X is in a vertical position'. This feature is not obligatory. Imagine, for example, a short-legged dachshund which, when standing, almost touches the ground with its belly: it can't possibly be said to be in a vertical position. At the same time, it is in an unsteady position and may fall (on its side) just like a long-legged hound, such that they both have to continuously maintain their balance. Thus, we consider the following feature to be functional: (1a) 'X, **supported by feet**, is in a **position of unsteady balance** (and continuously maintains its balance)'.

Now, let us take feature (2), 'X's feet are in contact with a surface', and show that, in the description of the function, it will have the following counterpart: (2a) 'X is mainly **supported by feet** touching a surface (X's main support)'. Indeed, if we consider an utterance such as *Ivan stoit, prislonivšis' k podokonniku* 'Ivan is standing, leaning on the window-sill', we will see that it is correct if most of Ivan's weight rests on his feet, i.e. if Ivan's feet are supported by the floor. Changing his posture slightly and moving the bulk of his weight over to the window-sill, Ivan ceases to be in a standing position and is already sitting, even though his feet continue to partially rest on the floor. Similarly, if Ivan is taking a ride on a streetcar holding on the overhead handrail, at times—for example, at sudden pull-ups or swerves, when the function of the main support goes from Ivan's feet to his arms and hands—he will be in a hanging, rather than standing, position. Therefore, the choice of the verb (*stands*, *sits*, *hangs*) depends not on X's outward (observed) position, which is the same in all the cases (X is in a vertical position touching the floor), but on an unobserved (interpretive) feature, how X is supported.

Finally, we come to feature (3), 'X is motionless relative to the surface of contact', which doesn't cover all the direct referents of the verb *stand*, either. Imagine an equilibrist standing on a ball and keeping his balance by oscillating with the ball, remaining at the same place. An utterance such as *X has been standing on the ball for 3 minutes already* would be quite correct, showing that X's slight movements in space are admissible. What matters is that these not be onward movements, i.e., they must occur in a **restricted space**. A similar situation arises in the case of X waiting for someone, tapping with his heels because of the cold. In view of what has been said, instead of feature (3) we will use in the description of the function feature (3a) 'X is **functionally** motionless (its local movements are unimportant)'.

Feature (3a) is quite important when we move from an analysis of current verbal meanings to an analysis of topical and background (i.e., metaphorical) meanings as in the following examples: *Ivan stoit v vorotax uže polčasa i do six por ne soveršil ni odnoy ošibki pri vyxodax na perexvat mjača* 'Ivan has been keeping [has been standing in] the goal for half an hour already and still hasn't made a single mistake coming out to intercept the ball'; *Ivan segodnja celyj den' stoit u stanka* 'Ivan has been standing at the machine all day today'. In both these examples the verb refers to the process not at the moment of observation (an on-going process over a short time-interval), but over a much longer (global) period of time. Over this period Ivan (a) **practically always** *stands*, in the current meaning of the verb (should Ivan, while operating the machine, sit rather than stand, the utterance in the above example would be incorrect in its "current" interpretation), and (b) **practically always** remains at the same place (by the goal, by the machine) and is, in this sense, globally (time-wise) motionless, as his movements in the vicinity of the locus of his standing are inconsequential. Leaving his workplace for a smoke, Ivan can say something like *Ja seičas stoju u stanka*, lit. 'I now stand at the machine', because, topically, his work on a machine continues (will resume shortly as a current process; for a more detailed treatment of these types of meaning, see p. 59).

Let us now formulate the functional meaning:

(8) *Z stoit* **'stands'** (Function) = Human (animal) X,

　(1a) is supported at the bottom part, **feet resting** on a surface (X's main support)

　(2a) is in a **position of unsteady balance** (continuously keeps his balance);

　(3a) is **functionally motionless** (can move only in the small vicinity of his support).

Adding up the prototype and the function, we get:

(9) *X stoit* **'stands'** (basic meaning) = Prototype (7) → Function (8).

Descriptions of the prototypical and functional components of the basic meaning of the verb *stojat'* 'stand' are shown in the table below:

PROTOTYPE (7)	FUNCTION (8)
Čelovek stoit, lit. 'The person is standing'	*Čelovek stoit*, lit. 'The person is standing'
Typical visual features	Obligatory functional features
(1) **feet are in contact** with a surface;	(1a) **feet rest** on a surface (X's main support);
(2) is in a **vertical position**	(2a) is in a **position of unsteady balance** (continuously maintains balance);
(3) is **visually** motionless relative to the surface of contact	(3a) **functionally** motionless (can move only in the small vicinity of his support)

2.2. The verb *ležat'* 'lie'. Consider dictionary definitions of this verb which show their prototypical character:

ležat' **1.** Be bodily on something in a horizontal position (Ozhegov: 311).
lie **1.** FLAT POSITION. to be in a position in which your body is flat on the floor, on a bed, etc.: *He was lying on the bed smoking a cigarette* (Longman 2009: 1006).

Let us formulate the prototypical component:

(10) *X ležit* **'lies'** (Prototype) = *Human (animal) X*
    1) is in a horizontal position,
    2) is in bodily contact with a surface,
    3) is visually motionless relative to the surface of contact.

Now let us examine the functional component of the meaning 'lie'. It is based on the feature 'X is in a quite steady position (it can't fall when a lateral force is applied, neither can it move lower towards the supporting surface)'; for all that, X's body does not have to be in a horizontal position. For example, a person can lie in an armchair slightly resting his feet on the floor and his head on the top edge of the armchair's back.

(11) *X lies* (Function) = Human (animal) X,
    (1a) is supported bodily **at the bottom** (there is a supporting surface), making full relaxation possible,
    (2a) is in a **quite steady position**,
    (3a) is **functionally motionless**.

As a final result, we get:

(12) *X lies* (basic meaning) = Prototype (10) → Function (11).

2.3. The verb *sidet'* 'sit'. Dictionary definitions of the basic meaning of this verb show similarities:

sidet' **'sit' 1.** Be in a position such that the lower part of the body rests on a support (Ozhegov: 706).
sit **1.** IN A CHAIR ETC to be on a chair or seat, or on a ground, with the top half of your body upright and your weight resting on your buttocks (Longman 2009: 1639).

We will proceed by assuming a wider scope of direct referents of the utterance *X sidit* ['X is sitting'] which also includes animals: *Sobaka sidit na kovrike* 'The dog is sitting on a mat' and the like. The question to ask is, what do they have in common with canonical uses, such as *Čelovek sidit na stule/na polu* 'The man is sitting on a chair/on the floor'? The answer seems obvious: they have in common X's partial steadiness of position, which is in between X's fully steady position when lying and X's unsteady position when standing (balance is still kept in this case but with a much bigger effort).

Therefore, just like in the previous analysis, we get:

(13) **X sidit 'is sitting'** (Prototype) = Human (animal) X

(1) is in contact with a surface by the lower (hind) part of the body,
(2) has the top (front) part of the body in a vertical position,
(3) is visually motionless relative to the surface of contact.

(14) **X sidit 'is sitting'** (Function) = Human (animal) X,
(1a) has a main support (supporting surface) **at the bottom part** (for the buttocks),
(2a) is in a **partially steady position**,
(3a) is **functionally motionless**.

(15) **X sidit 'is sitting'** (basic meaning) = Prototype (13) → Function (14).

2.4. A comparison of human motionless postures. As has been shown, the verbs *ležat'* 'lie', *sidet'* 'sit', *stojat'* 'stand', and *viset'* 'hang' prescribe for X (a) the type of support, and (b) the degree of the posture's steadiness determined by this support.

The results are summed up in the following table describing the classes of referents for these verbs.

The verb designating X's motionless posture	**Functional (causal) feature** of X's motionless posture	
	degree of X's steadiness	Type of X's support
X ležit ['is lying']	quite steady	lower
X sidit ['is sitting']	partially steady	lower
X stoit ['is standing']	unsteady	lower
X visit ['is hanging']	unsteady	upper

Here is an example. Consider a mountaineer climbing a steep (but not vertical) slope of a rock at the moment when he has secured his (precarious) position: he is pressing himself to the rock, using its juts as supports for his hands and feet. Depending on how the observer interprets his posture, any of the three references is possible: (a) *The mountaineer is standing* (his main support is his feet; the position is unsteady); (b) *The mountaineer is lying* (his main support is his entire body pressed to the rock; the position is steady); and (c) *The mountaineer is hanging on* (his main support is his hands and arms, the rest of the body tends to slide down; the position is unsteady).

It may be hypothesized that the classification given in the table possesses a universal character and reflects species-specific properties of humans (of their bodies). In particular, it is characteristic of Mandarin Chinese, cf. Aoshuan (2004/2012: 18):

> In Chinese… the verbs *zhan* 'stand', *zuo* 'sit' and *tang* 'lie' are used exclusively with reference to humans. This feature is inherent in the first two verbs, as their corresponding hieroglyphs include the element "man". The hieroglyph *tang* 'lie' with a determinative "body" may, at best, be used with reference to 'humanized' domestic animals such as a cat or a dog. In its canonical use, *tang* implies the kind of posture when a living being is lying on its back with its face up—a posture characteristic only of humans.

In the case of other species, the picture may be quite different. For example, for a macaque monkey capable of hanging on tree branches using both its hands and tail, a classification of motionless body postures would, apparently, differ from the one given above.

§ 4. The motion verbs *idti* 'walk', *bežat'* 'run', *polzti* 'crawl', *šagat'* 'step/stride', *prygat'* 'jump', and *exat'* 'go/ride/drive'

1. The motion verbs *idti* 'walk' and *bežat'* 'run'

1.1. Definitions of the verbs *idti* and *bežat'*. These verbs have already been considered, briefly, in § 1 section 1.4, where it was shown that their definitions are quite traditional: both dictionary and scientific definitions tend, first of all, to fixate the prototypes—characteristic visual appearances of walking and running as motion events. Let us return to these definitions in order to analyze them in more detail.

This is what we find in explanatory dictionaries:

idti **1.** Step, move by stepping, start moving by shifting from foot to foot (Dal', II: 9).

bežat' **1.** Move by stepping quickly, rapidly shifting from foot to foot (Ibid., I: 57).

idti **1.** Move by walking, making steps (about humans and animals) (MAS, I: 631).

***bežat'* 1.** By intensely speeded motion, and quickly shifting one's feet up and down, to move in some direction (MAS, I: 68).

***walk* 1.** to move forward by putting one foot in front of the other (Longman 2009: 1966);

***run* 1.** MOVE QUICKLY USING YOUR LEGS; to move very quickly, by moving your legs more quickly than when you walk: *He was running towards the door* (Ibid.: 1531).

Definitions from lexicographic research:

(1) ***idti* 1.** To move, shifting one's feet up and down, at a normal speed.
***bežat'* 1.** To move fast, shifting one's feet up and down (Gak 1977: 28).

(2) *Čelovek X idët iz Y-a v Z* [lit., 'A person, X, is walking from Y to Z''] ≅ 'Person X moves over a surface from Y to Z, shifting his feet up and down and never completely losing contact with the surface crossed' (compare, by contrast, *with bežat'*—'periodically losing contact with the surface') (Apresian 1974/1995: 108).

(2a) ***bežat'* 1.1.** *Ot lesa napererez banditu bežal policejskij* ['From the wood, a cop was running to intercept the bandit']; *Oleni begut na vodopoj* ['The deer are running to a watering place'].
MEANING: *A1 runs to A2 from A3 over A4 to (do) A5* 'A living being, A1, moves at a run to place A2 from place A3 over surface A4 in order to A5'.
***begóm* 'at a run; running', ADV. *Deti begom brosilis' iz klassa* (lit. 'The children, running, dashed from the classroom').
MEANING. 'Evenly moving by alternate pushes of feet from a surface so that, for a moment, the feet completely lose contact with it' (Aktivnyj Slovar' 2014, I: 177, 181).

At first sight, all these definitions appear to be quite adequate. They describe the typical visual appearances (kinematics) of walking and running, and they use visual features as the main distinctive features: either the speed of motion, which is higher for running and lower for walking (dictionaries, Gak), or "periodic loss/no loss of contact with the surface of motion", see (2).

1.2. How do the human walk and run differ? The seeming adequacy of the definitions in question may be put down to the fact that we have a very good idea of the visual prototypes of walking and running[15] which are easily recognizable (cf. Figures 1 and 2).

---

[15] I got these diagrams by fixating, frame by frame, the linear version of the point-light displays of the human walk and run available on the website of the Bio Motion Lab at

Prototypical walk   Prototypical run

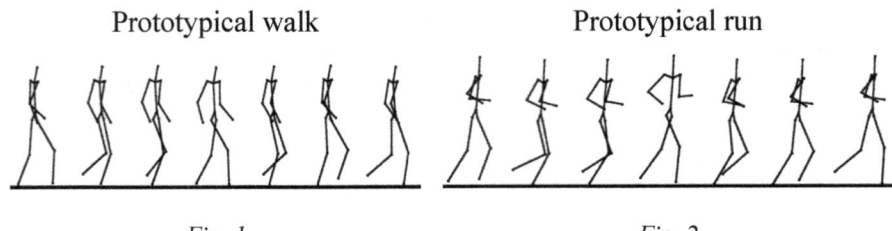

Fig. 1   *Fig. 2*

However, we shouldn't forget that, as visual prototypes, they reflect only the subclasses of typical movements. As a matter of fact, movements belonging to one category—for example, versions of a human run—may differ considerably in appearance, while movements belonging to different categories (such as running and walking), on the contrary, may be very similar. Yet a native speaker can always identify them easily and unambiguously. On the one hand, it doesn't matter to him "whether it is Carl Lewis circling a track or Grandma running to the telephone" (Golinkoff et al. 2002: 604). Both kinematic images are identified as running, regardless of how different they are. On the other hand, a native speaker doesn't have a problem distinguishing between "Grandma's" run and fast walk, although in either case her feet don't lose contact with the floor, and her run doesn't have any "flying" phases, which are typical features for distinguishing a walk from a run. In addition, there isn't much difference in speed between her fast walk and her slow run.

The speaker usually knows ("sees") when a person is running and when walking. In real life there aren't any "in-between" cases, when human locomotion could be called either running or walking at the same time. This begs the question, "What features does the speaker use to distinguish between a run and a walk?" As we have seen, the feature "high speed" doesn't serve the purpose (one person's walk can be faster than another's run), just as the feature "loss of contact with the surface" doesn't.

Queen's University (Kingston, Ontario), headed by Nikolaus Troje (cf. Troje 2002; http://www.biomotionlab.ca/Demos/BMLwalker.html; and http://www.biomotionlab.ca/Demos/BMLrunner.html, access 05.04.2018). The site shows not only typified animations of the human walk and run (both point-light and linear), but also more specific patterns for such locomotion of humans, determined by the sex, speed, etc. The animations demonstrate the human ability to instantly recognize not only the type of locomotion as such, but also its variable attributes: whether it is a man or a woman, stout or skinny, happy or sad, nervous or relaxed.

1.3. An analysis of prototypical definitions. Let us focus on definition (2). To show that it cannot perform the role of function and differentiate between a walk and a run, we will use a technique typical for the reference-based approach. We will think up several exotic, borderline examples of human locomotion that will fit the definition (2) *Čelovek idët* 'The person is walking' while referring to other types of motion: 'The person is running/crawling/riding'.

(a) *Čelovek bežit* 'The person is running'. An elderly person can run without losing contact with the ground. Pushing off from the ground, he maintains a contact with it which is of the touching type (a shuffling run). No native speaker of Russian would call this kind of motion a walk, in spite of the fact that all the conditions from the visual description (2) are satisfied.

(b) *Čelovek polzët* 'A person is crawling'. Imagine the following situation: a captive is lying on his back with his bound arms on his chest. If he started moving, each foot in turn pushing off from the ground, such motion would also satisfy definition (2). However, in reality, the man would be crawling, not walking.

(c) *Čelovek edet* 'A person is riding'. Imagine an adult sitting on a child's bicycle and propelling himself by pushing off with his feet from the ground; or, similarly, imagine a boy on a sled moving along an even, snow-covered road by pushing off with his feet. In either case the motion satisfies definition (2), but a native speaker will say *Čelovek/mal'čik edet* 'The person/boy is riding', not *Čelovek (mal'čik) idët* 'The person/boy is walking'. That a person uses an artifact as a means of locomotion is not an issue here; an old person may move his feet while using a special prop on wheels for support (a walker), but he would certainly be walking, not riding.

Of course, one could argue that (a)–(c) are rare, specially devised examples that may be ignored. However, such an argument cannot be accepted if our goal is to define the characteristic feature of **all** direct referents. Let us stress again: the sought feature cannot be singled out by 'adjusting' definition (2) and excluding examples (a)–(b). True, example (c) may be excluded if the component 'X is relatively tall' is added to definition (2). Yet this component doesn't help to solve the problem. Imagine a metamorphosis such as a fly growing the size of an elephant. In such a case it couldn't be said about the fly that it *crawls*. If, reversely, an elephant becomes the size of a fly, we still cannot say that it *crawls* (the number of legs doesn't matter—a turtle crawls, even though it has four paws).

1.4. Basic meaning of the verbs *idti* **'walk' and** *bežat'* **'run'.** Within the framework of a referential approach the meaning of a sensory (concrete) verb is represented by the pair 'Prototype → Function' (cf. definition (7) in § 1). Let us explore the functional components of the verbs *idti* and *bežat'*, taking definition (2) as a prototype. It should be reminded that the semantic distinction between these verbs consists in either retaining (*idti*) or losing (*bežat'*) contact with the surface.

A detailed referential analysis by Koshelev (1989) has shown that, in order to come up with adequate definitions for these verbs, causal features must be used that are not perceptually given: 'push', 'support', 'unsteadiness', etc. The resulting descriptions of a walk and a run are, essentially, as follows.

A walking person, A, **propels himself** over a surface (using his inner forces). While moving, he alternately **pushes off from the surface with his supporting foot**—the one that bears the weight of his entire body—and gradually, without losing support, transfers the weight of his body to the other foot, which now becomes a support, and so on. At the same time, and throughout the motion, A keeps his balance, being in an unsteady position (he may fall down on the surface over which he is moving), unlike in the case of steady motion by pushes described by the verb *polzët* 'is crawling'.

A phrase such as *Čelovek A bežit* 'Person A is running' designates a similar type of locomotion with one difference: the person **repeatedly loses support** when moving his body weight from one limb to the other.

These observations allow us to formulate the following functions:

(3a) *Čelovek A idët po poverxnosti v punkt Z* 'Person A is walking over a surface to point Z' (Function) =
   (i) Person A, pursuing his **spatial goal to get to** point Z, propels **himself**;
   (ii) he alternately **rests** his feet on and pushes off from the surface, each time moving his body weight from one foot to the other,
   (iii) not at any time **losing the support** of the surface;
   (iv) at any given moment the position of A is **unsteady**.

(3b) *Čelovek A bežit po poverxnosti v punkt Z* 'Person A is running over a surface to point Z' (Function) =
   (i) Person A, pursuing his **spatial goal to quickly get to** point Z, propels **himself**;
   (ii) he alternately **rests** his feet on and **pushes off forcefully** from the surface, each time moving his body weight from one foot to the other,

(iii) **momentarily losing the support** of the surface after each push;

(iv) at any given moment the position of A is very **unsteady**.

Description (3a) takes care of all three counterexamples given above. In situation (a) an elderly person is running and not walking because he periodically loses the support of the surface, maintaining only a **touching contact** with it (this is usually called a 'shuffling run'). The gliding run of a ballerina can be described in a similar way, as can the run of a goose about to attack its rival. At first, it walks slowly, then picks up speed, spreads its wings and starts to run. Although its feet still don't lose contact with the ground, to us it is undoubtedly a run: the wings give impetus to its pushing feet, and the goose's repeated loss of ground support becomes obvious.

In situation (b) the person is not walking but crawling because the **bulk of his body weight** does not move from one foot to the other. Finally, in situation (c)—a ride on a bicycle—the pushing foot never serves as a support and there is no transfer of the body weight from one foot to the other.

The example of the 'fly and elephant metamorphosis' can also be easily explained. A fly "grown" to the size of an elephant finds itself in an unsteady position as it needs special efforts to keep balance, while an elephant 'shrunk' to the size of a fly continues to be in an unsteady position, which means that the type of locomotion doesn't change: it is **walking**, not **crawling**. The function formulated above (3a) also covers the case of a person walking on crutches: the system of supports remains the same since the sore foot and the crutch function synchronously as a single paired support. A similar example would be the walk and the run of a skier who uses not only his feet (and skies) for support and for pushing off from the ground, but also the ski poles. In (3a)–(3b) it is specified that the supporting foot carries the weight of the **entire** (or **almost entire**) body, and with each push this weight moves to the alternate foot. If pushes with the ski poles play only an auxiliary role, the skier is walking (*idët*) or running (*bežit*). If, however, pushes with the poles are the skier's main propelling power, he is riding (*edet*).

Thus, a short list of distinctions between a walk and a run (as an answer to the question asked in the heading of sub-section 1.2) is as follows:

a desire (goal) to **quickly** move to location Z,

to push off **forcefully** with one's feet,

momentarily **to lose the support** of the surface,

to be in an even **more unsteady** position.

By coupling the functions (3a) and (3b) with the prototypes for a walk and a run (cf. Fig. 1 and 2), we get the final definitions:

(4a) *Čelovek A idët po poverxnosti v punkt Z* 'Person A is walking over a surface to point Z' (basic meaning) =

The Visual Prototype of a walk	→	Function (3a)
A does not move fast	→	(1a) Person A, pursuing his **spatial goal to get to** point Z, propels **himself**; (2a) he alternately **rests** his feet on and **pushes off** from the surface, each time moving his body weight from one foot to the other; (3a) not at any time **losing the support** of the surface; (4a) at any given moment the position of A is **unsteady**

(4b) *Čelovek A bežit po poverxnosti v punkt Z* 'Person A is running over a surface to point Z' (basic meaning) =

The Visual Prototype of a run	→	Function (3b)
A moves fast	→	(1b) Person A, pursuing his **spatial goal to quickly get to** point Z, propels **himself**; (2b) he alternately **rests** his feet on and pushes off forcefully from the surface, each time moving his body weight from one foot to the other, (3b) **momentarily losing the support** of the surface after each push; (4b) at any given moment the position of A is very **unsteady**

For a walk, a detailed schema of tying the causal features of the function to the visual features of the prototype is given in the table below. It contains pairs of visual features of the prototype (their verbal descriptions from Apresian's definition (2)) and causal features from (3a) that are attributed to the visual ones.

Čelovek A idët 'Person A is walking' PROTOTYPE (2) Typical visual features	Čelovek A idët 'Person A is walking' FUNCTION (3a) Obligatory functional features
(1) A is moving, not fast, to point Z,	(1a) A, pursuing his **spatial goal** to get to point Z, propels himself,
(2) **shifting his feet up and down** over a surface,	(2a) alternately **resting** his feet on and **pushing off** from the surface without losing support, each time moving his body weight from one foot to the other,
(3) not at any time **losing contact** with the surface;	(3a) not at any time **losing the support** of the surface;
(4) A is in a vertical position	(4a) at any given moment the position of A is **unsteady**

As it is, features (1a)–(4a) are hypotheses, causal interpretations of the visual features (1)–(4) perceived by the speaker when establishing reference. However, these visual features allow other interpretations prompted by the context of A's locomotion. For example, a person can, by shifting his feet up and down, not rest upon and push off from, but merely touch the surface, not propelling himself (as in a situation with a drunk or sick person being led while supported on both sides).

A historical digression. The force-dynamic features of walking and running used in our analysis were long ago identified and described by Bernstein (1990) within the framework of a different discipline, namely, physiology of human locomotion:

The walking locomotion consists for each foot in the alternation of the time intervals of **support** and **transfer**. The time interval of transfer for a walk is longer than the time interval of support (for running, it is quite the opposite); therefore, there are intervals when it is still the time of support for one foot, while the time of support for the other foot has already begun. We call these intervals times of **double support** (p. 341).

Our description, based on Bernstein's but adapted for the needs of cognitive semantics, illustrates the importance of data from other fields of research.

Another theoretical framework useful for cognitive semantics was developed within the theory of recognition of biomotions. Our interpretation of a physical action as a dual structure of the type "visual Prototype—

Function", offered in a number of publications (Koshelev 1989, 1990 and 1996), is close to the dynamics approach to action recognition (Runeson 1977; Runeson and Frykholm 1983; Bingham et al. 1995; Shipley 2003; Bingham and Wickelgren 2008). According to this approach, the specifics of an action's kinematics are determined by the action's dynamic features, in particular by its force-dynamic features (such as gravitation, shock, etc.) that are hidden from direct perception. However, humans identify perceived actions precisely by these dynamic, but not outward features (kinematics). Without going into more detail, it is sufficient to mention a curious fact from the history of cinematography. A good idea of the principles of perception of locomotion events is given by Hollywood's attempts to produce natural movements of fictitious creatures. For example, in the first versions of the *Godzilla* movie the monster, despite all the efforts of the animators, moved just like a mechanical toy. Only after Hollywood had learned to use good dynamic models to produce appropriate movements did the movements of such creatures—for instance, the dinosaurs in *Jurassic Park*—start to look realistic (Bingham and Wickelgren 2008: 276).

An observation made by Johansson (1976) directly bears on this fact: in the process of recognition of point-light displays of human motion it is not just the structure of connected segments that is perceived; it is something more, as the observers in the experiment distinguished between point-light displays of humans and similar displays of segmentally connected dolls.

1.5. An animal's run (quadrupedal locomotion). The function of a run (3b), formulated, for clarity, only for humans, remains in effect for any bipedal agent such as an ostrich, a chicken, a penguin, etc. For quadrupedal locomotion (*a cat/dog/horse is running*) the meaning of the verb *bežat'* 'run' has a **different prototype** but the **same function** (3b).

For evidence, let us consider the run of a horse as an example. For this purpose, we will use the concept of **paired take-off limbs**. If a horse is running at a trot, it simultaneously pushes off now with the first and the third legs, now with the second and the fourth legs, that is, alternately with one or the other paired take-off limb, each time losing contact with the surface and the support thereof.

If a horse is running at a gallop, it alternately pushes off from the ground now with forelegs and now with hind legs (the front and the rear paired limbs) and the support schema of its motion is the same. As a result, the basic meaning of the verb *bežat'* 'run' has two prototypes: Prototype 1 for humans and bipedal creatures (two single take-off limbs, vertical position of the body) and Prototype 2 for quadrupeds (two paired take-off limbs, horizontal position of the body). Both prototypes have the same function for interpreting the run of both bipeds and quadrupeds. The resulting definition can be stated as follows:

(5) *Čelovek/lošad' **bežit*** 'A person/horse is running (basic meaning) ≈
   (Prototype 1: A person is moving fast, **shifting his feet up and down** and periodically **losing** contact with the surface;
   Prototype 2: A horse is moving fast, **synchronously shifting pairs of legs up and down** and periodically **losing contact** with the surface) →
   Function: A person/horse, pursuing the goal to quickly get to a certain point in space, alternately **rests** his/its **single/paired limbs** on and **pushes off forcefully** from the surface (with one foot/leg or, synchronously, with a pair of legs), each time moving his/its body weight from one limb to the other and momentarily **losing the support** of the surface while **keeping unsteady balance**.

Thus, the basic meaning (5) specifies a single category 'X bežit', where X is a bipedal or quadrupedal individual.[16] This category is defined by one function and has two prototypes.

> **Note.** In the case of a running quadruped, loss of contact with the surface does not always happen. For example, if a dog is running at a gallop, the contact with the surface and the support thereof are lost; and if it is running at a trot or simply moving its legs chaotically, there may be no loss of contact while the support may be lost or greatly weakened (just like in the case of a shuffling human run). However, this not so obvious borderline between the walk and the run of a dog or cat does not make these categories fuzzy. For a dog or cat, just like for a human, walking and running are **different biomechanical systems of locomotion**, and transition from one to the other is abrupt. Outwardly it is manifested in the absence of what might be called a dog's or cat's fast walk. Unlike humans, a dog can't incrementally increase the speed of its walk; it either walks, moving its paws not fast,

---

[16] Such an integral interpretation is found in many explanatory dictionaries. Definition (5) simply substantiates it—compare the examples in the definitions of the verb *bežat'* 'run' above: *Ot lesa napererez banditu bežal policejskij* 'From the wood, a cop was running to intercept the bandit'; *Oleni begut na vodopoj* 'The deer are running to a watering place' (Aktivnyj Slovar' 2014, I). Cf. also **bežat' 1**. To move fast, by forceful pushes of the legs disengaging with the ground. *Lošad' bežala rysju* 'The horse was running at a trot' (Ushakov, I: 102).

or runs, rapidly shifting its paws. The run itself in this case may be either fast (at a gallop) or not (at a trot). Of course, a well-trained horse can shift between different speeds and types of walk in response to cues from its rider.

The verb *idti* 'walk' in its basic meaning can be used when speaking about not only bipedal, but also quadrupedal locomotion if it is not fast: *Koška/lošad' idët* 'A cat/horse is walking'. However, some languages do not allow for such extension of the basic meaning, cf.:

> In Modern Chinese [...] the verbs of autonomous locomotion (without the instrument of transport) remain exclusively the prerogative of mankind. Only a bipedal being with a vertically aligned body may become an agent of the verb *zou* 'walk'. Species from the animal world can only *pa* 'crawl', *pao* 'run', *tiao* 'jump', *you* 'swim' or *fei* 'fly' (Aoshuan 2004/2012: 20, 22).

1.6. The different goals of walking and running. Now the necessity to introduce the notion of A's spatial goal—'to move in space to some point Z'—will be illustrated. First of all, it should be kept in mind that, as far as the basic meanings of *walk* and *run* go,—'to move in space to some point Z' is **the main goal**. For example, an athlete circling a track at the stadium in preparation for the contest has a different main goal, which is not to move to a point in space but to exercise, grow some muscle, test his stamina, etc. Therefore, in our opinion, this kind of locomotion is named *run* only metaphorically, not in its basic meaning. If, however, a runner is taking part in a contest, a phrase such as *On bežit* 'He is running' is used in its direct meaning since the runner's main goal is to move across the finish line as fast as he can.

One of the reasons to distinguish between the basic and metaphoric uses of the verbs *idti* 'walk' and *bežat'* 'run' is that their primary meanings have to do with the goal of changing one's location in space. Under natural conditions a dog or an ape uses the locomotion technique of walking or running only for its intended purpose. This purpose remains the one and only for animals. A dog wouldn't run to exercise or show off before its master (as a young athlete might do in front of some girls to attract their attention). It may run around in excitement, though, greeting its master. As for humans, a great many derivative goals have emerged in the course of cultural evolution, and walking and running are used as a means to reach these goals.

As an illustration, consider some of these derivative goals and the actions caused by them. Imagine a gardener who has made a new path in the garden, covered it with a layer of sand, and is now trampling on it. While doing this, he is moving down the path in full accordance with points (2a)–(4a) from the function (3a), pushing off from the surface of the path with his feet, etc. However, a native speaker would not say in this case that *The gardener is* **walking** *down the path* (the manner of his locomotion would be somewhat different: he stamps his feet on the path, etc.). Something different would be said: *The gardener is* **trampling** *the path.* Similarly, a ballerina may run across the stage while doing some dancing pas, yet it would be inappropriate to say in this case that *The ballerina is running.* The phrase to be used would be *The ballerina is dancing.*

As can be seen, the manners of walking and running (as types of motion, cf. Talmy 1975) may be used by humans not only for locomotion, which is the primary goal, but also for other, non-spatial goals. Therefore, in description (3a) the spatial goal of a human using the manner of walking—to move to some point Z—must be explicit.

> **Note.** There may be a hierarchy of goals for a running person. For example, if a ballerina runs across the stage while doing some dancing pas she may be pursuing a spatial goal as well: she knows the direction and the place to which she must run. This goal, however, is subordinate to another, main goal: **to express** by means of a run **some aesthetic idea or a feeling**. It is for this reason that the locomotion of a ballerina using the manner of running may be called *run* only metaphorically. The same is true of the example with the gardener. Although he makes steps (shifts his feet) along the path, that is, uses the manner of walking, his main goal is not spatial and his motion, therefore, would not be walking.
>
> It should be noted that as soon as the main goal of locomotion becomes a non-spatial goal it radically changes the shape of the walk/run, including the pattern of steps, the position of the body, the movement of arms, etc. The ballerina does not think about how to best make a step or a jump but about how, by means of a step or jump, to express the grace and lightness of the movements, the aesthetic essence of her dance. That is why, from a trivial point of view, a ballerina's walk or run on the stage appear quite artificial. For example, she doesn't step on her heels but on the tips of her toes, turning her feet sideways, etc. Similarly, the actual movements of the gardener's feet change noticeably when making a step. He tries to raise his feet higher, stamp harder on the path, etc. It is these special features that help us identify the trampling of a path in the gardener's walk and the dance in the ballerina's run. It should be stressed that a walk or a run may be accompanied by other simultaneously pursued goals. For example, a

person may walk on tiptoes in order to sneak somewhere unnoticed, or to avoid waking someone up. While the shape of his walk changes quite substantially, the motion event remains, undoubtedly, that of a walk as its main goal is still locomotion.

The logic of the above argument necessarily leads to the following question: "Can such segregation of walking and running from other actions (dancing, trampling) be precise and discrete?" A simple analysis allows for a positive answer to this question. As a matter of fact, human goals possess a fundamental property, that of discreteness; one goal does not turn into another through a sequence of intermediate goals. This is what our examples show: the gardener moves, pursuing a spatial goal, but only to reach another, main goal—'to trample the path'. However, neither the goals nor their locomotive manifestations merge; we easily recognize the components of a stepping motion responsible for locomotion, and the components responsible for trampling. The same applies to the ballerina's motion on the stage.

Let us sum up the cognitive-linguistic definitions of the human walk and run and, accordingly, the semantics of the verbs *idti* 'walk' and *bežat'* 'run'. The structure of such definitions must, generally, have three hierarchical levels:

(1) kinematics—the outward appearance of the motion event without indication of its causes (lower level);

(2) force dynamics that generate it—the support-and-force schema of the motion event (mid-level);

(3) human goals that motivate the dynamics (upper level).

As a result, certain causal relationships emerge between these levels: **'a foot rests on a surface'** (dynamics) THEREFORE "the foot is in contact with the surface" (kinematics). Similarly, 'A person has a goal—to move to a different location' (the level of goals)—THEREFORE "his legs **alternately rest on and push off from the surface**" (dynamics). But the opposite is not true. If a foot is in contact with the surface, it may rest on it or it may not (when the contact is of the touching type); if a foot rests on and pushes off from the surface, the causes of this motion event may vary considerably.

Such a three-level representation of human locomotion shows that, in order for a walk or a run to be recognized (identified) by the appearance of a motion event (its kinematics), it is necessary to

(i) reconstruct the dynamics (the causal schema) of the motion event, and

(ii) identify the main goal of the motion event.

Only after this has been done can a native speaker establish whether a phrase such as *X idёt* 'X is walking' or *X bežit* 'X is running' is a correct reference to the observed locomotion.

Such complicated and subtle analysis of an observed motion event is done automatically and almost instantly by the human cognitive apparatus. Therefore, it eludes our attention, creating a false impression that an act of naming (reference) is quite simple and is based on the prototypical features of the action referent.

1.7. Metaphoric uses of the verbs *idti* 'walk' and *bežat'* 'run'. The verbs *idti* and *bežat'* have many figurative meanings as extensions of their basic meanings. This is not a topic covered in this book. Only a few examples will be analyzed to show the importance of **strict distinction between the prototype and the function** for the mechanism of forming 'semantic derivatives' (metaphoric meanings).

Uses such as *Poezd/mašina/paroxod idёt*, lit. 'The train/car/ship is walking' ('There's a train/car/ship coming'), are metaphoric. The motivating feature here is the function feature 'Person A, pursuing his spatial goal to get to point Z, propels himself' from (4a). Abstraction of this feature ('unidirectionality of the changes') serves as a motivation for uses such as *Časy idut*, lit. 'The clock is walking' and *Vremja idёt*, lit. 'The time is walking'.[17]

In a phrase such as *Čelovek šol na meste*, lit. 'A person was walking on the spot', the metaphoric use of *šol* is motivated by the resemblance between the action referent and the prototype from (4a). In a phrase such as *Kukla idёt*, lit. 'The puppet is walking', referring to a marionette moved by the strings tied to its legs, *idёt* is also used metaphorically as it corresponds to the prototype but does not correspond to the function. If, however, the strings cannot be seen and the viewer thinks that it is a 'live' puppet, such a use becomes basic.

Let us now look at the verb *bežat'* 'run' and recall its definition (2a) from Aktivnyj Slovar' (2014, I: 177, 181):

bežat' **1.1.** MEANING. *A1 runs to A2 from A3 over A4 to (do) A5* 'A living being, A1, moves at a run to place A2 from place A3 over surface A4 in order to A5'.

---

[17] It should be noted, for the sake of comparison, that in the northern dialect of Mandarin Chinese the verb *zou* 'walk', used exclusively with reference to humans ('a bipedal being with a vertically aligned body'), also allows for such metaphoric uses, cf.: *Biao bu zou le* 'The clock stopped walking' (Aoshuan 2004/2012: 22).

begóm ADV. MEANING. 'Evenly moving by alternate pushes of feet from a surface so that, for a moment, the feet completely lose contact with it'.

Clarifying this meaning, Iu. Apresian in his commentary specifically points at 'extended uses' applied to a very fast locomotion, especially in cases of an emergency:

> *K komu bežat', ot kogo ždat' pomošči?*, lit. 'Who to run to, who to expect help from?'; *Nado nemedlenno bežat' k vraču / v miliciju*, lit. 'It is necessary at once to run to the doctor [to the militia']; *I togda on pobežal k soavtoru, čtoby tot pomog emu xot' čto-to vspomnit'*, lit. 'And then he ran to his co-author, so he could help him to remember at least something' (G. Gorin) (Aktivnyj Slovar' 2014, I: 177)

However, this definition lacks the important feature "moves **fast**" usually found in explanatory dictionaries. Without it, the motivational underpinning of such extended (metaphoric) uses that would explain how they are derived from the basic meaning remains unclear.

Similar difficulties arise in explaining the motivation of metaphoric uses such as *Kofe/moloko bežit*, lit. 'The coffee/milk is running'. The definition given in Aktivnyj Slovar' (2014, I: 183)—'Liquid substance, A1, is flowing over the edge of the vessel, A2, which contains it, because it is boiling'—allows for incorrect phrases such as **Voda/ᵖsup bežit*, lit. 'The water/soup is running' (= 'The water/soup is flowing over the edge of the sauce-pan because it is boiling').

Here is a more precise definition of this metaphoric meaning (it is motivated by a similar feature of the basic meaning, 'X moves fast to a different location'):

(6) ***A bežit*** (metaphoric meaning: *kofe/moloko bežit*, lit. 'the coffee/milk is running') = 'Liquid substance A contained in a vessel, when starting to boil, quickly (and entirely or for the most part) moves from inside the vessel into the external space'.

This definition does not allow for a phrase such as *Voda bežit, lit. 'The water is running', because, unlike coffee or milk which, at boiling point, **quickly and entirely 'jump' out of the vessel**, water does not 'jump' out of the sauce-pan but overflows by small amounts. As for soup, it can overflow by substantial amounts if it is thick enough. This makes soup closer to coffee, which is why the phrase ?*Sup bežit*, lit. 'The soup is running', is less questionable. And the phrase, *Kaša bežit*, lit. 'The kasha is running', e.g. about cooked thin semolina, is already quite normal, because when it reaches boiling point it quickly spills out in even more substantial amounts. However, we cannot say this about thickly boiled pearl barley slowly pouring over the edge of a saucepan. As can be seen, in such explanations the degree of correctness of metaphoric reference can be traced to the referent's features—the amount and speed of its overflow when boiling.

The arguments given above show once again the subtlety and precision of the metaphorization mechanism. Native speakers, as if acting in unison (without any prompt or the help of a dictionary) automatically attribute the feature "quickly move to a different location" to boiling milk or coffee and don't attribute this feature to boiling soup or water.

1.8. Aphasiac loss of a word's figurative meanings. Another piece of evidence in favor of strict differentiation between the basic and figurative meanings of a word may be seen in examples of disorder in the use of figurative meanings by patients diagnosed with dynamic aphasia syndrome (Akhutina 2014: 34)—even though their ability to use a word in its basic meaning is fully retained. Thus, patient N. with dynamic aphasia syndrome, when tested for the preservation of the system of meanings for the word *idti* 'walk', did not have difficulties in producing phrases such as *Čelovek idёt* 'A person is walking', *Lošad' idёt*, 'A horse is walking', *Ljudi idut* 'The people are walking', but was unable to produce phrases such as *Avtobus/tramvaj/poezd idёt*, lit. 'A bus/streetcar/train is walking'. Moreover, he insisted that such phrases were incorrect or questionable and that it was more appropriate to say *Avtobus/tramvaj/poezd dvižetsja* 'A bus/streetcar/train is moving'. Akhutina (2014: 37) comes to the following conclusion: "Patients with dynamic aphasia retain, first of all, direct, nominative meanings, while meanings from the second group [context-dependent, derived from the basic meaning] tend to drop out".

After a series of lessons with N. aimed at restoring the system of the verb's figurative meanings (at these lessons he was told that phrases such as *Sneg idёt*, lit. 'The snow is walking', *Časy idut*, lit. 'The clock is walking', *Vremja idёt*, lit. 'The time is walking' were correct) it became obvious that not only had he lost the figurative meanings as such but also the ability to form them. For example, after the lessons N. "persistently argued that the expression *Zemlja idёt vokrug solnca*, lit. 'Earth is walking round the sun' is no less correct or commonly used than the expression *Zemlja dvižetsja vokrug solnca* 'Earth moves round the sun'" (Ibid.: 36). Apparently, what happened as a result of the lessons N. had had was an extension of the basic meaning of the verb *idti* 'walk' and **not a restoration of the mechanism for the formation of metaphorical meanings**.

2.   A comparative description of the verbs *idti* 'walk', *bežat'* 'run', *polzti* 'crawl', *prygat'* 'jump' and *šagat'* 'step/stride'

2.1. The verb *polzti* 'crawl'. Consider the phrase *A polzët* 'A is crawling'. Its referents can vary quite remarkably; not only humans, dogs, cats, etc. can crawl, but also insects, reptiles, worms, and pinnipeds. In some cases, as a result of a simple push, all of A comes into motion (e.g. a turtle or a fly); in other cases, only a part of A does (e.g. a snake, caterpillar or seal). The main specific feature of this manner of motion is A's **unquestionable steadiness**. As a rule, such steadiness is due to additional supports that retain their supporting function throughout the entire duration of the push. For a fly or caterpillar, these supporting parts are the temporarily inactive "limbs" (they do not participate in any push); for a crocodile, it is a permanently inactive part (the tail), and for a human, his belly.

Note that the ability of a fly or spider to crawl over the surface of a wall or a ceiling has to do with the inactive limbs which do not participate in the actual push but cling to the irregularities of the surface, thus preventing their bodies from falling down.

The following examples show the relevance of the supporting parts for language. As soon as a human doing the leopard crawl or a crawling dog raise themselves a little, thus losing the support of the body, or a fly raises itself on its rear legs, the utterance *A polzët* 'A is crawling' becomes incorrect because the steadiness of the position is lost (A may fall). This point of view also receives support from the following consideration: one cannot say about a beetle that has been crawling over a surface that it fell on this surface; it can only be said to have turned over. As a Russian saying puts it, "Polzja, upast' nel'zja" 'A crawl is safe from a fall' (lit. 'Crawling, one can't fall'). Yet we will say *upal* 'fell' about a tiny little gnome the size of a beetle, should we find him in a similar situation.

It is important to stress that an additional support is referentially relevant only on condition that it provides the motion event with the **required** steadiness. As soon as motion by pushes becomes unsteady, the crawling agent becomes a walking or a running one. Imagine a metamorphosis in which a mutant crocodile walks on long legs; in such a case we would use the verb *idët* 'is walking' regardless of the tail, which provides an additional support. Similarly, if a human has an additional support such as a handrail, crutches, a companion's arm, etc., his walk or his run cannot be called a crawl. All this gives us a reason to believe that in the mind of a native speaker of Russian at least three normative degrees of steadiness in the manners of impact-generated motion (by pushing off) are stored which determine the classification of such motion: low, medium, and high.

The functional component of the basic meaning of the verb *polzti* 'crawl' is thus formulated as follows:

(3c) *A polzёt po poverxnosti v punkt Z* 'A is crawling over a surface to point Z' (Function) =
   (1c) A living being, A, pursuing its **spatial goal to get to** point Z, propels **itself**;
   (2c) it alternately **rests** its limbs on and **pushes off** from the surface, each time moving **part of its body weight** from one limb to another and using the rest of the body to maintain **support**;
   (3c) at any given moment the position of A is **fully steady**.

2.2. Classification of the manners of impact-generated motions. Let us begin our consideration of this classification by giving some definitions.

The functional meanings of the phrases *A idёt/bežit/polzёt* 'A is walking/ running/crawling' possess the following property: they all describe an **impact-generated motion of A**, that is, a **sequence of elementary locomotions on a solid surface caused by pushes performed by A** (let us agree to call them **self-pushes**). Such iterative structure of the manners of motion caused by pushes allows us to assume that for their classification it is enough to describe (a) the type of self-push and (b) how these self-pushes relate to one another.

A comparison of self-pushes shows clearly that in (3c)—*polzti* 'crawl'— the self-push is the most steady, in (3a)—*idti* 'walk'—it is much less steady, and in (3b)—*bežat'* 'run'—it is the least steady (the support is periodically lost). Therefore, let us agree to call the types of self-pushes, as well as the manners of motion they constitute, **steady** (*X polzёt* 'X is crawling'), **locally unsteady** (*X idёt* 'X is walking'), and **globally unsteady** (*X bežit* 'X is running').

To understand how adjacent self-pushes are connected, let us introduce into our consideration the verbs *šagat'* 'step/stride' and *prygat'* 'jump' (in the sense 'repeatedly'). As a locomotion, *prygat'* differs from *bežat'* 'run' not so much in the type of self-push as in the degree of its separateness, its ability to be isolated from repeated movements as a motion event. In *running* self-pushes are short and continuously turn into one another, constituting a **com-**

plete motion. In *jumping* they are independent and separate (they may be long or short, continuous or interrupted by pauses), i.e. they constitute a **composite** motion. This is also true for the verbs *idti* 'walk' and *šagat'* 'step/stride'.

Let us draw a brief summary. The basic meanings of the phrases *A polzët/ idët/bežit/prygaet/šagaet* 'A is crawling/walking/running/jumping/stepping' define the classification of locomotion events (A's impact-generated motion) shown in the following table.

Motion verb	Type of impact-generated motion set by the functional meaning of the verb	
	Degree of A's steadiness when moving	Complete/composite motion
A polzët	steady	integral
A idët	locally unsteady	integral
A bežit	globally unsteady	integral
A prygaet	globally unsteady	composite
A šagaet	locally unsteady	composite

Comparing this table with the table of types of X's motionless positions set by the verbs *stojat'* 'stand', *sidet'* 'sit', *ležat'* 'lie' and *viset'* 'hang' given in § 3, section 2.4, we can see that the most important classification feature in both cases is the degree of A/X's steadiness. It may be hypothesized that this fact reflects the **universal human** (species-specific), rather than the **nation-specific** (Russian), classification of human locomotion and position in space.

3. Basic meaning of the verb *exat'* 'go/ride/drive'

3.1. Definitions of the verb *exat'*. Let us turn to the dictionary and scientific definitions of the verb *exat'* to see what kind of information they provide.

(7) ***exat'* 1.** To move in a certain direction using some means of transportation. *Exat' na paroxode, na poezde, na velosipede, na lošadjax, v sanjax* 'To go by boat, by train, on a bicycle, by horse, in a sleigh… (Ozhegov: 182).

(8) *X edet iz Y v Z na W* 'X is going from Y to Z by W' = 'X is moving from Y to Z because X is on W which is moving from Y to Z, and movement from Y to Z is among X's goals' (Apresian 1974/1995: 108).

The picture we see here is already familiar: both definitions describe the prototype (typical action referents) of this verb. There isn't a close lexical correlate to the verb *exat'* in English, which is why an Englishman learning Russian will have difficulty in acquiring this lexical item. Nevertheless, the above definitions will help him to quickly understand the meaning of the verb in a particular (con)text.

3.2. The Function of the verb *exat'*. Imagine now an opposite situation. An Englishman sees a person riding a horse at a gallop. Guided by definitions (7) and (8), he will designate the observed motion with the phrase *Čelovek edet na lošadi*, lit. 'A person is riding on a horse'. However, to a native speaker of Russian this phrase would sound at least odd, while if the horse is walking the phrase becomes correct.

As can be seen, to establish the reference of the phrase *Čelovek edet* (in its actual meaning) a native speaker of Russian uses some other property (the function) that characterizes **all** direct referents of the verb *exat'* rather than just its typical referents. What features constitute this function?

The example of a galloping horse suggests the first feature—"support of the surface for the moving object must be continuous". If a horse is walking or running at a trot one can say *Čelovek edet na lošadi* because the rider, through the intermediacy of the horse, has the continuous support of the road. If, however, the horse is running at a gallop (when the support of the road is periodically lost), to a native speaker of Russian such a phrase appears questionable, the more so the longer the horse's strides. In such a case the verb *skačet* 'is galloping' should be used.

A second feature that deserves attention is "**motion over a surface**" (not above or under a surface), hence the incorrectness of the utterance **X edet v podvodnoj lodke*, lit. 'X is going in a submarine'.

A third feature is 'for X, **the surface over which X moves must be solid**'. Indeed, it is not good to say about a person moving on a light raft down a river, *on* ['he'] *edet*. Note that the expression 'solid surface' is used terminologically, meaning 'the surface that serves as a support for X's steady motion, preventing X from falling through'. Thus, an utterance such as *My edem na paroxode*, lit. 'We are going on a ship', is acceptable (cf. this example in definition (7) above) even though the motion is on the water and not on the ground. Compare also the incorrect phrases **X edet na lëgkom parusnike / v lodke*, lit. '*X is going on a light sailing ship / in a boat*' (here the surface of the water is inevitably interpreted as not solid) and the correct phrases *X edet na voennom korable / na vodnyx lyžax / na vodnom velosipede*, lit. 'X is going on a man-of-war / on water skis / on a paddle boat'; here the surface may be interpreted as solid (= ensuring sufficient steadiness of the vessel and, therefore, of X).[18]

Let us now consider the role of 'means of transportation' mentioned in the scientific definition, (8). As a detailed analysis shows, while typical for the manner of motion designated by the verb *exat'*, it is not taxonomically relevant. Note, first, that X's use of a means of transportation does not mean that *X edet* 'X is going'. When an acrobat in a circus moves around the arena inside a rolling wheel, rotating with the wheel, it cannot be said about him, *on edet*. The acrobat has the continuous support of the arena but **his domain of support changes**. Examples like this suggest that, in the process of *ezda* 'going' as a manner of motion, the means of transportation serves as a **fixed area of support for** X.

Now we will show that it is important that the **area of support for the moving** X, provided by the solid surface, be **constant**. It is the means of transportation that serves as such a permanent area of support, an interlayer between X and the surface over which X is moving. However, such an interlayer may be absent, as in *Malyš edet s gory na spine / na nogax* 'The little boy is going down the slide on his back / on his feet'.

Here are some examples of the verb *exat'* used to refer to particular kinds of locomotion: a boy may be on a scooter, pushing off from the ground with one foot, or on a sled; he can be skating or riding a bicycle or an elephant, just as he can ride his friend, sitting on his back and using, so to speak, a 'walking', rather than 'going', means of transportation. Finally, he can go (*exat'*) down a slide on a piece of plywood. In all these examples the role of 'means of transportation' (a scooter, a pair of skates, an elephant, etc.) is virtually the role of a 'piece of plywood', providing the boy with a fixed area of support. Clearly, a pair of skates, scooter, sled, bicycle, etc. play the role of just such a 'piece of plywood', and a car, an elephant, or the boy's friend play the role of a self-propelled 'piece of plywood'. Thus, it is correct to say *Xokkeist edet (pod"exal) k treneru*, lit. 'The hockey-player is going (has gone) to the coach', if he is sliding by inertia while the ice under his skates provides constant support and his area of support, therefore, does not change. If this is not the case, one should say *Xokkeist bežit (k vorotam sopernika)* ('The hockey-player is running towards the rivals' goal').

---

[18] For a light X, the water surface may sometimes be interpreted as solid even in the case of impact-generated motion, cf.: *Pauk/vodomerka bežit po vode* 'A spider/water strider is running on the water'.

Thus, 'means of transportation' is an optional feature of the process of going (*ezda*) and should be excluded from the function. However, it must be present in the prototype in the form of a typical craft or vehicle.

Finally, one should emphasize the relevance of the feature 'movement from Y to Z is among X's goals', cf. (8). Indeed, if X is traveling against his own will, it is more appropriate to say that he is being transported (*ego vezut*). Neither can one say *on edet* if a person has slipped and is sliding down a slope.

The function may thus be defined as follows:

(9) *Čelovek X edet* **'Person X is going'** (Function) = X is moving
   (a) over a solid surface,
   (b) continuously using it as a support (direct or mediated)
   (c) for his fixed area of support;
   (d) this motion is X's goal.

The characteristics given in (9) set a clearly defined category of direct action referents 'Čelovek edet' of the phrase *X edet.*

3.3. Basic meaning of the verb *exat'*. In spite of its obvious simplicity, definition (9) is not intuitively transparent; it cannot be used in an explanatory dictionary because the expressions 'a solid surface' and 'fixed area of support' are, essentially, terms which require a special and rather detailed explanation. In other words, the function in (9) does not adequately explain how the perceived verb is understood. At the same time, it is capable of ensuring that the verb has reference, a transition from the 'live' image *Čelovek dvižetsja* 'A person is moving' to the phrase that designates this motion: *Čelovek edet.*

Now, the sought meaning may be formulated as follows:

(10) *Čelovek edet* (basic meaning) =
   Prototype: A person is moving, being on/in an object which is moving over a surface →
   Function: A person is moving over a solid surface, continuously using it as a support (direct or mediated) for his fixed area of support; this motion is X's goal.

3.4. Reference procedure. To continue our analysis, imagine the speaker observing a person on a bus which is in motion. In order to be able to say about this person *Čelovek edet*, the native speaker must make sure that in the "live image" he perceives all of the features listed in the function in (9) obtain: the person is moving over a solid surface using it as a support for his fixed area of support, this support is continuous, and he is moving of his own free will.

Such check-listing is performed by the cognitive procedure of reference which turns on automatically and gives an instant result—in this case, a positive one.

And indeed, firstly, the person has a **fixed area of support**—the floor and the wheels of the bus—by which means he is using the road for support. Secondly, via the wheels this area is **continuously supported** by the road. And, thirdly, the road is a **solid surface**.

Following this procedure, one can say about the moving bus *Avtobus edet*—only metaphorically, however, since the bus does not have a goal. But, apart from this, its motion meets the requirements of the function (9). Now the fixed area of support is the wheels of the bus which are continuously supported by the surface. True, there is no means of transportation in this case (an interlayer between the bus and the surface); however, it is not obligatory and is not mentioned in the function.

The same reference procedure tells us that it cannot be said about the wheels of a moving bus *oni edut* 'they are going' because the area of support of the turning wheel is constantly changing. Therefore, the utterance *Koleso edet 'The wheel is going' is incorrect.

Thus, we see that, in establishing the reference of a word to an observed motion event, not only the prototype and the function are used but also the cognitive procedure of reference that tests the correctness of the interpretation of the motion event by means of the function (9). In testing whether the given motion event corresponds to the function, this procedure relies on a whole arsenal of intellectual means such as various kinds of encyclopedic knowledge about the image, logical inference, formation of likely hypotheses, etc.

3.5. Impact-generated (*idti*) vs. nonimpact-generated (*exat'*) motion. Let us illustrate the linguistic relevance of the dichotomy "impact-generated vs. non-impact-generated motion".

The movement of a snake is very much like sliding. The metaphoric nature of the utterance *Zmeja skol'zit* 'The snake is sliding' is explained by the fact that a snake's motion is generated by impacts and not by low friction. The phrase *Lyžnik bežit* 'The skier is running' is correct if the skier moves by pushing off with his feet (skis). The moment such pushes cease, the phrase becomes incorrect. For example, if the skier pushes only with his ski poles the phrase *Lyžnik edet*, lit. 'The skier is going', is the sole possibility, since the poles perform only the pushing but not the supporting function (there is no transfer of the skier's body weight from one pole to the other). A similar example with a cyclist pushing off from the ground with his feet was given above.

Now let us consider the essential properties of the nonimpact-generated motion that the verb *exat'* refers to. This manner of motion constitutes the main opposition to impact-generated motion. As has been shown, the verb *exat'* designates the motion of an individual who (a) has **continuous** support of the surface and (b) retains a **constant** area of support from the surface.

Summing up the analysis of the manners of motion of X over a solid surface, we may conclude the following: one of the main features by which such manners of motion are classified in Russian reflects the type and the manner of X's support provided by the surface. Based on this feature, two types of locomotion are distinguished: (1) **impact-generated**, whereby X's means of support on the surface is **not constant** and X 'rolls over', that is, travels in space moving the weight of his body from one place to another by self-pushes; and (2) **nonimpact-generated**, whereby X's means of support on the surface in the course of his movement to a new location is **constant**. Impact-generated motion falls into several subtypes (*polzët* 'is crawling', *idët* 'is walking', *bežit* 'is running') depending on how X's support changes, while nonimpact-generated motion falls into subtypes (*edet* 'is going', *skol'zit* 'is sliding', *katit* 'is rolling') depending on the type of X's constant support (for *edet* and *skol'zit* the area of support is constant, while for *katit* and *katitsja* (reflexive) the area of support changes).

The above arguments may be illustrated by the utterance *Mašina edet*, lit. 'The car is going'. The car's motion on wheels, while impact-generated **from the point of view of physics** (the wheels keep pushing off from the surface), does not correspond to the **linguistic type of impact-generated motion** since there is no transfer of the weight from one wheel to another.

§5. The structure of lexical polysemy

1. Reference in lexicology

Our starting premise is that the lexical polysemy of a notional word is founded on its basic meaning, which "reflects our understanding of a 'piece of the world'" (Vinogradov 1977: 163). However, as was shown in chap. 2, the basic meaning can be explicated only through a detailed analysis of the word's referential function. Meanwhile, the issue of how this function should be described in lexicological theories has been given hardly any attention. This is true, for example, in regard to the framework developed by the Moscow School of Semantics (MSS) led by Apresian, the lexicological research carried out by Talmy (1975 and 1985), Lakoff and his co-researchers (Lakoff 1987;

Brugman and Lakoff 1988; Norvig and Lakoff 1987), Evans (2009 and 2015), and others.

Iu. Apresian, explaining the specificity of *The Active Dictionary of Modern Russian* (Aktivnyj Slovar' 2014, I), compiled by a group of linguists under his leadership, points out that "the purpose of active dictionaries is to meet the needs of spoken communication" (p. 6). This contrasts with the purpose of passive dictionaries, which is to provide information about a word necessary for understanding this word in any randomly chosen text. At the same time, there is no mention of the information necessary for the correct reference of a word in each of its meanings. Yet, as has been shown above (§ 4, section 1.7), absence of such information may lead to incorrect use of a word.

To describe the semantics of motion verbs (their basic meanings), Talmy (1985: 57, 61) used the following elements: 'Motion' (change of location), 'Figure' (the moving object or agent), 'Ground' (the reference-object), 'Path' (the course followed by the Figure object), 'Manner' (the mode of motion: shifting one's feet, flapping one's wings, etc.), and 'Cause' (the cause of motion). But all these elements are visual characteristics of a motion event; and as we have seen more than once, visual characteristics cannot serve as a basis for strict differentiation of the various types of motion events described by motion verbs. These elements are also too general. For example, the difference between walking and running lies in a rather subtle distinction between the manners of these motion events and requires a completely separate analysis, see § 4.

In Lakoff's (1987) theory of radial categories, the structure of a category includes a central subcategory and noncentral subcategories that are predicted from the central subcategory—the analogues of basic and derived (= figurative) meanings. At the same time, "there are no general principles that can predict the noncentral cases [subcategories.—*A. K.*] from the central case" (Lakoff 1987: 379). Consequently, the issue of correctness in predicting noncentral categories is ignored. This issue is also present with regard to Evans's (2009 and 2015) framework, which ignores the issue of a word's reference when it is used in its basic and figurative meanings ("sense extensions"). As noted by Murphy (2011) in his review of Evans (2009), the following "intriguing problem" is not discussed by Evans:

> [...] some sense extensions are possible but others are not. [...] It is common to use an author's name to refer to his or her work but not the publisher's name (*I have been reading Dickens/*Knopf*). In a book-length treatment of how words take on different meanings in different contexts, one would expect some mention of the limits on this phenomenon. [...] e.g.

newspaper can be used to refer to the company that publishes it, but *book* cannot [...] (Murphy 2011: 393, 394).

An answer to Murphy's question may be found in section 4.2 below. A more detailed discussion of the approaches used by Apresian, Lakoff, and Evans will be offered in section 4.

2. Lexical polysemy

2.1. The unbounded character of lexical polysemy. Words are not just polysemous in the sense of having several customary meanings that are well known and given in dictionaries. The essential feature of lexical polysemy is its potential unboundedness. In communication speakers often use words **impromptu**, in new senses which they haven't known or come across previously (cf. Leshchëva 2014: 37, 192). However, despite the novelty of such occasional word use, the listeners do not, as a rule, experience problems in understanding the speaker's meaning.

For example, a boy may run up to his mother, almost out of breath, breathing rapidly, and hear her say: *Ax ty, moja sobačka* 'Oh, my little doggie'. The mother in this case likens her son to their little dog whose breath is also rapid and shallow. Note that this is not a feature typical of dogs. It is typical of a particular dog that both the mother and the son know well. Therefore, there may be as many such occasional uses of the word *sobaka* 'dog' as the number of individual features identified by the dog's owners, which is infinitely many.

A minute after the occasional use of the word *sobaka* described in the example above it will be forgotten, and no one will remember about it afterwards. It will not be used repeatedly in other situations and will not be committed to memory by the speakers; that is, the word will not acquire a new customary meaning. Maslov (1987: 104) called such word uses "transient".[19] Sometimes, however, such uses may become frequent and "take root" in the long-term memory of the speakers, thus becoming a new customary meaning. And vice versa, if a customary meaning stops being used regularly, it becomes forgotten and falls out of use.

This begs the question: why does language need such a unique feature that sets it apart from all other sign systems—the employment of its units in occasional uses? The answer is that language needs this feature because it uses a

---

[19] In the English literature the terms "irregular" and "regular polysemy" are used (for a detailed discussion see: Pinker 2007: 114).

finite set of linguistic means to describe the infinite diversity of the world around us. The attention of humans is continuously drawn to the new phenomena of the perceived and conceived world (objects, actions, aspects, states, etc.), and we must be able to describe them using the available linguistic means.

That being said, it becomes clear that one of the central problems in cognitive semantic theory is explanation of the mechanisms responsible for new occasional uses of linguistic items. In this context, the pioneering research conducted by Paul (1970: chap. IV) in the late 19th century should be mentioned. He studied the types of changes of lexical meanings and the mechanisms responsible for such changes: metaphor, hyperbole, litotes, euphemism, metonymy, irony, etc. Out of the great number of derivational mechanisms identified by Paul the most important are the mechanisms for metaphor and metonymy. By applying them to the components of the basic meaning of a linguistic item, represented as a dual structure in (1) below, the speaker forms all other meanings, including the occasional uses of the given item.

2.2. Where do derivative meanings come from? A number of lexicographic definitions discussed previously (on p. 43) have shown that the **basic meaning of a sensory word** (concrete noun or action verb) may be represented in the form of a dual structure:

(1)   Basic meaning = visual Prototype → Function

where 'Prototype' defines the typical visual (more broadly, perceptual) feature of word referents, and 'Function' the functional (causal, intentional) feature characteristic of all word referents.

Our approach to the problem of polysemy may be briefly described as follows. **Derivative word meanings**, without exception, **are metaphors, metonymies, or synecdoches that arise from the basic meaning. All other mechanisms for the generation of derivative meanings, mentioned by many linguists starting** from Paul (Ibid.) and Bloomfield (1973: chap. IX), boil down to these three. This speaks to the uniqueness of the basic meaning of a word, with its "genetic" function with regard to other meanings. Evidently, this explains the tradition according to which word entries in explanatory dictionaries usually give basic meanings first, followed by derivative meanings; metaphoric meanings are often marked as *fig.* (figurative), while metonymic meanings are not marked in any way. For example, the word *cel'* 'target' has three meanings (Ushakov, IV: col. 1211)—one basic and two derivative:

(2) *Cel'*
  a. 'target—object for hitting when shooting or throwing';
  b. 'front sight—a small protrusion at the end of the barrel of a gun, used for aiming';
  c. *fig.* 'that which a person wishes to achieve'.[20]

For comparison, let us look at the referential definition of the basic meaning of the word *cel'*. For a concrete noun, the visual prototype in definition (1) is a paired entity: Prototype (typical image) of the referent + Typical Interaction with the referent, while the function is a causal characteristic of this pair (interactions with the referent): its relevance and value to the speaker. Accordingly, we get the following:

(2') *Cel'* (basic meaning) ≈
  'Prototype: "A visual image of a circle or some object (shooting mark) + A person aims a gun or pistol at this circle or object with the help of the front sight located at the end of the barrel (typical interaction)"[21]
  → Function: "A person wishes to shoot and hit this object (target)"'.

Let us elaborate on how both extended meanings are derived from the basic meaning. First, it should be noted that the mechanisms of metaphor and metonymy use non-verbal cognitive units. Metonymy is usually defined as the use of the name of one object (the referent) for that of another object (which is not the referent) contiguous to the former in space or time. In meaning (2b), the word *cel'* is metonymically transferred from the target to the front sight. The contiguity of the front sight and the target is not trivial: it is their temporary alignment on the line of sight. It is impossible either to understand this fact or to make a metonymic transfer guided only by the verbal explication of the basic meaning of the word *cel'* given in (2a).

Metaphor is the transfer of the name of an object (in its basic meaning) to another object (which is not the referent) which possesses a feature somehow similar to the feature of the referent object, thus suggesting comparison. In

---

[20] These three meanings, and in the same order, are given in the *Russian Academic Dictionary* (Slovar' Akademii Rossijskoj 1794, VI: col. 642–643]; the third meaning— 'Namerenie; konec, kotorago kto dostignut' želaet' [Intention; result that someone wishes to achieve]—is preceded by an asterisk *, the meaning of which is explained in the first volume of the dictionary as 'V smysle perenosnom' [in a figurative sense] (Slovar' Akademii Rossijskoj 1789, I: col. XVI).

[21] Other kinds of actions are not mentioned here, such as shooting with a bow and arrow, spear throwing and the like, because what is at issue is a typical action.

meaning (2c) it is the function that motivates the metaphor: 'A person wishes to shoot and hit this object (target)'. Used in this meaning, the word *cel'* names a similar but more general property characteristic of any purposeful action: 'that which a person wishes to achieve'. Clearly, in this case a metaphor cannot be generated without (a) a cognitive (non-verbal) description of basic meaning, as in (2'), and (b) a strict isolation, within this description, of the semantic (causal) function.

2.3. The system of meanings of the word *tarelka* 'plate'. The above framework can be well illustrated by the system of meanings of the word *tarelka*.

Basic meaning of the word *tarelka* =
　　　'Prototype: "a round flat object with slightly raised sides (referent prototype) + a person, using a spoon or a fork, puts small portions of food placed therein in his mouth + (typical interaction with the referent)" →
　　　Function (roughly): "a container made to be filled with a portion of cooked food (liquid or solid) for one person immediately before consumption"'.

　　The function explains the function of the referent and the cause of a typical interaction with it: a person puts apart his portion of food to consume it in a certain manner—by putting small portions of it in his mouth and eating them. On the one hand, the function helps eliminate the objects that do not correspond to the prototype. For example, a frying pan has the shape of a plate and one can eat off it, for example, fried eggs. But a frying pan cannot be called *tarelka* 'plate' because the function specifies that the container should hold 'a portion of cooked food'.

　　On the other hand, owing to the function, we use the word *tarelka* 'plate' to refer to objects that do not correspond to the prototype or typical interaction. For example, (a) pancakes may be served on a completely flat disposable plate, and (b) on a hike, baked potatoes are often taken from the plates with fingers and not with forks. The definitions found in dictionaries, such as "*Tarelka* ['plate']—a piece of tableware with a flat bottom and raised sides" (MAS, IV: 341) or '*Plate*—A flat and usually round dish that you eat from or serve food on' (Longman 2009: 1322)—are not suitable for describing these functions.

　　Here is a short list of figurative meanings and uses of the word *tarelka* 'plate'.

　　Metonymies
　　1. 'The contents of a plate'. *Dve tarelki s"el*, lit. 'He's eaten two plates' [He's had two platefuls].

2. 'The volume of a plate'. *Miska v tri tarelki*, lit. 'A bowl of three plates' [A bowl for three platefuls].

Metaphors

3. 'The flat brass plate of a percussive musical instrument' [cymbals].

4. 'An unidentified flying object of round shape'. *Letajuščaja tarelka* 'A flying plate [saucer]'.

5. 'A satellite aerial in the shape of a dish'. *Sputnikovaja tarelka*, lit. 'A satellite plate'.

6. 'A mechanical part that has the shape of a flat disc'. *Tarelka klapana* 'The poppet of the valve'.

To these customary meanings (usually given in dictionaries) a great number of occasional uses may be added; one could use the word *tarelka* to refer to a hat with flat sides, or a chandelier of a similarly flat design, etc.

It should be noted that a satellite aerial or a chandelier may resemble a bowl or saucer more than a plate; however, it would not be good Russian to say **miska antenny*, lit. 'the bowl of the aerial' / **bljudce ljustry*, lit. 'the saucer of the chandelier', while the expressions *tarelka antenny/ljustry*, lit. 'the plate of the aerial/chandelier', are quite acceptable, because metaphoric transfer works only for the most typical name of this kind of tableware, which is *tarelka*.

That such organization of polysemy is natural for language is proven by the fact that it may also be observed in the sign language of deaf-mutes. As Vygotsky (1986) observed,

> ...in the sign language of deaf-mutes touching a tooth may have three different meanings: "white", "stone", and "tooth". All three belong to one complex, whose further elucidation requires an additional pointing or imitative gesture to indicate the object meant in each case. [...] A deaf-mute touches his tooth and then, by pointing at its surface or by making a throwing gesture tells us to what object he refers in a given case (p. 134).

Thus the separate (non-contextualized) gesture "tooth" is used in its basic meaning 'tooth', which does not require additional elucidating gestures. The other two meanings are figurative meanings. The meaning 'white' is metaphoric (the motivating property "white" is the color of a prototypical tooth), and the meaning 'stone' is metaphoric-metonymic. In the latter case, the metaphor (the "tooth" gesture) is used to refer to something hard (it is motivated by the property 'the hardness of the tooth'), and the metonymy (indicating a stone by the "throw" gesture) is motivated by spatial contiguity and functional connection between the stone and the hand that throws it. All these meanings may be assumed to be customary as well.

The ability of a word to have occasional uses as well as customary ones, is a crucial feature of lexical polysemy. Occasional uses are not stored in the mental lexicon of the speaker; they are "invented" to meet the current communicative task and may be understood by others only via the knowledge of (a) the general mechanisms of such uses and (b) the context or referent situation. As an illustration, consider the dictionary entry for the word *obez'jana* 'monkey' (Ushakov, II: col. 629), with additional meanings (d) and (e) taken from other dictionaries.

Obez'jana 'monkey'.
Basic meaning.
    a. 'A four-handed mammal closest to man in body structure'.
Figurative customary meanings.
    b. 'a person given to imitating or mimicking others // that who makes faces, gives himself airs' (metaphor);
    c. 'a very unattractive person' (metaphor);
    d. 'a tactless, wild person' (metaphor).—*Ax ty, **obez'jana**! Ty u kogo sprosilsja-to?* [A. Ostrovskii] 'What a monkey you are! Who did you ask for a permission?';
    e. 'nutria, dressed to look like monkey fur' (metonymy).

Meanings a.—e. are customary. Apart from these meanings, the word *obez'jana* has many occasional ('transient') uses:

    f. 'a stooping person with long arms';
    g. 'an unusually hairy person';
    h. 'a person living in a tree';
    i. 'a person who scratches his left ear with his right hand';
    j. 'a person making a monkey's face', etc. [22]

The speaker's ability to generate, and the listener's ability to understand, new occasional uses of words show that we do not necessarily use a ready-made (customary) meaning of a word stored in the lexicon. Using the mecha-

---

[22] "This traditional view is exposed perhaps most fully, though quite laconically, in (Maslov 1987: 101–106), in the part dealing with lexical polysemy; all three types of word meaning are mentioned: basic, figurative, and occasional or "transient" (see also: Reformatskii 1996: 44–48). An alternative to this approach is the modern, or 'listing', tradition to view all meanings of a word as genetically equal and give them in dictionaries in the order of high to low frequency (see Apresian 2010a, 2010b and 2014).

nisms of metaphor and metonymy and the basic meaning of a word, the speaker generates an occasional use as needed for the purposes of communication. Then, this use is either quickly forgotten or, in other cases, remembered, and gradually becomes a new customary meaning (is committed to the speaker's lexicon).[23]

In summing up this brief exposition of our approach to lexical polysemy, its two distinctive features should be emphasized: (1) basic meaning is the basic concept the child originally forms over the first 12 months (before language acquisition begins) as a result of perceptual and interactional experience of the world, and (2) metaphor and metonymy are the main mechanisms of deriving figurative meanings from basic meaning.

Since basic meaning, as one of the central concepts of this book, will be discussed throughout its entire length, we will touch on it here only by way of illustration. Basic meaning defines a rather narrow class of objects or actions, and for this class all components of the function (interpretation), and only these components, are retained. For example, the basic concept-action ČELOVEK BEŽIT 'A PERSON IS RUNNING' includes the component 'the main goal of the motion is to move to another point in space'. For a child, in the course of formation of this concept (based on the child's own experience and observation of others running) this component is always present. Therefore, if we know that an athlete running on the track at the stadium is preparing for a contest (that is, the main purpose of his run is training, not reaching the finish line), the use of the verb *bežit* 'is running' to designate his motion will be metaphoric. It will be a new use of the verb, with a different final goal of motion. The outward resemblance of these motions will be the motivating feature in this case. Similarly, if a ballerina runs across the stage to express, through motion, her feelings, it will be more natural to designate her movement by the verb *tancuet* 'is dancing' and not the verb *bežit* 'is running'.

Our approach is close to the work of such contemporary researchers in this area as Kustova (2004) and Leshchëva (2014). Not attempting to give a detailed analysis of their work, we will mention only some points of disagreement.

---

[23] It is this ability of speakers to generate and understand occasional uses of word that makes the range of its meanings **potentially unlimited (unbounded, or endless polysemy)**. Leshchëva (2014: 193) quotes Stachowiak (1985), according to whom the average speaker of English uses close to 3,000 new occasional meanings per week (cf. Kustova 2004: 20, 22).

Consider the interpretation of the verb *sorvat'* 'pluck' given by Kustova:

> When a person plucks a flower or a fruit, he does not just detach it from the root or the branch; he irreparably SEVERS the organic ties between the object and the point of its attachment, bringing the natural growth of the object to a stop. This causes DAMAGE to the object [...] it is this implied damage on which a wide range of meanings of the verb **sorvat'** is based (*sorvat' kožu na pal'ce* '[lacerate] the skin on a finger' / *rez'bu* '[strip] the thread' / *golos* '[strain] one's voice' / *urok* '[disrupt] a lesson' / *peregovory* '[derail] the talks'); these meanings absolutely cannot be derived from the source meaning 'by pulling and detaching from the root, to begin to have (in one's hand)' (Kustova 2004: 39; original emphasis).

However, severing an organic tie does not always cause damage, cf.: *sorval speloe jabloko* '[he] plucked a ripe apple'. Therefore, the component 'cause of damage', which is the result of an interpretation of the outcome of the action "sorvat", is not part of the basic meaning of the verb *sorvat'* 'pluck'. This meaning may be specified by using a reference-based approach. Let us ask the question: to what parts of a plant can the action *sorvat'* 'pluck' be applied? The expressions *sorvat' plod/cvetok/list* 'to pluck a fruit/flower/leaf' are quite correct; by contrast, the expressions **sorvat' sučok / makušku / torčaščij koren'* 'to pluck a twig / the top / the protruding root' are not. It may be hypothesized that the action designated by the verb *sorvat'* is applicable only to an integral part of the plant. Yet, although a branch is an integral part of a plant, the expression **sorvat' vetku* 'pluck a branch' is incorrect. It may be inferred that the object must be not only an integral, but also a renewable, reproducible part of the plant. As a result, we arrive at the following interpretation:

(3)   *Čelovek sorval Y (cvetok, jabloko, list)* 'A person plucked Y (a flower/ apple/leaf)' (basic meaning) ≈ 'a person has a goal to be able to freely handle Y, a reproducible part of the plant (≈ to begin to hold Y in his hand) THEREFORE he takes this part in his hand and by a sudden strong movement detaches it from the rest of the plant'.

The use *sorvat' kožu na pal'ce* 'lacerate the skin on a finger' mentioned in the quote above is motivated by the same feature as in (3): 'by an abrupt movement a person detached a reproducible part (piece of skin) from the rest of his body'. For the other figurative uses—*sorval rez'bu* 'stripped the thread' / *golos* '[strained] one's voice' / *urok* '[disrupted] a lesson' / *peregovory* '[derailed] the talks'—the characteristic feature is not the detachment of Y, but its destruction: there is no thread, the voice is lost, the lesson is interrupted.

These metaphors are motivated by another feature in (3): 'the plant loses its part Y'. Now, consider the metaphor *Kartočnyj igrok sorval bank* 'The gambler broke the bank'. It is motivated by a third feature of the basic meaning in (3): 'by an unexpected (≈ sudden) move the gambler comes in possession of the entire prize sum (≈ gets the ability to manipulate it)'. While in the previous cases the object that lost its part, Y, was damaged, in this case it is the opposite: the gambler, breaking the bank, came into possession of it, profiting from it.

Consider another metaphor: *Veter sorval šljapu s golovy proxožego*, lit. 'The wind plucked the hat from the passerby's head'. Here, the passerby and the hat are interpreted by the speaker as a whole, and the hat as an integral part of this whole. To blow the hat off the head, some force must be applied; this makes this case similar to (3). As soon as this similarity disappears, the metaphor becomes incorrect, cf.: *Veter *sorval šljapu so stola*, lit. 'The wind plucked the hat from the table'.

As can be seen, the various motivating features singled out in the basic meaning of the verb *sorval* allow the speaker to use this verb to designate new actions that are not covered by its basic meaning.

While agreeing with many of Leshchëva's (2014) propositions, we cannot subscribe to her general thesis about what word meanings are represented in the speaker's lexicon: "The word is in the mind with its entire system of meanings, customary and potential, ready 'to surface on the first occasion' (Vinogradov 1977: 17)" (p. 194). As we have tried to show, potential meanings are not in the mind of the speaker such that they can 'surface' on the first occasion. Instead, in each use special mechanisms generate them from a word's basic meaning.

The structure of grammatical polysemy is discussed in chap. 4.

3. Supplement. Three contemporary approaches to lexical polysemy

In a brief survey of the three approaches used by Apresian (2005, 2010b and 2014), Lakoff (1986 and 1987), and Evans (2009 and 2015) given below, we will focus solely on an analysis of the principles of describing lexical polysemy. This will allow the reader to compare—on this parameter—these frameworks with the approach described above.

3.1. Iurii Apresian and the Moscow Semantic School's (MSS) framework.
There is a tradition in lexicography to give a definition of the basic (≈ most concrete) meaning of the word in a word entry first, followed by definitions of other meanings. In some contemporary dictionaries—for example, Longman

Dictionary (2009)—a quite different, synchronic principle is used to describe lexical polysemy. Basic meaning is not identified as primary, from which other meanings are derived; all meanings of a word are treated as typologically similar. The most frequent meaning is given first, followed by all other meanings in the order of their frequency, from high to low. Similarly, in a textbook by Shaikevich (2005: 141–154) one finds, along with the traditional approach, a modern understanding of basic meaning as the "most frequent" meaning.

The MSS has been developing a similar approach, treating all meanings of a word as typologically homogeneous and genetically indistinguishable. The list of a word's meanings defined in a dictionary starts with the meaning that is most "topical and elaborated in a given language", cf.:

> In most Russian explanatory dictionaries, the word CEL' has, as its first meaning, 'target, that which a person intends to hit using a weapon' [basic meaning.—*A. K.*], while the second meaning is 'that which a person intends to achieve' [figurative meaning.—*A. K.*]. However, […] in modern Russian the second meaning has an indisputable advantage over the first [it is more "topical".—*A. K.*], and it is this meaning that is given preference in the AD [Active Dictionary.—*A. K.*].[24]
>
> The main lexeme is followed by other word lexemes [its other meanings.—*A. K.*] depending on their semantic closeness to the main lexeme and to each other (Apresian 2010b: 72).

Thus, the dictionary entry for *Cel'* begins with the most elaborated in the [Russian] language (but also the most abstract) meaning: 'that which a person intends to achieve'. It is followed by the semantically close meaning 'target, that which a person intends to hit using a weapon' and, finally, by a third, semantically remote meaning, 'front sight—a small protrusion at the end of the barrel of a gun, used for aiming'.

Recall that in the framework of the reference-based approach, which leans on the lexicographic tradition, it is the "visual" meaning 'target' that is interpreted as basic. And it is this meaning that is the source of two figurative meanings: 'front sight' (metonymically linked with the target), and 'that which a person intends to achieve' (a metaphoric extension of a shooting action to a whole range of resultative actions; for more details, see section 2). Thereby

---

[24] Similarly, in Longman Dictionary (2009: 1803) in the word entry for *target* the meaning 'something that you practice shooting at', which is basic and should come first, comes only fourth according to its frequency.

the phenomenon of lexical polysemy is explained in a natural way, both as a synchronic state of the system of customary meanings of a word, and a process of diachronic change of this system, i.e. the possibility for a word to develop new meanings (to form occasional metaphors and metonymies). Moreover, this explanation makes clear why figurative meanings, which may be very far from the basic meaning, nevertheless fall within its scope—why, for example, the meaning 'front sight' belongs to the scope of meanings of the word *cel'* 'target'. It also makes clear the origin of such an abstract meaning as 'that which a person intends to achieve'.

The MSS lexicographic framework does not have answers to such questions. Rather, the MSS approach is oriented only towards representation of the synchronic state of lexical polysemy—**"taking stock" of the current range of customary word meanings** that exist at the time of their description. It is appropriate to mention here Potebnia's (1976) words:

> Usually, we study words in the very form in which they appear in dictionaries. It is tantamount to studying a plant as it appears in a herbarium—that is, not as a real living plant, but as something artificially prepared for the purposes of a study (pp. 465–466).

3.2. George Lakoff's theory. Unlike the MSS framework, Lakoff's radial semantic categories framework does not ignore the genetic relationships between word meanings. Lakoff distinguishes a central subcategory (an analogue of basic meaning) from noncentral subcategories derived from it. At the same time, he claims that "there are no general principles that can predict the noncentral cases from the central case" (Lakoff 1987: 379). An example of a radial category is provided by the category *Mother*: "there is a *central subcategory* ['mother' as such.—*A. K.*] […]; in addition, there are *noncentral extensions* […] (*adoptive mother, birth mother, foster mother, surrogate mother*, etc.). These variants are not generated from the central model by general rules; instead, they are extended by convention and must be learned one by one" (p. 91; original emphasis).

To describe the relationships between the central and peripheral subcategories, what is needed is, firstly, a *theory of motivation* (which has not been worked out) and, secondly, "cognitive models of various sorts: propositional, metaphoric, metonymic, and image-schematic" (p. 153). As can be seen, along with the metaphoric and metonymic models, two more general models are involved: propositional and image-schematic. It is these models that complicate the entire picture.

According to Lakoff, the meanings of the word *window* are formed on the basis of an "idealized cognitive model", cf.:

> In our cognitive model of a window there is both an opening in the wall and a glass-filled frame fitting into it. This correspondence provides *motivation* for using the same word to refer to both. In isolation, an opening in the wall doesn't have much if anything *in common* with a glass-filled frame. Independent of any knowledge about the way windows happen to work, there would be no objective reason to place these two very different kinds of things in the same category. The fact that the opening in the wall and the glass-filled frame have been brought together to fit one another physically and to correspond to one another in the same cognitive model seems to make them members of the same cognitive category—so much so that in sentences like the following the word *window* doesn't seem to distinguish between them.
>
> How many windows are there in your living room?
>
> Here *window* seems to refer, not to either the opening or the glass-filled frame, but to the combination (Lakoff 1987: 417; original emphasis).

However, here we are dealing with typical metonymy, which mysteriously escapes Lakoff's attention: the name of the opening in the wall made for letting in light and fresh air (and this is the basic meaning of the word *window*) is extended (by "contiguity") to the glass-filled frame fitted in the opening. This is quite similar to the classic metonymy *Kastrjulja kipit*, lit. 'The pan is boiling', where the verb *kipit* 'is boiling' is extended to refer to a contiguous object containing boiling water—a pan. It must be emphasized that in both cases the contiguous objects function as a single whole. For a metonymic transfer it is usually not enough to indicate spatial contiguity. For clarification, let us look at the same example, *kastrjulja kipit* 'the pan is boiling'. If the pan is sitting on a hot stove and the water in it is beginning to boil, it is quite correct to say *Kastrjulja kipit* because the pan is linked to the water not only by contiguity but also functionally, as it is involved in the process of heating the water. However, if the water in the pan is brought to a boil by an immersion heater, the phrase **Kastrjulja kipit* becomes incorrect. The contiguity of the pan and water is still there, but the functional link between them is lost.

In another part of his book Lakoff (1987) describes the formation of a noncentral category by image-schema transformation. Considering the examples, *The man ran into the woods* and *The road ran into the woods*, he argues that in the first case *run* is used for a case where there is a (long, thin) trajectory, while in the second case *run* is used for a long, thin object (a road). Thus, there is an image-schema transformation: TRAJECTORY SCHEMA $\leftrightarrow$

LONG, THIN OBJECT SCHEMA; "[t]his image-schema transformation is one of the many kinds of cognitive relationships that can form a basis for the extension of a category" (p. 106).

Yet this interpretation doesn't explain why, for example, the phrase *Uzkaja proseka bežala k reke* 'The narrow glade ran towards the river' is incorrect—considering that the aforementioned schema covers the glade as well. We see the cause of such incorrectness in that a glade doesn't have the function of a road, because a glade isn't made for running on; therefore, the verb *bežit* doesn't allow for a metonymic transfer to the glade.

This property of metonymy also explains the examples given by Murphy (2011) (see section 1 above), who observed that, for some reason, (1) an author's name can be used to refer to his work while the publisher's name cannot (*I have been reading Dickens*/*Knopf*), and (2) *newspaper* can be used to refer to the company that publishes it, but *book* cannot. This is because an author and his book form a functional whole, while a publishing company and a book published by it don't. A book is created by its author, but to the publisher it is an external, alien object, accidental to a certain degree. In the case of a newspaper the situation is different: the publisher of the newspaper is also its creator, therefore the metonymy is correct.

3.3. Vyvyan Evans' theory. According to Evans (2009; 2015), his theory of lexical concepts and cognitive models (LCCM) can easily explain generation of lexical meanings with the help of such notions as "lexical concept" and "cognitive model".

A lexical concept is associated with a word (a word form) and is a component of linguistic knowledge, the semantic pole of a symbolic unit that encodes a range of various types of schematic linguistic content (Evans 2015: 359). Lexical concepts provide direct access to various cognitive models.

A cognitive model is a complex of multimodal knowledge derived from experience, interoceptive systems, and propositional information (achieved via language, cultural learning, and so forth). There are two kinds of cognitive models in the LCCM framework: primary (directly accessed via the lexical concept) and secondary (sub-structures of primary models, indirectly accessed via the lexical concept).

The formation of lexical meanings is illustrated by the following examples containing the word *France*:

(3)   a. France is a country of outstanding natural beauty.
      b. France is one of the leading nations in the European Union.
      c. France beat New Zealand in the 2007 Rugby world cup.

As pointed out by Evans, the meanings of the word *France* vary across these sentences. In (3a) it is 'a geographical landmass', in (3b) 'a political entity, a nation state', and in (3c) 'the 15 players who make up the French Rugby team'. Such variation of meaning is explained, briefly, as follows. The word (form) *France* is associated with the lexical concept [FRANCE]. This concept is directly related to the first-level cognitive models GEOGRAPHICAL LANDMASS and NATION STATE. In addition, the latter is related to the second-level cognitive models NATIONAL SPORTS and POLITICAL SYSTEM.

The differentiated meanings of the word *France* arise as follows. In example (3a), the lexical concept [FRANCE] is related, due to the context, to the first-level cognitive model GEOGRAPHICAL LANDMASS, which is interpreted as a geographical region. In (3c), again because of the context, another first-level cognitive model is activated, NATION STATE, which is related to the second-level cognitive model NATIONAL SPORTS; and the latter model is interpreted as a team of French players who represent the French nation on the rugby field.

Here is one of the concluding propositions made by Evans:

> One reason for the distinction in literal versus figurative interpretations is a consequence of the cognitive model profile, and a distinction, therefore, in terms of the range of analogue concepts directly and indirectly accessed by the lexical concept. Literal interpretations involve activation of a primary cognitive model [...] while figurative interpretations involve activation of secondary cognitive models. [...] While there is unlikely to be a neat distinction between primary and secondary cognitive models, and while the distinction is likely to vary from individual to individual, and indeed across discourse communities, there appears to be a sound basis for making a qualitative distinction of this sort (Evans 2015: 366–367).

In keeping with this proposition, the meaning of the word-form *France* in (3a), 'a geographical landmass', may be interpreted as basic, and the meaning in (3c), 'the 15 players who make up the French Rugby team', as figurative (metonymic).

As Evans pointed out, because there isn't an explicit rule for the isolation of cognitive models and their hierarchical distribution, there is hardly a distinct division between primary and secondary models and, as a result, between literal and figurative word uses. This may easily be shown with some examples. In the sentence *France is a state with a democratic form of government* the word *France* is used in its basic meaning. However, a secondary cognitive model is activated in this sentence: the lexical concept [FRANCE] → NATION STATE → POLITICAL SYSTEM. Thus, in the framework proposed by Evans, the word *France*—in this case—must have a figurative meaning.

§ 6.   Appendix 1.
Excerpts from the email correspondence between
A. D. Koshelev and I. A. Mel'čuk (February—March 1995)

This Appendix is primarily of historical interest, and there are two reasons for this. First, it shows that the reference-based approach was formed about 20 years ago. In 1996, *Moskovskij lingvističeskij al'manax* (The Moscow Linguistic Almanac) published my article "Referentsial'nyj podxod k analizu jazykovyx značenij" ("A reference-based approach to analysis of linguistic meanings", p. 82–185), in which a detailed analysis of many typologically different linguistic meanings was offered, both lexical (concrete and abstract) and grammatical (aspect and tense). Second, the polemics in the correspondence clearly outline the antagonistic positions taken by each side and the impossibility to somehow reconcile one with the other. As may be seen from the contents of chapter 1, the situation has not changed in the years that followed.[25]

Letter № 1

From A. Koshelev to I. Mel'čuk
27 February, 1995

Dear Igor'!

[...]
I am glad that you asked me to read the volume and give some comments, because I was going to do it anyway. I doubt, however, that my comments will be very much to the point. You know, my interests lie in the field of semantics, which, I imagine, is hardly touched upon in your volume.

Speaking of semantics. Here (at a workshop at RGGU [Russian State University for the Humanities]) we've been engaged in semantic battles around semantic primes, definitions, and the like. At the latest workshop meeting (where Iu. D. Apresian's recent 1994 article "On the language of definitions and semantic primes" was discussed) I quoted your book "Opyt Teorii...", p. 22: "[...] the meaning [now I call it conceptual representation.—*I. M.*]

---

[25] Other excerpts from this correspondence are given in § 6 of chapter 2, where the concept ŽIVOJ—ŽIVOE [ANIMATE masc.—ANIMATE neut.] is analyzed.

of utterances […] lies outside the model 'Meaning ⇔ Text' and […] is formed by a separate mechanism (some other model) in the motion from meaning to text. If, for example, we speak about a verbal description of a particular situation, the procedure for correct translation of such a situation (which is the 'meaning content', or meaning, of the corresponding texts) must be supported by a special model 'World ⇔ Meaning'." And, finally, the crucial point (p. 12): "[…] At the same time, semantic representation must be a natural outcome of the function of the model 'World ⇔ Meaning' when the motion is reversed— when the given automaton somehow formalizes particular visual and other auditory 'impressions' from the world […]. Therefore, a semantic representation is also determined by the efficacy of the models 'World ⇔ Meaning' that use it." I used these quotations as an additional argument in support of my main thesis: A DEFINITION OF A NOTIONAL WORD MUST ADEQUATELY DESCRIBE A SET OF ITS DIRECT REFERENTS. [By no means!— *I. M.*] In other words, a human-like robot (one that has a body and a sensory apparatus similar to those of a human [along with the similar knowledge of referents.—*A. K.*]) should be capable of correctly relating a word to a fragment of the world (the referent) by using such a definition. An implementation of this thesis is the first step to the model 'World ⇔ Meaning' from the side of language (semantics).

Arguments in brief:

1. A child learns the semantics of notional words mainly through references (made by those around him along with his own), not through definitions. [Right, but that is HOW he learns, not WHAT he learns!—*I. M.*]

2. Throughout his adult life his referential capability is sustained and doesn't change [I'm totally unconvinced! I don't think this is the case!—*I. M.*] (therefore, the referential component of a word's meaning, which plays, in this respect, the role of the meaning nucleus (function), doesn't change, either). [It is the function that doesn't change, because it is 'recorded' in the language of 'human' interpretations of reality (predetermined by the abilities and needs of the human body and its psyche and thus independent of the knowledge a human has). And this is true not only of concrete lexical items (*derevo* 'tree', *dom* 'house', *stol* 'table', *lošad'* 'horse', *bežat'* 'run', *čitat'* 'read'), but of quite abstract items as well (*obman* 'deceit', *igra* 'game', *xoxma* 'gag', *izučat'* 'study', *vospityvat'* 'bring up'), not to mention grammatical meanings. It is sets of words' referents that change (are extended), because the correctness of relating a function to a referent depends on knowledge about the referent.—*A. K.*]

3. It becomes possible to verify, in a relatively objective way, the accuracy of a definition: it must cover all direct referents, and only those referents (whether an object or process belongs to the set of referents of a noun or a verb does not, as a rule, cause much controversy). [Linguists don't need such verification—this is not language.—*I. M.*] [Such verification makes it possible to study linguistic meanings by studying the linguistic categorization of the world these meanings induce.—*A. K.*]

4. In this regard, well-known definitions are substantially inadequate; there are, however, examples of adequate definitions (they have been discussed in detail at the workshop).

5. It becomes possible (a) to go over and beyond language boundaries when defining the meanings of words [And this is something that should NOT be done (by linguists!).—*I. M.*], and (b) to understand what meanings should be considered as primes: namely, those that would be elementary to a human-like robot (and not those that are most frequent in the definitions of linguistic meanings, according to Apresian).

Yours,

A. K.

Letter № 2

From I. Mel'čuk to A. Koshelev
2 March, 1995

Dear Alexey,

[...]

In your debate with Apresian, I'm 100% on Apresian's side. It all depends on WHAT semantic primes you're looking for. If those are mental or perceptual primes, then, of course, they should be sought in the world around us [in our mental representation of the world, to be more precise.—*I. M.*]. If, however, they are primes used to define the word MEANINGS (and NOT to define things!), they exist only in language. All smart non-linguists make the mistake of confusing LINGUISTIC meaning with PERCEPTION RESULTS.

Funny that you should quote me in the opposite sense! I'm convinced (have always been, and am quite sure now) that the definition of a word should NOT describe a set of its referents! To me, this is the central belief of a linguist. To be able to identify a horse, I must define the horse, and NOT the word *horse*. I think this is precisely what I tried to say in 1974.

I can't agree with your propositions—alas!—either globally or minutely. People identify things and actions very precisely, often being unable to name them even in their native tongue. Try and describe a complete stranger to me so I could identify him! Or express verbally how Georgians differ outwardly from Armenians or Jewish brunettes—even though the difference is quite obvious. No, language is a very singular matter.

Yours,

I. M.

Letter № 3

From A. Koshelev to I. Mel'čuk
3 March, 1995

Dear Igor',

I failed to make myself clear. The point in question is not at all the definition of the perceptual image of a set of referents. And not because it is hard to define verbally, but because IT IS NOT THE IMAGE that is the characteristic feature of a referent. Making reference to something, the speaker ATTRIBUTES a characteristic feature [= generalized interpretation.—*A. K.*] to an object/process based on its perceptual properties, observed behavior, and what not. There are Georgians who don't look like typical Georgians at all (for example, they may be the spitting images of Armenians or Jews), and there are Jews that look like Arians (fair-haired and blue-eyed). [But then they won't be identified as such by their looks!—*I. M.*] [Of course! *Georgian* ≈ '1) a typical appearance (prototype) and 2) a specific (to Georgians) system of behavioral stereotypes (function)'.—*A. K.*] It is not the appearance that defines a 'set of referents' for a nation. Let's consider an example.

Take a typical definition of the verb *dogonjat'* 'overtake':

(1)   *A dogonjaet* ['is overtaking'] *B* =
      '(1) A and B are moving in the same direction
      (2) A is behind B;
      (3) the distance between A and B is shortening'.

Doesn't it seem like a good definition?

Let's begin its referential analysis by identifying the process-referents this definition doesn't cover. [I can't see anything referential here; you keep speaking about meaning!—*I. M.*]

1. On some sections of the path, A and B may be moving in different, even opposite, directions (parallel streets racing), but the correctness of reference may still hold. Therefore, property (1) is not obligatory.

2. Athletes on the running track at a stadium. B may be ahead of A (locally, visually) but at the same time overtaking him. Property (2) is not obligatory, either (if we assume the usual meaning of the word *pozadi* 'behind').

3. The distance between A and B may grow on some sections of the path without affecting the correctness of reference (take the very same parallel streets racing). Property (3) is not obligatory.

Thus, what we have is a definition of the prototypical referent, or prototypical meaning: A and B are moving over a straight section of a highway (and this definition is similar to the definition of a Georgian by their typical appearance); but it is not a definition of the characteristic property of the referent (= description of the meaning sought for). [I absolutely don't understand the relevance of this!—*I. M.*]

Counter-example referents prompt the definition in (2) below. Let us begin by illustrating some novel concepts: let A be moving along a sinusoid toward a greater value of X, while B moves along axis X in the same direction. In this case, the sinusoid will be the path of A, axis X the path of B, and the points of intersection of the sinusoid and axis X will constitute the shared (congruent) path of A and B. Thus we have:

(2)   *A dogonjaet* ['is overtaking'] *B* =
      '1) A and B are moving along a SHARED PATH; [The concept (meaning) of 'shared path' should be defined linguistically!—*I. M.*] [But of course! *Sinusoid* and *axis* X are used for brevity.—*A. K.*]
      2) at every point on this path B arrives LATER than A;
      3) B's delay time is shortening, and it is very likely that A and B will reach some farther point at the same time'.

I believe that a 5-year-old child watching cartoons and establishing the reference of the verb *dogonjat'* 'overtake' makes use of a schema close to (2), and not to (1). [I don't know! I doubt it.—*I. M.*] And he ATTRIBUTES this schema to the perceived dynamical image, thus making it a referent.

Yours,

A. K.

Letter № 4

From I. Mel'čuk to A. Koshelev
6 March 1995

Alexey,

Your arguments are of much interest to me; but, alas, not all may be made clear in an email.

The point is that you've formulated a good [and quite linguistic.—*I. M.*] criticism of definition (1). But: if I can say about something, *X is overtaking Y*,

I can ALWAYS say that *X is behind Y*, and that the distance between them is shortening; this is inferred from language and has nothing to do with something in the real world.

BESIDES, people have a way to 'pull' clear and (relatively) simple linguistic meanings onto wild referents: that's a totally different tune!

No, I still insist—just as in 1974—that referents should not be taken into account (not generally, of course, but in LINGUISTIC semantics; then rules for matching meanings with referents will be needed, and this is where your considerations would become applicable).

[The following are what I would like to be distinguished. There are referents in the world: external reality; there are mental representations of these referents: conceptual representations; and there are linguistic representations of conceptual representations: linguistic meanings. The roles of referents and knowledge about referents may be different, depending on lexemes. For example, interpretations of *lošad'* 'horse' or *koška* 'cat' are based on knowledge about the referents, whereas interpretation of *podtalkivat'* (*kogo k čemu*) 'urge (sb. to do sth.)' isn't based on it at all!—*I. M.*]

[I would define the external world (referents) as a two-layered structure: (1) a layer of perceptual (available for perception) images, and (2) a layer of interpretations of such images—hypotheses about the images based on one's knowledge about them. Linguistic meaning has a similarly binary structure: prototype (generalized image)—function (generalized interpretation). Reference is a correct mapping of the function onto a suitable INTERPRETATION of the referent.—*A. K.*]

Yours,

I. M.

Letter № 5

From A. Koshelev to I. Mel'čuk
9 March, 1995

Igor',

[...]

Turning to the topic of semantics, I'd like to emphasize that, knowing how busy you must be, I don't NECESSARILY expect answers to the questions raised.

Let me give a response to your answer first. I agree that "if I can say about something, *X is overtaking Y*, I can ALWAYS say that *X is behind Y*, and that the distance between them is shortening; this is inferred from language and has nothing to do with something in the real world". And here's why:

The meaning of a notional word is made up of two components: the FUNCTIONAL component that defines the set of ALL direct referents (meaning (2) *A dogonjaet* 'is overtaking' *B*), and the PROTOTYPICAL component that defines the image of a typical referent (meaning (1)). Prototypical meaning (1) is the result of numerous performed or observed direct references (mappings of meaning (2) onto external world) crystallized in the linguistic consciousness of an individual. Thus, (1) is the superficial and CONSCIOUS component of meaning. Therefore, in a sentence (in the absence of a referent [to the hearer, who simply can't see this referent.—*A. K.*]), prototypical component (1) represents typified external reality (the typical referent). [Alas, I don't understand any of this.—*I. M.*]

As for your second proposition, "people have a way to 'pull' clear and (relatively) simple linguistic meanings onto wild referents: that's a totally different tune!", it isn't quite clear to me. Prototypical meaning (1) cannot be "pulled" onto "wild" referents [Hwhiiiyy cain't et? 'The distance is shortening, but in just such a wild sense'.—*I. M.*], while functional meaning (2) covers all of them. It seems reasonable to assume that this component belongs to the realm of the subconscious knowledge of a word's meaning and reveals itself only when "wild" referents are analyzed. [I don't understand.—*I. M.*]

Yours,

A. K.

Letter № 6

From I. Mel'čuk to A. Koshelev
17 March, 1995

Alexey,

[...]

I have a difficulty understanding you but am convinced that linguistic meaning should be defined WITHOUT any recourse to referents (although it is, of course, formed [in the speaker's brain.—*I. M.*] on the basis of referents both direct and indirect, just as you claim).

What you call "the subconscious knowledge of a word's meaning" is, to me, NOT a word's meaning (even a subconscious one); rather, it is a mechanism for mapping [the meaning of a word onto a concept, and then.—*I. M.*] onto a referent.

Yours,

I. M.

Letter № 7

From A. Koshelev to I. Mel'čuk
19 March, 1995

Igor',

[...]

About meanings. I agree that the referential component of a word's meaning should not be viewed as PURELY linguistic. It may be viewed as referential meaning, let us say. [Concept!—*I. M.*] But its direct relationship to language is beyond any doubt to me.

[Surely concepts relate to language (directly!).—*I. M.*] [In the chain, Word—Meaning—Concept—Referent that you suggest, the status of Concept ('mental representation of referents') is not clear to me. Why, not being a component of meaning, does it directly relate to language? If it is directly related to Meaning, where is the border between them (the boundary defined by the function of Concept)?—*A. K.*]

And here's why. Along with the function of communication, language also has another function which is no less important: to describe the perceived external world (a witness's tale, a reporter's account, and the like); this function cannot be performed without referential meanings [True!—*I. M.*].

It is these meanings (and not PURELY linguistic meanings) that lie at the basis of linguistic categorization of the world [True!—*I. M.*]. Hence the inevitability of going over and beyond the boundaries of language IN A STUDY OF LANGUAGE (analyses of referents, human perception specifics, etc.) [But this is not true. In such a case the object of study is not language, but linguistic behavior.—*I. M.*]

Letter № 8

From I. Mel'čuk to A. Koshelev
20 March, 1995

Alexey,

[...]

I absolutely agree that language doesn't function separately from the referents. I also agree that the function of description/analysis of the world is no less important for language than the function of communication. I would only like to SEPARATE (into levels) meanings and their relationship with words on the one side [This, and only this, is LANGUAGE.—*I. M.*], and referents [Via concepts; this is not language.—*I. M.*] on the other [Of course, it doesn't really matter WHAT is included WHERE and WHAT is named HOW. But the techniques of description in language (discrete, like algebra) and outside of language (continuous, like analysis) are QUITE DIFFERENT.—*I. M.*].

[I call the Function "meaning", because, just like the Prototype(s), it is DIRECTLY connected with Word: Function—Word—Prototype(s). With its functional meaning Word is oriented to the external world (referential function), while with its prototypical meanings it is oriented to text (communicative function). Moreover, Function, in fact, made concrete in Prototypes, plays the role of MEANING INVARIANT.—*A. K.*]

It would be fascinating to talk to each other, wouldn't it?

It seems the time has come for me to start planning a trip to Moscow again.

Yours,

I. M.

§ 7. Appendix 2.
An infant's early acquisition of the laws of nature

1. An infant's view of the physical world

Early on, infants begin to understand and use verbs of physical action and spatial orientation (posture verbs) such as *udarit'* 'hit-PF', *tolknut'* 'push-PF', *padat'* 'fall-IMP', *brat'* 'take-IMP', *stojat'* 'stand', *viset'* 'hang', *bežat'* 'run', etc. Meanwhile, the meanings of these verbs contain non-trivial conceptual components. For example, the meaning of the verb *udarit'* 'hit-PF' contains invisible force-dynamic characteristics, such as 'one object transfers the force of motion to another object', and a causal relationship THEREFORE that connects the effects of these invisible forces: 'THEREFORE the other object suffers a shock'. Similarly, to understand the verbs *padat'* 'fall-IMP' or *stojat'* 'stand', infants must have some ideas of the invisible force of gravity, the support a motionless object must have, the locus of an object's center of gravity, conditions under which an object falls, etc.

It is only natural to ask: how and when does an infant acquire such knowledge? The data from numerous experiments show that these and many other conceptions of the laws of the physical world are formed by the age of 13–14 months—much earlier than one would think. Thanks to such formed conceptions, infants can already at an early age understand force-dynamic interactions and cause-effect relationships between objects in the surrounding visible world. It must be emphasized that the fact that infants can grasp such interactions and relationships between objects is determined exclusively by infants' cognitive development. Acquisition of the lexicon of the child's mother tongue does not substantially affect this process.

Supportive evidence can be found in how infants view the world in general. As recent cognitive research has shown, already during the first year an infant acquires diverse and detailed knowledge about objects, living beings, and interactions between them (Spelke et al. 1992 and 1995; Baillargeon 1994, 1999 and 2002; Carey 2009; Murphy 2002; Sergienko 2006; Subbotskii 2007, *inter alia*). Thus, at 6 months, infants begin to distinguish between inanimate objects and living beings. They already understand that, unlike humans and animals, inanimate objects are incapable of self-propulsion (for example, they cannot begin to move without some external influence from another object, or come to an abrupt stop in the absence of an obstacle), nor can they move purposefully: circumvent an obstacle, halt before it and move in reverse, etc.

> For example, in an experiment by the psychologist Elizabeth Spelke, a baby is shown a ball rolling behind a screen and another ball emerging from the other side, over and over again to the point of boredom. If the screen is removed and the infant sees the expected hidden event, one ball hitting the other and launching it on its way, the baby's interest is only momentarily revived; presumably this is what the baby had been imagining all along. But if the screen is removed and the baby sees the magical event of one object stopping dead in its tracks without reaching the second ball, and the second ball taking off mysteriously on its own, the baby stares for much longer.[26] Crucially, infants expect inanimate balls and animate people to move according to different laws. In another scenario, people, not balls, disappeared and appeared from behind the screen. After the screen was removed, the infants showed little surprise when they saw one person stop short and the other up and move; they were more surprised by a collision (Pinker 1994: 423ff.).

Quite remarkably, infants begin to acquire such knowledge very early, not later than 2 months of age. From that moment on, their knowledge expands and grows in depth extremely quickly, following a number of steps in infants' cognitive development. It involves, among other things, the dynamics of acquisition of the laws of the physical world and, in particular, the nature of

---

[26] See (Spelke et al. 1992 and 1995). On how infants, at 12 months, interpret perceived motion as purposeful and optimal, see (Csibra et al. 2003; Gergely et al. 1995).— *Author's note.*

force-dynamic interactions between physical bodies. These phases in the cognitive development of infants are so distinct that they can be easily observed by conducting simple experiments.

Consider two examples directly bearing on acquisition of semantics of the verbs *udarit'* 'hit-PF' and *padat'* 'fall-IMP':

1) Collision of objects. At 2.5 months infants reason that if a ball rolls down a gently sloping ramp and hits an object standing at the foot of the ramp, the latter must move even if the ball is very small and the object very large. However, at 6 months infants understand this kind of interaction much better. They already know that the larger the ball, the farther the object is expected to move, and vice versa.

2) Object's stability before fall. At 3 months (but not earlier), infants expect an object which has no contact with any other object to fall, for example, like a box that was placed on a platform but, after being pushed, loses contact with it. If, however, the box has contact with the platform (for example, it is placed against the side of the platform) it isn't expected to fall. By 5 months infants can already distinguish between two types of contact between the box and the desk (ensuring support or not ensuring support), but they still do not take into account the amount of support required for the stability of the box. Infants believe that the box will be stable if only 15% of its bottom portion rest on the platform while the rest of it hangs in the air (Baillargeon 1994: 134). At 6.5 months infants already take this factor into account and expect the box not to fall only if most of the box's bottom part rests on the platform. However, infants still cannot predict stability of objects that are more complex in shape. For example, infants will expect a wooden object shaped like the letter F to remain stable when placed on the platform, because the entire bottom portion of the stem rests on the platform. At 12.5 months, however, they already don't think this will be the case, as they can predict stability of an object of a complex shape—which inevitably involves identification of the object's center of gravity (Carey 2009: 90–93; Baillargeon 2002: 52–54; Kognitivnaja psixologija 2002: 367–369).

2. Formation of causal relationships

Let us take a closer look at how infants perceive a "hitting" event—collision of a moving object with a motionless object that is in the moving object's path. Here, a similar picture can be seen: infants become aware of regularities in the behavior of colliding objects by stages.

In a series of experiments conducted by Leslie (1984), infants at 2.5 to 3 months of age watched as one object (a red block) moved up to another object (a green block) and stopped, while the green block slowly came into motion ("direct impact"); this did not cause any surprise in infants (they ceased to pay attention to the event rather quickly). However, if the red block stopped just a little short of the green block and the latter, nevertheless, started to move ("impact without collision"), infants were surprised by such a development. After 3 months of age, infants were also surprised to see one object (a red block) come up to another object (a green block) and stop, while the latter started to move not at once, but with a delay ("deferred impact"). Infants showed the same reaction when they watched a similar motion of squares of light instead of blocks (which is understandable because, at this age, infants do not make much of the shape, size, and color of the object observed). These and many other similar experiments allowed the researchers to conclude that a **necessary condition for perceiving a direct impact as the bearer of causal relationship between the subsequent motions of the blocks is the spatio-temporal continuity of their motions**.

It has also been shown, in another series of experiments, that at 7 months infants distinguish a 'direct impact' event from the continuous motion of a block that changes its color from red to green in the course of motion. Taken together, these data indicate that, from 7 months, infants **perceive two subsequent motions of two colliding discrete objects as 'direct impact'**, i.e. **as two motion events that are in a causal relationship to each other** (Leslie 1984; Subbotskii 2007: 177–178).

> **Note.** The data described above allow us to conclude that infants develop an ability to spontaneously make causal "subconscious inferences"[27] as follows: if infants perceive two visual images whose subsequent motions satisfy the condition for "direct impact" (spatio-temporal continuity of "motion transfer"), they automatically attribute a causal relationship to this motion. Importantly, rational reasoning that may show this subconscious inference to be false in a particular case cannot cancel or repudiate this relationship. Michotte (1962), in his pioneer study (based on similar experiments) of how adults perceive direct impact and interpret the inherent causal relationship, produced screen projections of direct impact, not of colored blocks, but of squares of light. The adults in the experiment, who understood very well the true mechanism of the squares' motion, could not

---

[27] This is the term used by H. Helmholtz; for its explanation see, for example, (Sechenov 1952: 356ff).

get rid of the impression that one square gave a "slight push" to the other. The impression that there was a causal relationship between these motions was, apparently, false, yet it persisted (for a more detailed discussion of this property of subconscious inferences see Koshelev (2015a: 226–231)).

Note also that, according to Leslie (1984), who elaborates on Michotte's (1962) ideas (see also Carey 2009: 217–221), and some other researchers (see references in Subbotskii (2007)), the direct mechanical impact discussed above encapsulates a causal relationship and is, to the child, the source of a more general understanding of the cause-effect relationships between objects. Cf.:

... at 2 to 3 years of age, children recognize, as a cause of a phenomenon, only such an event which is materially connected to the phenomenon one way or another (that is, it sort of "passes on" its "energy"); thus, if, in the presence of two working fans, a burning candle goes out, to identify the cause children point to the fan blowing air in the direction of the candle. In other words, this module [the direct impact.—*A. K.*] brings the child to the idea of the necessity of spatio-temporal continuity between cause and effect (Subbotskii 2007: 180)

For a detailed discussion of this view see Carey (2009: 221–246).

Notice the remarkable subtlety with which infants classified different types of interactions between blocks. Not only did they single out direct impacts as a special, central class, they also identified three other independent classes of "impacts": "impact without collision", "deferred impact" (infants did distinguish between them), and "deferred impact without collision", which integrated the two deviations from "direct impact". If infants saw that the red block stopped short of the green block (first deviation from direct impact) and the latter started to move only after several moments have passed (second deviation), their surprise (an eagerness to see such an event again) was greater than in the case of only a single deviation (Subbotskii 2007: 177–179; Leslie 1982 and 1984).

Chapter 3

Basic-level concepts
as the neurobiological codes for memory

§ 1. Concrete concepts and motor concepts

1. Introduction. Two interpretations of basic-level concrete concepts

In the area of cognitive research associated with the names of R. Brown, E. Rosch, C. Mervis, B. Berlin, and G. Lakoff, among others, an important discovery has been made concerning how children acquire **generic categories**. By making use of contrasting categories, it was shown that a child acquires generic categories first, and that these categories are maximally distinct (cf. Lakoff 1987: 58–67). Therefore concepts—cognitive structures that shape generic categories—are called basic, or basic-level, concepts.

As has been found by Rosch and her colleagues (Rosch et al. 1976), the basic level is, among other things, the highest level at which category members have similarly perceived overall shapes and at which a person uses similar motor actions for interacting with category members. It is also the first level named and understood by children (cf. Lakoff 1987: 46).

Leaning on previous research by his predecessors, Lakoff (1987: 36) identifies two interconnected features that form a basic concept: overall shape and typical motor interactions, "the possibilities for which are also determined by overall shape". Thus, a typical interaction with chairs is to sit on them, with flowers to smell them, with cats to pet them, with a ball to play with it in a certain way. In other words, according to Lakoff, a basic concept is constituted as follows:

(1) Concept = overall Shape + physical Interaction.

> **Note**. A similar schema is also given in Gallese and Lakoff (2005: 466). They extend the use of this schema, as described in the following excerpt:

We believe that the same basic structures—schemas structuring senso-ry-motor parameterisations—can be used to characterise all concrete con-cepts. Take, for example, the basic-level concepts [...] chair, car, etc. As we saw, basic-level concepts are defined by the convergence of (1) gestalt ob-ject perception (observed or imaged) and (2) motor programmes that define the prototypical interaction with the object (again, performed or imaged). Thus, a chair looks a certain way (and we can imagine how it looks) and it is used for sitting in a certain position (and we can imagine sitting that way) (Gallese and Lakoff 2005: 469).

According to this definition, the basic-level concept STUL 'chair' is con-stituted as follows:

(2) concept STUL (basic meaning of the word *stul* 'chair') =

Shape	&	Human interaction with it
Video clip		Video clip
	&	

As can be seen, schemas (1) and (2) provide visual identification of the basic-level concept; both of its components are easily stored in a native speak-er's memory.

According to another, similar view (Nelson 1973; Mervis 1987; Rakison 2000), basic-level concepts have binary structure:

(3) Shape — Function.

Here, the overall shape of an object is matched with its general function rather than interaction.

2. Functional schema of basic-level concepts

It seems that the formula for a basic concept given in (2) should include two more functional features. An object's shape must be complemented by its function (the pair "Shape → Function"; see the definition of the Function on pp. 41 and 43), and visually perceived human interaction must be comple-mented by the psychophysical state of the interacting person (the pair "human

Interaction ← psychophysical State"; for a definition of psychophysical state see § 2 section 2). Let us use the symbol "&" to designate the relationship of association between these two pairs. Then we get the following:

	Object	Interaction

(4)   Basic-level concept = (Shape → Function) & typical (human Interaction → psychophysical State).

Or, in a shorter version:

(4')   Basic-level concept = Object (Shape → Function) & Typical motor concept.

The arrow (→) designates a relation of interpretation: the visual property (Shape) is ascribed a functional property (the initial job done by the shape), which is a feature of a different nature. The word 'typical' indicates that the associated interaction is probable and potential, but not actual; it will often be omitted in the subsequent discussion.

The above definition may be clarified using the basic-level concept STUL ('chair') as an example. The general function of a chair (the function of its shape) is to be sat on by a person in a certain posture: the person leans on the back of the chair, his buttocks rest on the seat of the chair, and his feet are supported by the floor. The state of a person sitting on a chair ('half-steady position of the body') is a range of his typical sensations caused by his interaction with the chair. Clearly, the function of a chair and the state of a person sitting on this chair are two interrelated but completely different features. The first function characterizes the chair, while the second function characterizes the person.

As a result, we come to the following:

(5) concept STUL (basic meaning of the word *stul* 'chair') =

(Shape	→	Function)	&	(Interaction	→	Psychophysical state)
	→	Allows a person to sit like this:	&	A person's back and buttocks are supported by the chair:	→	1) With the objective to do some work at a desk/table, a person 2) takes this body posture and 3) is in a **half-steady (semi-relaxed)** state

Some clarification is in order here. The definition features the same "picture" twice. However, in the first case the picture explains **the function of a chair**—to allow a person to take a certain posture, while in the second case it explains **the psychophysical state** of a person taking such a posture. In the first component of the concept invisible properties—durability, stability, ability to support a human body—are attributed ($\rightarrow$) to a visually perceived shape. If, for example, we take a chair made of papier-mâché, we will see that these properties do not always come with the shape of chair. In the second component, it is the human activity of "sitting on a chair" to which a 'semi-relaxed state' is attributed, caused by the interaction. That such an interpretation is not obligatory may be illustrated by the following circus act: a clown is sitting on a chair in the middle of the arena in the posture of Rodin's "Thinker". The clown's mate sneaks up from behind and pulls the chair from under him. But the clown continues to "sit" in the Thinker's posture (to the delight of the laughing audience). The sitting posture is now practically the same (except there is no support from the back of the chair) but is not associated with any, even partial, relaxation of the clown's body.

It is crucial that the component 'psychophysical state' be included in the definition of basic concept. As will be shown in § 2 section 2, it is precisely the different psychophysical states of a sitting person that distinguish the categories 'Stul'ja' ('Chairs'), 'Kresla' ('Armchairs'), and 'Taburety' ('Stools') as strictly separate from one another. At the same time, neither the difference in shape between chairs and armchairs nor the different sitting postures associated with them allow for a strict differentiation.

3. The function of an object and a linguistic explanation of this function

The function of an object (the initial job it does) is its most important taxonomic characteristic. It is closely connected with the object's shape but dominates it in the following sense: the shape of objects belonging to the same category may vary to a certain extent, while their function always remains the same.

That an object has a certain function may easily be determined, since it is the function that defines the parts into which the object can be divided. For example, the function of a chair—'make it possible for a person to sit in a certain manner'—defines its division into three parts: the back of the chair, with the particular function 'support for the back of the sitting person', the seat, with the function 'support for the person's buttocks', and the legs of the chair, whose function is to ensure 'the position of a person's legs and the support of the floor for the feet'.[1] **The sum of these three particular functions constitutes the general function of a chair**. An armchair features additional parts: armrests as supports that provide for a much steadier state of the body of a sitting person.

Because of an object's general function, a native speaker always knows which physical part of the object is its functional part proper and which part is not. For example, the function of a knife '≈ to cut something holding a knife in a hand' determines its division into two constitutive parts, the blade (with the particular function 'to cut') and the handle (with the function 'for holding in a hand'). These particular functions together define the general function of a knife.

Importantly, an object's parsing structure is verified linguistically. In Russian, the relationship 'Y is a part of X' is usually expressed by a noun phrase *Y X-a* ('Y of X'), which consists of two nouns; one of these nouns is in the Genitive case, e.g.: *lezvie (Y) noža (X-a)* 'the blade of a knife-Gen', *ručka (Y) kastrjuli (X-a)* 'the handle of a pan-Gen', *spinka (Y) kresla (X-a)* 'the back of an armchair-Gen', etc. (for more details see chap. 4, § 1). Notably, noun Y refers not to just any physical part of object X, but specifically to its **functionally relevant** part, that is, the part whose function directly contributes to the object's general function.

Therefore, expressions such as *lezvie noža* 'the blade of a knife', *ručka noža* 'the handle of a knife' are correct. However, a corkscrew or fork in a Swiss Army knife, being its physical parts, are not its functional parts as they don't contribute to the knife's general function ('to cut'). Consequently, expressions such as **štopor noža* 'the corkscrew of a knife', **vilka noža* 'the fork of a knife' are incorrect (in Russian the correct phrasing would be *vilka u noža* 'the knife's fork'). Similarly, the general function of a door is 'to open and close the doorway', therefore a handle is its functional part. But an eyehole in a door does not contribute to this function (the function of an eyehole is 'to show who is behind the door'); therefore, it is quite correct to say *ručka dveri* 'the handle of a door', but one cannot say **glazok dveri* 'the peephole of a door' (it should be *dvernoj glazok* 'the door-ADJ peephole').

The correctness of the expressions *spinka/siden'e/nožki stula* ('the back/seat/legs of a chair') is explained in a similar way: each of these parts contrib-

---

[1] One of the most felicitous definitions of an object's shape has been offered by Pereira and Smith (2009: 68): "objects are perceptually parsed, represented, and stored as configurations of geometric volumes ('geons'). Within this account, object shape is defined by two to four geometric volumes in the proper spatial arrangement, an idea supported by the fact that adults need only two to four major parts to recognize instances of common categories [...]".

utes to the general function of a chair. But imagine that a head-rest has been attached to the back of a chair, and a foot-rest to its legs. The incorrectness of the expressions *podgolovnik stula* 'the head-rest of a chair' and *podnožnik stula* 'the foot-rest of a chair' shows that, becoming physical parts of a chair, they don't become its functional parts (they don't contribute to the general function of chair but rather limit the required degree of mobility of the sitting person). For an armchair, however, these parts are natural and functionally significant because they increase the steadiness of the person sitting in it. Therefore, the similar expressions *podgolovnik kresla* 'the head-rest of an armchair' and *podnožnik kresla* 'the foot-rest of an armchair' are quite correct. These, as well as other examples (see below), show that a native speaker is well aware of the functions of objects. Only by taking these functions into account can he easily "compute" the functional parts of objects. This enables him to identify the correct and incorrect uses of expressions that designate parts of objects.

4. A linguistic explanation of the concept functional schema

As shown in (4) and (5), a basic concept includes four interrelated components: [Shape → Function] & [Interaction → State].

There is evidence of various kinds that each of these components is differentiated and possesses an independent status. As an illustration, consider Schema (5).

1. Shape. In Rene Magritte's painting "The Legend of the Centuries" (see Fig. 5 in chap. 2, § 1, section 2.3), a gigantic stone object is depicted that resembles a chair by shape. This resemblance is quite sufficient for naming the object metaphorically: *This is a chair*.

2. Function. Consider a chair (Fig. 1) whose shape is not typical (it does not fit the prototype). If it were made of papier-mâché, the phrase *This is a chair* would also be metaphorical, but for a different reason: this object would not possess the function of a chair as it would be crumpled should someone sit on it.

Fig. 1

3. Interaction. One could say, metaphorically, about the clown who continues to keep the posture of the thinker after the chair has been pulled away

from under him, that he is sitting. The action 'to sit on a chair' (its manner, outward appearance) is, therefore, quite independent and separate from the other components of the schema in (5). It is this action that motivates the metaphor *The clown is sitting*, even though the clown's state is obviously not semi-relaxed.[2]

4. State. One could say about a stack of bricks propped against a wall in such a way that one could sit on it, leaning on the wall: *This is a chair.* This metaphor, by contrast with the previous ones, is motivated solely by the ability of the construction described to produce the required (semi-relaxed) state in a person sitting on it.

The concept schema introduced in (4) and (5) defines the algorithm for recognizing (identifying) an object perceived by a person as a chair. The object's shape prompts an initial hypothesis: this might be a chair. Then the possibility of a specific interaction with this shape ('to sit') is tested. If there is such a possibility, the person performs such an action in his mind to check if the object can keep him in a sitting position (the function of a chair) and whether the person sitting on it finds himself in the required psychophysical state. If that is the case, then the perceived object is a chair. If, however, a similar but different psychophysical state is obtained—'almost completely relaxed position of the body'—then it is an armchair.

The proposed four-component schema of a basic-level concept was recently corroborated by unexpected, even though circumstantial, evidence: it seems that similar schemas form the basis for object taxonomies of animals, briefly discussed in the following section.

5. Neurobiological grounds for the basic concept schema

Joe Tsien's (2008) innovative research on human memory studies gives reasons to believe that the components of the concept STUL ('chair') in (5), which define the category "Stul'ja" ('Chairs'), are directly encoded in human memory as an ensemble of specific groups of neurons (neural cliques). Neural

---

[2] Consider an example of a child's metaphor motivated solely by the form of interaction with an object. Jacqueline (aged 2 years and 3 months), holding a comb over her head, said: *This is an umbrella* (Eliseeva 2008: 86). The correctness of such an occasional use of the word *umbrella* is due exclusively to the fact that the interaction with the comb is the kind of interaction typical for an umbrella. Had the girl held the comb in a different manner (not in the manner an umbrella is held), the phrase would have been incorrect. Therefore, in a child's mental schema of the meaning of the word *umbrella*, the component 'interaction with an umbrella' is featured as quite independent.

cliques are groups of neurons that respond similarly and selectively to an event; this makes them the coding units of memory. Subscribing to Tsien's theory, it may be hypothesized that one clique fires when an object resembling the **prototypical chair** (image) is perceived, another clique fires when the body of a person takes the posture (enters an **interaction**) 'sitting on a chair', and a third fires when a **semi-relaxed state** obtains following the interaction. If this is in fact the case, it may be claimed that the totality (an ensemble) of such cliques encodes the concept STUL ('chair'), as shown in (5), in the long-term memory, and the concept defines the category "Stul'ja" ('Chairs').

Tsien's theory cannot be described here in detail for space considerations. However, it can be illustrated by a significant example—a description of the mouse's "concept" NEST (a mouse's idea of a nest). As it turns out, this concept is quite similar to the human concept BED, with a structure shown in (5). It is stored as an ensemble of neural cliques of the net-work CA1 of the mouse's hippocampus. Below is a short discussion of the experiment, with a picture that illustrates it (Fig. 2).

> Consider, for instance, the concept of "bed". People can go into any hotel room in the world and immediately recognize the bed, even if they have never seen that particular bed before. It is the structure of our memory-encoding ensembles that enables us to retain not only an image of a specific bed but also a general knowledge of what a bed is. Indeed, my colleagues and I have seen evidence of this in mice. During the course of our experiments, we accidentally discovered a small number of hippocampal neurons that appear to respond to the abstract concept of "nest". These cells react
>
> vigorously to all types of nests, regardless of whether they are round or square or triangular or made of cotton or plastic or wood. Place a piece of glass over the nest so the animal can see it but can no longer climb in, and the nest cells cease to react. We conclude that these cells are responding not to the specific physical features of the nest—its appearance or shape or material—but to its functionality: a nest is someplace to curl up in to sleep (Tsin' 2007: 58)

Fig. 2. Mouse relaxes in a dish it views as a nest
(adapted from Tsin' 2007)

Thus it was not just the shape of the encountered object (with a hollow) that the mouse perceived. The mouse (1) made an initial hypothesis that it was a nest, (2) performed a mental action of 'lying in the hollow' (the glass blocked this action), (3) tested the ability of the nest to hold it (thus a dry leaf with turned-up edges was rejected), and (4) whether it (the mouse) would gain the required comfort and safety (the psychophysical state). Thus it was the state of lying in a nest, represented in the memory by a specific clique, which defined the 'abstract idea' of a nest. Therefore, NEST is a nameless basic-level concept that has the same structure as the human basic-level concept given in (4). This concept is activated in the mouse's memory if, while perceiving the object, an ensemble of cliques which encodes the concept NEST begin to fire together—all four cliques which represent, respectively, the shape of a nest (a "hollow"), the functions of the shape ("fixation of the body"), the interaction itself ("lying in the hollow"), and the state ("rest and comfort").

It should be noted in conclusion that, in contrast to the human concept STUL ('chair') in (5), the mouse's concept NEST is, apparently, not a system of independent components but rather a gestalt structure.

6. Motor concepts

Concrete basic-level concepts are usually taken to be the primary units of the human taxonomy of the world. From the arguments presented above, however, it follows that despite all their simplicity they are secondary because, in the end, they seem to be defined by more elementary cognitive units, i.e. the concepts of human interaction, or human **motor** concepts.

The grounds for this hypothesis (about the primacy of human interaction with objects compared with the objects themselves) are quite clear: it is through interactions with objects that humans solve tasks and fulfill their desires. To humans, the surrounding objects exist only as potential (role-playing) participants in such interactions that help achieve the desired goals. Moreover, natural dynamic phenomena—the flow of water, the heat of the sun, the blow of the wind, etc.—are also relevant to humans and thus receive functional interpretations from the point of view of a human being (safety, usefulness, etc.).

To begin with, let us consider the concepts of human interactions.

A human motor concept has the following structure:

(6)   Motor concept = Human interaction (visual Shape) → psychophysical State.

Now, the basic-level motor concept should be defined. Bear in mind that a basic-level concept is a concept that, first of all, has a visual prototype or generic shape (superordinate concepts such as PLANT, ANIMAL don't have this). Secondly, this shape is the most general. TREE, DOG, are basic-level concepts, while the subordinate concepts BIRCH, HUSKY are not because their prototypical shapes are not generic.

The above is also true for motor concepts: ČELOVEK SIDIT ("a person is sitting") is a basic-level motor concept. Its prototypical interaction—"a relatively vertical position of a person's body whose buttocks are in contact with a horizontal seat"—is the most generic, as is the function "a person's body has a main support at the bottom part and is in a partially steady position" (cf. the basic meaning of *sidet'* 'sit' in chap. 2, § 3, section 2.3). Similarly, the motor concepts ČELOVEK STOIT/LEŽIT ('A PERSON IS STANDING/LYING'), ČELOVEK IDËT/BEŽIT ('A PERSON IS WALKING/RUNNING') are also basic-level concepts.

The concepts ČELOVEK SIDIT NA STULE / V KRESLE / NA POLU ('A PERSON IS SITTING ON A CHAIR / IN AN ARMCHAIR / ON THE FLOOR') are subordinate.

Consider, as an example, the motor concept given earlier in (5):

(7)　Motor concept ČELOVEK SIDIT NA STULE (the meaning of the phrase *Čelovek sidit na stule* 'A person is sitting on the chair') =

Human Interaction	→	Psychophysical State
A person's back and buttocks are in contact with the chair:	→	1) (goal) With the goal to do some work at a desk/table, a person 2) (dynamics) takes this body posture and is in a **half-steady (semi-relaxed)** state

It must be noted that a human motor concept possesses an independent status that is not determined by the object with which a person interacts. Thus, in the human basic-level concept ČELOVEK SIDIT both the shape and the state are strictly the features of a human interaction; they do not include the features of the object sat on. The same is true for the concept in (7). Here the left-side component—physical interaction—is, rather, of an illustrative, explanatory nature because the posture of the sitting person registered by the receptors in the human body (proprioceptors) is stored in the psychophysical state (in the coded memory of a typified interaction "sit on a chair", cf. §1 section 2). The chair itself is not part of this state.

Now consider the basic-level concept ČELOVEK IDËT 'A PERSON IS WALKING'. The object with which a person interacts is a hard level surface (a road, a trail). Taking into account the meaning of the phrase *Čelovek idët* (cf. chap. 2, § 4, section 1.4), we get the following:

(8) Motor concept ČELOVEK IDËT 'A PERSON IS WALKING'—
the meaning of the phrase *Čelovek idët* =

Human Interaction	→	Psychophysical State
A person is moving down the path, but not quickly 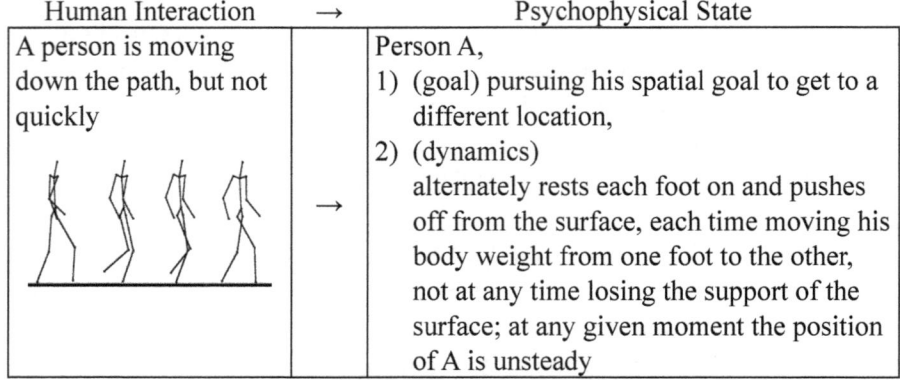	→	Person A, 1) (goal) pursuing his spatial goal to get to a different location, 2) (dynamics) alternately rests each foot on and pushes off from the surface, each time moving his body weight from one foot to the other, not at any time losing the support of the surface; at any given moment the position of A is unsteady

Here the psychophysical state (memory code) of the walking person is likewise an internal feature of the person's psyche which does not include the features of the surface with which the person interacts. The kinematics of walking is also stored in this memory code (in the proprioceptive data). As for the left-side component (visual prototype), it is included in the definition of the concept (and basic meaning) to clearly show this component of the state.

Along with the concepts that describe human actions there are motor concepts that describe actions of objects: KAMEN' LETIT ('THE STONE IS FLYING'), VODA TEČËT ('THE WATER IS FLOWING'), etc. They possess a similar structure except that instead of a psychophysical state an affective constituent (a person's interest in the action, expected outcome (negative or positive) from it, etc.) is ascribed to the shape of the action.

7. Concrete concepts TROPINKA 'FOOTPATH', DOROŽKA 'TRACK', DOROGA 'ROAD'

Following the approach to the definitions of CHAIR and ARMCHAIR, we can now define some types of surface over which motion takes place—a footpath, track, or road—guided by their functions and the psychophysical state of the walking/running/moving persons, respectively.

We will begin with the concept TROPINKA 'FOOTPATH' and define it in a way similar to that in which we defined the concept STUL 'CHAIR'. While a chair is a man-made object used by a person for sitting on, *tropinka* 'footpath' is an entity that comes into being spontaneously and is used for the passage of a single person.

In explanatory dictionaries the word *tropinka* 'footpath' is defined with the help of the word *dorožka* 'track', cf.:

***Tropinka* ['footpath'] 1.** Uzkaja pešexodnaja dorožka, protoptannaja lud'mi ili životnymi v lesu, v pole, po snegu i t. p. ['A narrow pedestrian track beaten by people or animals in a forest, field, snow, etc.'] (Ushakov, IV: col. 808).

This definition is in need of specification. First, unlike a track, a footpath is made exclusively by humans; compare the correctness and incorrectness of the expressions *zverinaja tropa* 'wild animal track' and **zverinaja tropinka* 'wild animal footpath', respectively. Second, in its basic meaning the word *tropinka* 'footpath' refers to a strip of ground beaten in a forest, field or highland, but not in snow—consider the questionability of the phrase ? *tropinka v snežnom pole* 'a footpath in the snow-covered field'. Third, a footpath is a very narrow track, just wide enough for one person. And, finally, the words *dorožka* 'track' and *tropinka* 'footpath' are semantically very close and one feels reluctant to explain one word with the help of the other. The following definition will be accepted here:

(9) ***Tropinka* ['footpath'] 1**
  a) is a narrow strip of beaten ground used by people in an area inconvenient for walking;
  b) it is hard and even, convenient for walking;
  c) it is used by people for walking alone or in single file.

As can be seen, the entity 'tropinka' [footpath] is defined through (a) its prototypical shape ("narrow strip of ground surface") and (b) its function ("hard and plane, convenient for walking"), as well as (c) the motor concept ČELOVEK IDĖT 'A PERSON IS WALKING' ("used by people for walking alone or in single file"). This is quite consonant with the definition of a concrete concept presented in the schemas in (4) and (5). As a result, only one potential motor concept is associated (&) with the pair "Prototype → Function" as one of an object's components:

(10) The concrete concept TROPINKA 'FOOTPATH' (basic meaning of the word *tropinka*) =

(Prototype	→	Function)	&	Motor concept
	→	Narrow strip of ground surface, hard and plane enough for a person to walk conveniently	&	ČELOVEK IDĖT (8)

The function of the footpath defines its parts: the middle, which can be walked on, and the edges, which separate it from the adjoining surface (which is unfit for walking); hence the correctness of the expressions *seredina/kraja tropinki* 'the middle/edges of the footpath'. A rut or a bump on a footpath, for instance, are not parts of it as they do not contribute to its function, hence the incorrectness of the expressions **rytvina/*bugor tropinki* 'the rut/bump of a footpath'.

Dorožka 'track', which is already an artifact, has a man-made hard surface and is usually designed not just for walking, but also for running and cycling. Therefore, the concrete component of the concept is associated with a set of three potential motor concepts: ČELOVEK IDËT ('A PERSON IS WALK-ING), ČELOVEK BEŽIT ('A PERSON IS RUNNING'), and ČELOVEK EDET NA VELOSIPEDE ('A PERSON IS CYCLING'). As a result, we get the following:

(11) The concrete concept DOROŽKA 'TRACK' (basic meaning of the word *dorožka*) =

(Prototype	→	Function)	&	A set of motor concepts
	→	Narrow strip of ground with a hard even surface made for convenient travel for one or two persons	&	ČELOVEK IDËT, ČELOVEK BEŽIT, ČELOVEK EDET NA VELOSIPEDE

A still greater number of motor concepts is associated with the concept DOROGA 'ROAD'. On a road people can walk, run, drive (a car, tractor, etc.) and, at the same time, transport something in either direction. Note that a crosswalk marked by white stripes is not part of the road (it impedes traffic), while traffic lane markings (which facilitate traffic) are, cf.: **perexod dorogi* 'crosswalk of a road' vs. *razmetka dorogi*, lit. '(lane) markings of the oad'.

In our further discussion the second component of the concrete concept shown in (4')—the typical motor concept (or a set of such concepts)—will often be omitted for the sake of simplicity, and a simplified formula will be given:

(12) Basic-level concept = Shape of object → its Function.

8. Concepts OZERO 'LAKE' and REKA 'RIVER'

A similar approach will now be used with regard to a lake and a river. Their prototypes are evident, and their general function may be formulated as follows: 'a continuously sustained large mass of fresh water which naturally appears on the surface of the ground, completely covering the area'. The distinctive features are, briefly, these: a river is 'a mass of fresh water moving continuously and unidirectionally', and a lake is 'a mass of still fresh water'. This allows for the following representation of the concept OZERO 'LAKE':

(13) Concept LAKE = Prototype (Shape) of a lake → its Function

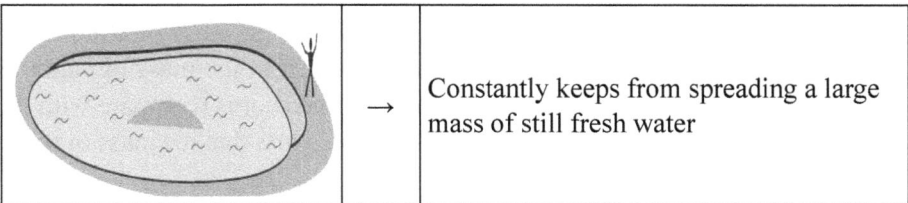

| | → | Constantly keeps from spreading a large mass of still fresh water |

A few words must be said about the second component of the concept OZERO, omitted in (13) but associated with the first component, namely, a set of potential motor concepts. Among other things, they determine the human scale of a lake relative to a sea on the one hand, and to a pool of water on the other. A lake is relatively small and can be swept by a single glance together with its shores. It is a water barrier for passage to the other shore, and it is deep enough for a person to drown while trying to swim it. Its width is relatively small, such that a person can swim across it at some points or easily reach the opposite shore in a boat. One can swim in a lake, relax on its shore, drink its water, go fishing, wash oneself, wash and rinse linen, etc.

By contrast, a sea is so large that a person cannot take it in at a glance, see the opposite shore, or reach the opposite shore by swimming or in a boat. A person sees only a part of the seashore on which he is standing, and the adjoining part of the sea. Drawing an analogy, one could compare the difference between the motor concepts PLYT' PO OZERU 'SWIM/SAIL OVER A LAKE' and PLYT' PO MORJU 'SWIM/SAIL OVER A SEA' with the difference between the motor concepts SIDET' V KRESLE 'TO SIT IN AN ARMCHAIR' and SIDET' NA STULE 'TO SIT ON A CHAIR'. Sea water is salty and cannot be used to quench thirst, etc.

A pool is a small, temporarily appearing mass of fresh still water. It can be stepped over or crossed at a few steps. One cannot swim in it, etc.

A river, in its magnitude, is between a lake and a sea. Its depth and width are relatively small; a person can see both its banks (the one he is standing on and the opposite one) at a single glance and swim across it or cross it in a boat.[3] However, the length of a river is great: one cannot see the source and the mouth of a river at the same time or swim its entire length. Standing on the bank of a river, one can see only a small section of both its banks.

Clearly, a lake and a river invoke largely similar but different kinds of human interactions with them. As natural objects, they define different sets of potential motor concepts associated with them.

Let us now consider the general function of a lake. Like a chair or a road, a lake also possesses partial functions which add up to its general function. This general function is, essentially, to prevent a large mass of water from draining away and disappearing. Therefore, apart from the mass of water as such, a lake has two more parts, the bottom and the shores (compare with the bottom and the sides of a cup). It is thanks to these parts that the mass of water remains still and keeps its shape.

This inference is supported by the correctness of the expressions *voda/ dno/berega* **ozera** 'the water/bottom/shores of a lake'. However, neither a river flowing into a lake, nor the fish living in it, nor an isle jutting up in the middle, nor a pier on its shore are functional parts of a lake. This accounts for the incorrectness of the expressions **reka ozera* 'the river of a lake', **ostrov ozera* 'the isle of a lake', **pristan' ozera* 'the pier of a lake' (for more details about these and other natural entities see chap. 4, § 1).

Similarly, a river also has parts which contribute to its overall function: the bottom and the banks that sustain the shape of water flow, the source (where the water comes from), the mouth (where the water goes), and the riverbed over which the water flows; cf. the correctness of the expressions *berega/ruslo/istok/ ust'e/dno/voda* **reki** 'the banks/bed/source/mouth/bottom/water of the river'. A waterfall, ford, bridge, dam or rapids have nothing to do with the function of a river; hence the incorrectness of the expressions **vodopad/*brod/*porogi/ *most/*plotina* **reki** 'the waterfall/ford/rapids/bridge/dam of a river'.

---

[3] Of course, there are bodies of water called 'lakes' even though their size by far exceeds the size mentioned above. Such names should be considered metaphoric. For example, the width of Lake Baikal varies from 25 to 79 km, therefore it is often called "sea". Similarly, the banks of the Amur may be as far apart as 40 km. However, in popular experience the banks of a river are accessible for direct observation, which finds proof in the line from a popular song: "you and I are just two sides of the same river" (i.e. 'we can see each other, but cannot connect').

9. The concept DEREVO 'TREE'

Heretofore we have discussed only categories of inanimate objects. In the case of an animate object the concept schema given in (12) **does not change**. Consider the concept DEREVO 'tree' as an example; this is what it looks like as a first approximation (the prototype of a tree is shown as extended over a time period):

(14) Concept DEREVO = Prototype of a tree → its Function ('grows from the ground by itself, blossoms, and bears fruit')

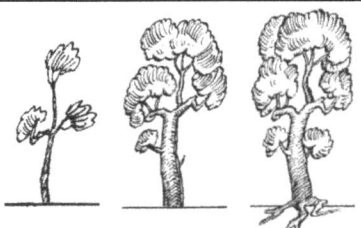

The trunk of the tree stands vertically and motionlessly on the ground; the roots are in the ground. The tree gradually grows in size, its trunk gets taller and thicker, and the branches get longer and thicker. Every spring new branches shoot forth from the trunk and the older branches; blossoms appear on the old branches to be followed by fruit, which falls to the ground in autumn	→	Bears fruit periodically, i.e. grows fruits and seeds. This is done as follows: from the roots in the ground, which provide nourishment, a hard thick sprout (trunk) grows; from the trunk hard thinner sprouts (branches) grow in different directions; periodically (in spring) buds appear on the branches; from the buds come blossoms, and from the blossoms come fruit (seeds) which ripen (in autumn) and fall from the tree

The prototype of a tree is shown as three chronologically ordered "profiles" of a tree: a sapling, a young tree, and a grown tree. The text below these profiles describes the typical visual characteristics of growing, blossoming, and fruit bearing, while the function explains these observable characteristics, i.e. our intuition about the tree as a living organism whose growth and development depend on its internal activity and interaction with the ground. One might think that this function, which gives an idea of the vital functions of a tree, reflects not the trivial knowledge of a native speaker but a truncated projection of our knowledge gained from a school course in botany. To show that this is not the case, we turn to the functional parts of a tree; as can easily be seen, their composition and structure are defined by the function of a tree as formulated above.

Indeed, just as parts of a chair—the seat, back, and legs—conjointly define its function, the roots, trunk and branches define the function of a tree. The roots procure nourishment from the ground; the trunk supports the branches, and the procured nourishment is delivered via the trunk and branches to the buds and fruits. The functional relevance of this parsed structure is manifested in the correctness of the expressions *korni/stvol/vetki der-eva* 'the roots/trunk/branches of a tree' in contrast with the incorrectness of similar expressions referring to alien objects physically connected with a tree, cf.: **gnezdo dereva* 'the nest of a tree' or **skvorečnik dereva* 'the starling-house of a tree' (of a nest built on a branch of the tree or a starling-house nailed to the trunk).

Quite a few human motor concepts are associated with trees: SAŽAT'/ POLIVAT'/UDOBRJAT' DEREVO 'TO PLANT/WATER/FERTILIZE A TREE', SREZAT' VETKI / SRYVAT' PLODY / LAZIT' NA DEREVO 'TO CUT OFF BRANCHES / PICK FRUITS / CLIMB A TREE', SIDET' V TENI DEREVA 'TO SIT IN THE SHADE OF A TREE', PILIT' DEREVO 'TO SAW A TREE', etc. These constitute a second, motor component of the concept DEREVO.

A shrub has a different parsing structure. It has multiple trunks which are low and thin, and therefore the scope of potential human interactions with it is different: one doesn't have to climb the shrub to pick its fruit; it will not provide shade to hide from the sun, etc.

Let us summarize what we have looked at in this chapter. Lakoff (1987: 31–32), following Brown (1965: 318–319), believes that, just like a man-made object, a living object is defined by a single characteristic interaction: with flowers—to smell them, with cats—to pet them, etc. However, there are reasons to believe that the category of living objects is defined by two sets of interactions: the object's interaction with its surroundings and the interactions of humans with the object. For example, the following actions are characteristic of a cat: to climb trees, to walk on fences and roofs, to stalk prey and then catch it with its paw. Quite different actions are characteristic of a dog. A dog joyfully greets its master coming home, it likes to be taken out for walks, it can guard the house—all of these are quite alien to interactions between a human and a cat. Another example would be that of a feral cat and a lynx, which show similar parsing structures and habits; however, a cat is not a danger to man, while a lynx is.

10. Appendix. On the dual nature of human categories

The formula for a concrete concept in (12) gives grounds to believe that the semantic category of noun, i.e. the category of referents defined by the basic meaning of a noun (concrete concept), is simultaneously defined by two criteria of different nature: the prototypical shape of an object, and the object's function. The prototype criterion assigns an underspecified fuzzy category of referents, while the function criterion sets a rigid category. Specifically, the function criterion, which appears at a later stage, does not cancel the prototype criterion, but it has a higher priority. Thus, the principal controversy between Lakoff and Wierzbicka is resolved in a natural way.

Since the 1970s, research done by Eleanor Rosch, George Lakoff and other cognitive scientists has led to the development of a new theory of natural categories which are defined, for example, by notional words such as *bird*, *boat*, *cup*, *bachelor*, *mother*, *game*, *healthy*, *climb*, etc. Leaning on works by Wittgenstein (1953: 66–71) (his analysis of the word *game* and his notion of "family resemblance"), Austin (1961: 71) (who discussed the fuzzy semantics of the word *healthy*), and using the results of some psycholinguistic experiments, Lakoff (1987) proposed a new approach to human categorization. The core claim of his proposal was that human categories are defined on the basis of "embodied" basic-level concepts which reflect a child's imaginative perception and motoric conceptualization of the world. Therefore, human categories are prototypical by nature and, as a consequence, essentially fuzzy, as they are based on prototypes defined by cognitive models. Thus, the classical Aristotelian view of category as a set defined by the properties shared by all its members could no longer be considered adequate.

Wierzbicka (1990) disagrees with Lakoff and claims the opposite: semantic categories of the very same notional words (*bird*, *boat*, *cup*, *bachelor*, *mother*, *game*, *healthy*, *climb*) are quite strict.

The definition of a concrete concept given in (12) resolves this contradiction. It allows us to claim that natural human categories are at least dual, i.e. they are **simultaneously** defined both as prototypical and fuzzy (based on prototypes) and as classical and strict (based on functional features).

§2. On the psychophysical state and the neurobiology of human actions

1. Events and their storage in memory (the neural codes of memory)

Our definition of the term 'psychophysical state' (of a human) will lean heavily on the research on human and animal memory structure conducted by Joe Tsien and his colleagues (Tsien 2008; Tsien et al. 2013).

A brief overview of some of their findings is given in Tsien (2007), which discusses the results of experimental investigation on how memories of staged dramatic events are encoded in the episodic memory (in the hippocampus) of a mouse. The tests consisted in the following. Using a technique for simultaneously recording the activity of 260 neurons in the hippocampus (in the CA1 region, which is important to forming memories in both people and animals), the experimenters subjected mice to seven stressful episodes separated by periods of rest for several hours. Among such events were (1) a lab version of an earthquake, induced by shaking a small container holding a mouse, and (2) a brief vertical free fall inside a small "elevator" (provided by a cookie jar). The researchers reasoned that such dramatic events should produce memories in the mouse by forming new patterns of neuronal activity (firing) in the hippocampus, which would later manifest themselves during perception or recall of such events. And indeed, new patterns of activity in the CA 1 neural ensembles were found within a computer-monitored population of 260 neurons.

As it turned out, the basic units of memory (functional coding units) are the so-called neural cliques—ensembles of neurons in the neural population of the CA 1 region—which show similar features and selective response reactions. In other words, a clique is a group of neurons that respond similarly to an event and thus operate collectively as a robust coding unit. For example, in the course of the experiments a "general startle" neural clique was activated in a mouse's hippocampus which responds to all types of startling stimuli, including the elevator drop, earthquake, and air-blow (Tsien 2008: 407). Furthermore, cliques were activated that encode more specific types of startling events. Thus, a subgeneral startle clique responds to a combination of only two types of startling events: free fall and earthquake. Finally, highly specific cliques encode various features of an event: one encodes shaking, another location of the shake, etc.

According to Tsien and his colleagues, their findings show that a perceived event is encoded in the memory of a mouse by a whole assembly of cliques which represent a range of varying common features of the event. To understand the process of remembering, it is important to know how new cliques are formed and what are the sources of information about the event. It appears that the new cliques that encode the features of an event receive input from particular subsystems of the brain:

> The CA 1 region of the hippocampus receives inputs from many brain regions and sensory systems, and this feature most likely influences what type of information a given clique encodes. For example, the clique that responds to all three startling events could be integrating information from the amygdala (which processes emotions such as fear or the experience of novelty), thereby encoding that "these events are scary and shocking"; the cliques that are activated by both the earthquake and the elevator drop, on the other hand, could be processing input from the vestibular system (which provides information about motion disturbance), thus encoding that "these events make me lose my balance" (Tsin' 2007: 56ff).

As a result of multiple occurrences of similar events, their typified memory code (ensemble of cliques) moves from episodic memory (the CA 1 region of the hippocampus) to long-term memory.

Some of the collected evidence allowed Tsien to hypothesize that such a mechanism for the organization of neural cliques may also be found in humans:

> The categorical and hierarchical organization of neural cliques most likely represents a general mechanism not only for encoding memory but also for processing and representing other types of information in brain areas outside the hippocampus, from sensory perceptions to conscious thoughts. [...] In the visual system, for example, researchers have discovered neurons that respond to "faces", including human faces, monkey faces or even leaves that have the shape of a face. Others have found cells that respond only to a subclass of faces. Back in the hippocampus, researchers studying patients with epilepsy have discovered a subset of cells that increase their firing rates in response to images of famous people. Itzhak Fried [...] made the fascinating observation that one particular cell in a patient's hippocampus seems to respond only to the actress Halle Berry. (Perhaps it is part of a Halle Berry clique!) (Ibid.: 58).

For more detail on the memory code see Tsien 2008; Tsien et al. 2013.

2. Psychophysical state as a memory code for interaction

Going back to the notion of "psychophysical state" and its interpretation, **a psychophysical state** is a neural code of long-term memory (an ensemble of cliques) that encodes a typified immediate interaction of a human, that is, a motor concept. In other words, a psychophysical state is a complex of polytypic data generated by various regions of the human brain in the course of performing a concrete physical action. The following are examples of various kinds of such interactions (motor concepts): SIT ON A CHAIR, SIT IN AN ARMCHAIR (these interactions cause different psychophysical states of the sitting person), DRINK WATER, DRINK BRANDY, SHAVE WITH AN ELECTRIC RAZOR, SHAVE WITH A RAZOR, RUN, WALK, RIDE A BICYCLE, RIDE ON A BUS, CUT BREAD WITH A KNIFE, CUT CARDBOARD WITH SCISSORS, etc.

A psychophysical state integrates input from different subsystems of the nervous system (limbic, vestibular, somatic, the cerebellum, etc.) which register human motives and goals as well as various kinds of sensations (physical and emotional) that accompany a particular physical interaction. Each subsystem contributes to the psychophysical state, activating its neural clique: the limbic system is responsible for the emotional-motivational aspect of the interaction, the vestibular system deals with the information about balance (sustainment of vertical orientation of the body), acceleration or deceleration of motion, and the like, the cerebellum coordinates the motions that require sequential contractions of multiple muscles, controls the balance of the body, forms the current plan of interactions and adjusts its implementation.

Let us focus on the somatic system, which is comprised by the afferent (sensory) and efferent (motor) neurons. The afferent constituent (proprioceptors) provides for the muscle-joint feeling which helps to control the position of the body and its interrelated parts in space, sustain awareness of the direction and speed of motion, and define the muscular strength required for a given motion or for keeping the joint in a particular position. The efferent constituent (the motor efferent neurons found in the spine and brain), processing the input from proprioceptors, sight, and hearing, provides for control over the body and its locomotion by causing contraction and relaxation of the skeletal musculature.

As we already know, an immediate human interaction has a three-component structure: (1) the motive (goal), (2) the dynamics (force-dynamic schemata), and (3) kinematics (changes in the spatial orientation of the body and its parts). The goal of an interaction is represented in the psychophysical state by a clique that receives input from the limbic system. The interactional dynamics are represented by the input from the efferent constituent of the somatic subsystem which, among other things, controls implementation of the force-dynamic schema of motion.

Of special interest to us is the motion kinematics input. The memory code receives this input from the afferent constituent of the somatic system—a system of proprioceptors located in the muscles, ligaments, and joint capsules of a human body. Thus. speaking of locomotions such as walking, running, and so forth, Bernstein noted:

> The *main afferents* on this level [...] are proprioceptions of joint-angular and geometric velocities and positions, to which a vast complex of general exteroceptive sensations of pressure reception, deep sense of touch and friction is added [...], with exact 'local marks' characteristic of such receptions (Bernshtein 1990: 71; original emphasis).

Thanks to this input humans are constantly aware of the position of their limbs and joints, whether they are in motion or at rest; they possess a feeling of body posture (position of all their limbs in space), a feeling of locomotion (awareness of the direction and speed of their joints in action), and a feeling of force (ability to assess muscular strength required for moving or keeping a joint in a particular position). Therefore, it is input from the afferent system of the somatic subsystem that serves to register a human's current activity (or inactivity).

As an illustration of what has been said above, compare two motor concepts and their respective psychophysical states (these concepts have been discussed in detail in § 1, section 6).

(1) Motor concept ČELOVEK SIDIT NA STULE 'A PERSON IS SITTING ON A CHAIR' (the meaning of the phrase *Čelovek sidit na stule*) =

A Person's Interaction	→	Psychophysical State
A person's back and buttocks are in contact with the chair: (kinematics):	→	1) (goal) With the goal to do some work at a desk/table, a person 2) (dynamics) takes this body posture and is in a **half-steady (semi-relaxed)** state

(2)   motor concept ČELOVEK IDËT (po doroge) 'a person is walking (on the road)' (the meaning of the phrase *Čelovek idët*) =

A Person's Interaction →	Psychophysical State
A person is moving down the road, putting one foot in front of the other, but not fast (kinematics) →	1) (goal) A person, pursuing his spatial goal to get to a different location, 2) (dynamics) → alternately rests his feet on and pushes off from the surface, each time moving his body weight from one foot to the other, not at any time losing the support of the surface; at any given moment his position is unsteady

Note the specific distinctions between the memory codes for motor concepts (1) A PERSON IS SITTING ON A CHAIR and (2) A PERSON IS WALKING. In the latter case, there are full-fledged interactional dynamics that result in the locomotion of the body, its acceleration and deceleration. Therefore, there is, along with other cliques, a clique in the memory code that stores input from the vestibular system. In the former case, the role of proprioceptors is also important; they register the position of the motionless body, that is, the specific location of its parts such as the back, buttocks, and legs/feet with their specific supports. There are also cliques that store input from the cerebellum (the state of partial stability of a motionless body) and the limbic subsystem (motivation for the interaction). At the same time, the vestibular subsystem does not contribute to the psychophysical state 'sit on a chair' because its receptors are not activated if the body is motionless.

Note 1. All that being said, it becomes clear how visual prototypes (kinematics) of a person's actions (shown in Fig. 1 and 2), as parts of the definitions of the motor concepts (1) A PERSON IS SITTING ON A CHAIR and (2) A PERSON IS WALKING, are connected with the psychophysical state of a person sitting on a chair or a walking person. They are reflected in the proprioceptive input and represented in the memory code of the motor concepts by a corresponding neural clique that stores this input. It has already been discussed above (chap. 2, § 1, section 1.9) why, when explaining the meaning of a word to a native speaker, it is enough just to describe the prototype (outward appearance, or the kinematics) of the word's referents. It is enough, it has been argued, because the prototype (the visual component of basic meaning) triggers activation of the function in the native speaker's memory—the main component of basic meaning. But what is the actual mechanism of connecting the prototype and the function? Now this mechanism becomes clear: during perception of a motion's kinematics a corresponding clique in the memory code is activated in which proprioceptive data about these kinematics are stored, and this activation is followed by activation of the other cliques of the memory code (the function).

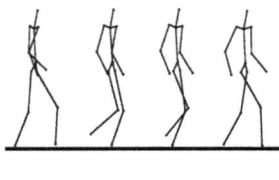

Fig. 1   *Fig. 2*

Gallese and Lakoff (2005) argue that the "neural substrate" used in imagining a motion is the very same substrate used in its understanding. This hypothesis is illustrated by the simple sentence *Harry picked up the glass*:

If you can't imagine picking up a glass or seeing someone picking up a glass, then you can't understand that sentence. Our hypothesis develops this fact one step further. It says that *understanding is imagination*, and that *what you understand of a sentence in a context is the meaning of that sentence in that context* (Gallese and Lakoff 2005: 456; original emphasis).

In other words, a claim is made that the meaning of the given sentence is a "neural substrate" that provides only the visual component (kinematics) of the basic meaning of the verb *pick* (*up*), that is, only the proprioceptive component of the memory code of the action "pick up". Thus, the second component of the meaning—the function—is overlooked. Moreover, as has been shown, a single kinematic component is not enough to understand an action (its goal), because there may be several memory codes with similar kinematics but different dynamics or goals.

The notion of psychophysical state may be explained with the help of a simple example. It should be remembered that the basic meaning of a sensory verb is its current meaning (see the definition in chap. 2, § 2). Imagine a marathon runner approaching the finish line. He can be described by a phrase such as *Čelovek bežit k finišu*, lit. 'The man is running to the finish line', in its current (basic) meaning. This phrase expresses the psychophysical state of running. However, if the runner has stopped for a moment to grab a bottle of water offered by a spectator and take a few gulps, his psychophysical state will change dramatically; it will be expressed with the help of the phrase *Čelovek p'ët vodu*, lit. 'The man is drinking water'. In this case, what changes is, in the first place, the runner's proprioceptive input; it registers that the runner is now standing, holding a bottle at his mouth and swallowing. Inputs from other subsystems also change: the limbic system registers that the thirst is being quenched, and the cerebellum that the body is in a steadier position now, etc.

Similar psychophysical states determine the basic meanings of such verbs as *udarit'* 'hit', *padat'* 'fall', *brat'* 'take', *vzbirat'sja* 'climb', *risovat'* 'draw', *stojat'* 'stand', and others.

> **Note 2.** In discussions of the essence (or invariant) of verbal meaning, such properties as 'motion' and 'energy expenditure' are those often considered. However, none of them is a universal property. Thus, a man holding a suitcase may be motionless but expending energy. A man who is lying down is motionless and doesn't expend energy, yet the verb *ležat'* 'lie' is no less a verb than the verb *bežat'* 'run'. One might think of 'time' as a universal property, but it is rather opaque. We believe that the essence of verbness and of the physiological sense of time is expressed by input from the human proprioceptive subsystem; this continuously updated input signals at every moment about the position of the body and its parts, regardless of whether it is in motion or at rest. By reducing verbal meaning to a psychophysical state that includes proprioceptive input, the expression *tekuščee vremja* 'current time' acquires an explicit cognitive property; that is, it becomes a term of the cognitive metalanguage of linguistics.

3. Biomechanical models of walking and running

A rather detailed description of particular dynamic components of human locomotion has been given above, as well as their cyclic occurrence (pushing, losing support, transfer of support from one foot to the other, etc.). However, to describe locomotion in full it is necessary to view it as an entire process, i.e. as an integrated biomechanical model.

This notion may be discussed using walking and running as examples. As has been noted earlier, an increase in the speed of a walk does not turn it into a run. Indeed, a person may be walking very fast (faster that a person running slowly), yet his manner of locomotion will not qualify as a run. For example, playing a film of a walking man in 'fast forward' mode does not turn the man's motion into a run. Bernstein viewed locomotion as a live *morphological object*:

> [...] The idea that motion is, in many respects, not unlike an organ (that exists in the coordinates of x, y, z, t, just like anatomical organs) seems to

be very fruitful, especially when such a durable and universal kind of motion as locomotion is at issue. [...] As studies of walking have shown, motion displays very selective reactions. To changes in one component it reacts by changes in a number of other components, which are sometimes quite far from the former in space and time; at the same time, those components which, normally, are right next to the initially changed one, almost merging with it, remain unaffected. Therefore, *locomotion is not a chain of components, but a structure differentiated into components*; an integral structure characterized by high differentiation of its components and various-selective forms of the relationships among them. [...] A run as a *biomechanical structure* is, by and large, the opposite of a walk [...]; walking and running solve the mechanical task of moving a body in space in almost opposite ways (Bernshtein 1990: 336, 337, 353; original emphasis).

This insightful claim may be elucidated by a simple experiment the reader can easily perform himself. If you begin to walk at a normal pace and then increase the speed of motion incrementally, you won't feel any substantial changes in the motion's biomechanics except greater pushing efforts. But the moment you start running, even if it is a very slow jogging run, the biomechanics of your locomotion change abruptly. Now your feet push off from the ground not only in a forward direction, but in an upward direction as well to make you 'fly' over the ground just a little bit. Your arms will bend at the elbows and start moving as counterbalances not only back and forth, helping to keep the already unsteady balance of the body, but also up and down to counter the pushes of your feet, to ease takeoff and soften landing. In sync with the pushes, your shoulders and torso will turn now left and now right, facilitating your motion forward; landing after a push will shake your entire body, and you will need special shock absorption provided by the legs (the leg, taking the role of support, bending slightly at the knee), something completely absent during a walk; your body will involuntarily lean forward, facilitating motion, etc.

Thus, during walking and during running the human locomotive system works in two different modes, using two different biomechanical models of motion. It doesn't matter who the runner is—a sprinter, a child, or an old lady. Of course, in the case of an old lady all these changes in motion will be much less noticeable; however, the totality of her running movements will readjust in a systemic way just as in the case of a sprinter. Her arms may not be bent at the elbows, but to keep better balance they (especially her elbows) will be more prominently drawn apart than in a walk, moving more actively in sync with the legs; ground support will be periodically lost or considerably weakened, and so on.

It may be hypothesized that the biomechanical models of walking and running are stored in human psychophysical states. Therefore, the psychophysical states of walking and running are strictly different and discrete, which means that the categories "A person is running" and "A person is sitting", set by these states, are likewise discrete.

4. On recognition of observed actions

The arguments given above allow for a step-by-step description of the process of recognition of an observed action. As has been repeatedly mentioned, an action has a three-level structure: goal => dynamics (force-dynamic schema) => kinematics (changes in the position of the body and its parts in space, reflected by proprioceptors and the visual image of the motion). It has also been shown that both the dynamics and the goal are reflected in the kinematics, which contain their input (imprints). An action cannot be recognized without taking into consideration these inputs. For example, it has been shown that it is very hard to distinguish between a walk and an old person's shuffling run by kinematics alone. However, if the dynamics input is taken into account, such differentiation becomes easier. For example, during a shuffling run a person periodically loses ground support, and to keep balance he often draws his elbows apart. In a similar fashion, the effect of the motive of locomotion on its kinematics should also be taken into account. Thus, if a gardener is *trampling* a newly laid path, he raises his feet higher and brings them down with a greater force than when he is simply *walking* on it.

Going back to the psychophysical state of a human, i.e. the memory code of an action, it can be said in somewhat general terms that this code includes three components (three neural cliques). One component lays down the kinematics of the action (input from proprioceptors that reflects changes in the position of the body and its parts in space throughout the action), another the dynamics (input from the efferent system that controls motor neurons), and the third component stores the data about the motive (goal) of the action (input from the limbic system).

It may be hypothesized that during perception of an action the recognition procedure involves three phases. First, using kinematics as a template, all memory codes with a similar kinematic component are found. Then, if there is more than one memory code, the dynamic aspect of the kinematics is assessed (contribution of dynamics to kinematics). If after that there are still several memory codes left, the action's goal component is checked. If only one memory code is left in the end, it means that the perceived action has been recognized—that is, it has been included in the category defined by this code. And since the memory code of a typified action is none other than the basic meaning of a corresponding verb, the phrase designating this code and, by inference, the perceived action are recognized simultaneously.

5. Mirror neurons and action recognition

The explanation of the process of action recognition offered above draws on Tsien's theory of memory codes. The process is interpreted somewhat differently in the theory of mirror neurons. Mirror neurons begin to fire when a person sees another person performing a purposeful physical action:

> In humans, as in monkeys, the sight of acts performed by others produces an immediate activation of the motor areas deputed to the organization and execution of those acts, and through this activation it is possible to decipher the meaning of the "motor events" observed, i.e. to *understand* them in *terms of goal-centred movements*. This understanding is **completely devoid of any reflexive, conceptual, and/or linguistic mediation** as it is based exclusively on the *vocabulary of acts* and the *motor knowledge* on which our capacity to act depends[4] (Rizzolatti and Sinigaglia 2008: 125) (original italics, emphasis added.—*A. K.*).

For Rizzolatti and Sinigaglia, to "decode the meaning" of an observed action is to understand, guided by its kinematics, its goal; it is specifically emphasized that mirror neurons don't react to certain goalless movements such as a wave of an arm (Ibid.: 84). Thus, a direct connection is assumed between the kinematics of an action (its 'live' image) and its goal. This makes an action appear as a two-component structure: kinematics—goal. Such an interpretation is at the basis of the hypothesis that it is possible to compile and use a dictionary of actions.

Let us recall that, according to our hypothesis, an action is at least a three-level hierarchical structure: kinematics—dynamics (force-dynamic schema)—goal; the dynamics of an action play an important role in its recognition. For example, walking and running are distinguished, primarily, by their dynamics (the support-and-push motion schema). If, however, a two-level interpretation of an action is accepted, the dynamic aspect of its recognition is lost.

Let us clarify the issues that arise here. We have already mentioned the well-known fact that many physical actions—walking and running in particu-

---

[4] Actually, mirror neurons react to a wide spectrum of human actions, even to point-light animation displays of walking and jogging (Fogassi and Ferrari 2011: 31).

lar—are instantly recognized by a single static image (see Fig. 3a that shows a fragment of a painting on an ancient vase; the image of the runner is slightly skewed because of the shape of the vase).

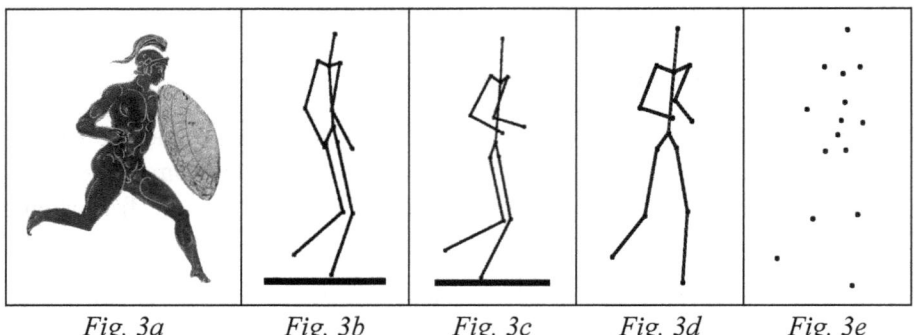

Fig. 3a	*Fig. 3b*	*Fig. 3c*	*Fig. 3d*	*Fig. 3e*

Moreover, we instantly recognize single "linear frames" of walking and running (see Fig. 3b and 3c). But this is probably the limit of what humans can do, as we cannot recognize running by a separate point-light frame (see Fig. 3d and 3e).

Mirror neurons also respond to static images (fragments) of actions, for example, to a single 'frame' of the grasping movement of a hand (Kourtzi and Kanwisher 2000; Urgesi et al. 2006). Thus, it appears that mirror neurons respond not only to observed actions but also to point-light animation displays (which look like apparently chaotic motions of a set of point-lights[5]) and to single static images of actions. It is not quite clear how recognition, guided by such poor (and, therefore, ambiguous) visual stimuli, can be "based exclusively on the *vocabulary of acts* and the *motor knowledge*", since even full-blown images of some actions are often ambiguous.

That being said, a claim may be made that the explanation of how actions are recognized, offered by the mirror neuron theory, is not quite adequate. It seems that the issues that emerge here go back to the reduced two-level representation of a physical action (kinematics—goal). As a matter of fact, such oversimplification involves at least two aspects of an action. First, the intermediate level of action **dynamics**, which connects the kinematics and the goal, is not taken into account. Second, it is ignored that, unlike for macaque monkeys, for humans a single action may have not only a **primary** (main) goal but also a **secondary** goal. For example, one can eat to satiate hunger

---

[5] See, for example, the following links: http://www.biomotionlab.ca/Demos/BMLwalker. html, and http://www.biomotionlab.ca/Demos/BMLrunner.html.

(primary goal) or to oblige one's hostess (secondary goal); see chap. 2, § 4, section 1.6.

The above said can be illustrated with the help of an example of how the type of human locomotion is recognized. Imagine a ballerina moving on the stage as if she were gliding, her feet keeping contact with the floor. Is her motion a fast walk or a dance? If we exclude the context (which is absent in Fig. 3c), much will depend on the reconstructed dynamic (support—take off) schema. If, after the next push of her take-off foot, the ballerina's body loses support (for a fleeting moment her feet only **touch** the floor), then she is running. If, however, the support is not lost, then it is a fast walk. Suppose we have identified it as a run—to be more precise, while moving on the stage the ballerina uses the **manner** of running. Now we must understand the goal of using this manner, whether it is primary or secondary. If the ballerina is trying to use the manner of running as a means to express some emotional state (secondary goal), then she is dancing; it would be odd to call it running. However, if the ballerina's main goal is a primary goal—simply to move to a different spot on the stage—then she is really running. And this goal is "computed" by taking the dynamics into account.

Building on the arguments above, it should not be difficult to describe the process of recognition of a single (but typical) frame of an action, i.e. to explain how it happens to be so informative as to define the action as a whole, including its kinematics, dynamics, and goal.

Consider again the image in Fig. 3c. First of all, we automatically build its dynamic (support—take off) schema. In this case it is clear that the person lands on his left foot after a rather strong take-off push and a short "flight". The arms bent at the elbows, the right foot raised high, and the torso leaning forward are all typical signs of landing after a short jump. Clearly, it is not a walking step (compare to Fig. 3b); neither is it the final phase of stepping over a puddle; in that case the motion dynamics and, consequently, kinematics would be different. In particular, the arms would be in quite a different position. Obviously, the main goal of this jump is just to move forward. For example, the light jump of a ballerina in a dancing run would have different dynamics and kinematics. It is most likely not the final phase of landing in a single long jump; therefore, it should be a fragment of some cyclical motion. But what kind of motion? Were the person hopping on one (left) foot, then, in accordance with the dynamics of this motion, the right foot would also be in a different position. There is no choice but to assume that this is just a sequential mini-jump with the goal of moving forward, and, by inference, that it will be instantly followed by just another such mini-jump. Therefore, what we see is running. A sequence of its separate frames is so tightly **integrated systemically**—is an "integral structure", according to Bernstein (see the quote above in section 3)—that a single frame defines this structure as a **whole**.

Thus, a single frame (Fig. 3c) allows us to recognize a person running, i.e. to reconstruct the **three-level** structure of locomotion: kinematics—dynamics—goal. Every component of the structure, including kinematics, is chosen from several alternatives in the course of cyclical comparison of the intermediate results of the recognition process.

In the mirror neurons approach, recognition of a perceived action is seen as a result of mirror neurons firing during perception of this action ("action simulation"). Based on our conclusions, it may be hypothesized that the mirror neurons' response is **collateral** to the independent process of recognition of an observed action. Indeed, during perception of an action's kinematics a clique that stores proprioceptive input is activated in the memory code for the action. This is followed by activation of other cliques in the memory code, including the clique that stores efferent input from the motor neurons that fire while the action is being performed. It is the activation of this clique that produces the mirror neurons effect.

6. Canonical neurons and object recognition

The recognition procedure for an observed object—its inclusion into one or another category of objects—is based on formula (4) given in § 1, which defines a concrete object as a system of visual and functional components. The process has been briefly described in section 4 of the same paragraph. It will be recalled here by considering perception of a chair with armrests as an example. We need to decide whether we are looking at a chair or an armchair. Guided by the object shape, we advance an initial hypothesis: this is a chair. This instantly activates the motor concept associated with the chair—SIT ON A CHAIR. In our mind, we sit on the perceived "chair" and test whether the psychophysical state 'semi-steady position of the body' pertains. If this state is acknowledged (as potentially experienceable) by the sitting person, then the perceived object is a chair. If it cannot be acknowledged, another hypothesis is tested: this is an "armchair", because the shape of the perceived object resembles that of an armchair. Now a different concept is activated—SIT IN AN ARMCHAIR. In our mind, we sit down as we would sit in an armchair and test whether the (potential) state of 'almost fully steady position of the body' may be acknowledged. If the answer is "yes", then the perceived object is an armchair. If the answer is "no", it is neither a chair nor an armchair.

A neurobiological interpretation of the relationship between the image of a perceived object and a typical interaction with this object is well known. This relationship is established by the so-called canonical neurons in the pre-motor region of the cortex (Rizzolatti and Sinigaglia 2008: 79; Gallese and Lakoff 2005: 461). They fire not only when the subject performs a certain interaction with an object, but also when the subject perceives an object with which he could actually perform such an interaction. For example, if a human subject sees a chair that is easily available, the canonical neurons instantaneously respond to the action "sit on a chair" (not by launching it automatically, but by "simulating" it).

The above discussion allows us to assume that the object recognition procedure is not in any way related to the canonical neurons effect. This effect is secondary and appears to be collateral to the independent process of object recognition.

Chapter 4

Elements of a sensory grammar

§ 1. On the basic and derivative meanings of nominal genitive constructions in Russian (*ručka dveri* *handle*-Nom *door*-Gen, *vetka dereva* *branch*-Nom *tree*-Gen)

1. The 'part-whole' relationship and its linguistic representation

Parsing an object (X) into parts (Y, Z, etc.) is something a native speaker can do easily (for relevant references, see Tversky et al. (2008)). In Russian, to state a fact that Y is a part of X a nominal genitive construction, *Y X*-Gen, is usually used (cf. Kategorija posessivnosti 1989; Kibrik 2003), where *Y* and *X* are concrete nouns: *stena doma* wall-Nom house-Gen ('the wall of the house'), *nosik čajnika* spout-Nom teapot-Gen ('the spout of the teapot'), *golova Ivana* head-Nom Ivan-Gen ('Ivan's head'[1]). It is generally assumed that in such cases the genitive expresses the 'part-whole' relationship 'Y is a part of X' (cf. Rakhilina 2000: 37, 39), for example, "parts of the body (*ruki* 'arms/ hands', *glaza* 'eyes', *pal'cy* 'fingers') and parts of artifacts (*guby ploskogub-cev* 'the lips of the pliers', *linzy očkov* 'the lenses of the glasses', *klaviši pišuščej mašinki* 'the keys of the typewriter')" (Liashevskaia 2004: 61).

However, a simple analysis shows that such an interpretation is in need of clarification. When speaking about lenses and keys, one can say *linzy očkov* 'the lenses of the glasses' or *klaviši pišuščej mašinki* 'the keys of the type-writer'. But when speaking about hands or fingers as body parts one cannot say **ruki tela* 'the hands of the body' or **pal'cy tela* 'the fingers of the body'. The interpretation given above falls short of explaining other uses as well.

---

[1] For the sake of readability and ease of understanding, only the literal translations of the Russian examples will be given in the rest of the chapter.—*Translator's note.*

The expression *dver' doma* 'the door of the house' can refer only to the entrance door, not to the door that leads, for example, from the corridor to the kitchen, in spite of the fact that it is also a part of the house. Gates are part of a fence, yet the expression **vorota zabora* 'the gates of the fence' is incorrect.

Clearly, for the nominal genitive to be used correctly in the construction *Y X*-Gen, it is not enough for Y to be a physical part of X. As will be illustrated further, for the construction *Y X*-Gen (where *Y* and *X* are concrete nouns) to be used correctly, the following condition must be met: Y, being a physical part of X, is also X's functional part; that is, the function of Y directly contributes to the general function of X. Thus, the entrance door is a functional part of the house (it opens and closes access to the house), while an interior door is not a functional part of the house as it does not contribute to the general function of the house. Therefore, one can say, for example, *dver' doma* 'the door of the house' about an entrance door but not about a kitchen door. Note that the expressions *dver' kuxni/komnaty* 'the door of the kitchen/room' are quite acceptable, while the expression **dver' koridora* 'the door of the corridor' is questionable (the correct expression is *koridornaja dver'* 'the corridor-Adj door') as it is not quite clear how the door contributes to the function of the corridor (after all, there may be corridors without doors). The function of a fence is to prevent trespassing, so it does not have to have a garden gate or gates—as in the case of a fence separating two adjoining gardens. Therefore, the expressions **kalitka/vorota zabora* 'the garden gate/ gates of the fence' are incorrect. Similarly, a door handle is operationally connected with the function of the door, helping to open and close the door. A peephole in the door, on the other hand, performs a different function which is not directly connected with the function of the door: it allows one to see who is standing outside the door. Therefore, the expression *ručka dveri* 'the handle of the door' is correct, while the expression **glazok dveri* 'the peephole of the door' is not. For the same reason, speaking about a mailbox attached to the entrance door or gate, one cannot say **počtovyj jaščik dveri/ kalitki* 'the mailbox of the door/gate'.

The walls also perform a direct and obvious function of a house (*stena doma* 'the wall of the house'), but a window in the wall does not have a function associated with the wall (**okno steny* 'the window of the wall'). Like a wall, a window has its own (and different) function contributing to the function of the house. Speaking about a prop holding up the leaning wall of a barn, one can say *podporka steny saraja* 'the prop of the wall of the barn', thereby acknowledging that it is a functional part of the wall; however, one cannot say something similar about a hook for work clothes nailed to the same wall; the expression *krjučok steny saraja 'the hook of the wall of the barn' is incorrect, as the hook has nothing to do with the function of the wall. For the same reason, the expressions kryl'co/podval/čerdak **doma** 'the porch/basement/attic of the house' are correct, while the expressions *veranda/prixožaja/pogreb/balkon doma 'the veranda/hallway/cellar/balcony of the house' are not. It is correct to say podporki doma 'the props of the house' but not *otmostka doma 'the perimeter pavement of the house', just as it is incorrect to say *garaž doma 'the garage of the house' about a built-in garage.

Consider the functional structure of a living-room. The expressions okna/dver'/potolok/pol/steny/ugly/ventiljacionnaja rešëtka **komnaty** 'the windows/door/ceiling/floor/walls/corners/ventilator grating of the room' are correct, but the expressions *balkon/časy/stol/škaf/batarei/ljustra/kovër **komnaty** 'the balcony/clock/table/wardrobe/radiators/chandelier/carpet of the room' are not. It may be concluded that the latter referents of Y (the noun that designates both a physical and functional part of the room such as a balcony, table, chandelier, etc.), in contrast with the former referents (the windows, ceiling, ventilator grating), do not perform any particular functions of the room. The expressions *gazovaja plita /mojka **kuxni** 'the gas stove/sink of the kitchen' do not sound natural in Russian because the function of the kitchen is much broader than cooking and having meals or washing the dishes. Similarly, the function of a bathroom is broader than having a bath in it, therefore the expression *Vanna našej vannoj komnaty udobnee, čem vanna vo fligele 'The bathtub of our bathroom is more comfortable than the bathtub in the wing' sounds odd.

The examples given above suggest that the incorrect use of the nominal genitive in the construction Y X-Gen—and, correspondingly, the functional dependency of Y on X—may entail one of the following: either Y is functionally connected not with X itself but with some functional part of X (the expressions *fortočka doma 'the ventilation pane of the house' or *pol doma 'the floor of the house' are incorrect as compared to the correct expressions fortočka okna 'the ventilation pane of the window' or pol komnaty 'the floor of the room'), or Y, while remaining a physical part of X, is functionally independent of X. For example, a balcony or an aerial are functionally independent of the house. It is incorrect to say *balkon doma/komnaty 'the balcony of the house/room' or *antenna doma/kryši 'the aerial of the house/roof', but the expression naružnaja antenna televizora 'the outdoor aerial of the TV' is quite correct.

2. Objects and their functional parts

It goes without saying that native speakers of Russian cannot learn all the possible cases of distribution of functions between an object and its physical parts. How, then, do they know when the construction *Y X*-Gen can be used and when not? The ease and certainty with which they do it give grounds to assume that the speaker computes, automatically and subconsciously, the function of a newly perceived object, which then helps to compute the structure of the object's parts.

That there is a functional relationship between objects X and Y, of which the latter is smaller than and functionally connected with the former, is tested by the speaker as early as the perception phase. For example, when a handle is attached to the door or a peephole is made in it, there emerge in the doer's experienced image of the door the relationships 'the handle is now a functional part of the door (it becomes functionally subordinate to it)' and 'the peephole sustains its functional independence (it is functionally independent of the door')—all this regardless of whether the doer wishes to say anything at all about the new objects and their relationships. However, should he wish to do so, the new relationships have already been established and are "ready" for linguistic reference: the expression *ručka dveri* 'the handle of the door' is correct, while **glazok dveri* 'the peephole of the door' is not.

> **Note.** The above considerations allow us to infer that humans, recognizing and categorizing the surrounding world, spontaneously attribute functions to all objects—not only things, but also landscape entities such as a river, mountain, forest, etc. Therefore, we know that expressions such as *morja i okeany / lesa i gory* **Zemli** 'the seas and oceans / forests and mountains of **Earth**', *reki i doliny / poleznye iskopaemye / atmosfera / zelёnyj pokrov* **Zemli** 'the rivers and valleys / mineral resources / atmosphere / green mantle of Earth' are correct, because their referents are immediate functional constituents of Earth. By contrast, expressions such as **ovragi / rečki / rošči / neboskrёby / neftjanye skvažiny / ugol'nye kar'ery* **Zemli** 'the gullies / brooks / groves / skyscrapers / oil wells / coal quarries of **Earth**' are incorrect; however, the following expressions are correct: *ovragi/rečki/rošči* **našej mestnosti** 'the gullies/brooks/groves of our country', *neboskrёby / neftjanye skvažiny / ugol'nye kar'ery* **Sibiri** 'the skyscrapers / oil wells / coal quarries of Siberia', and the like. It is incorrect to say **zvёzdy neba* 'the stars of the sky' because stars are independent of the sky both physically and functionally; by contrast, the expression *zvёzdy nebosvoda* 'the stars of the firma-

ment' is quite correct because stars are an important part of the concept 'firmament'.

In a similar fashion, we understand ('compute') that for a small private house the lowest level of its functional parts will be the level of the room (*komnaty doma* 'the rooms of the house'), while for an apartment building it will be the level of the apartment rather than the level of the room (*kvartiry neboskrëba* 'the apartments of the skyscraper', not **komnaty neboskrëba* 'the rooms of the skyscraper').

3. The basic meaning of the nominal genitive construction *Y X*-Gen

Thus, the genitive construction *Y X*-Gen, referring to object X and object Y when Y is physically connected to X, is correct only on condition that Y possesses one of the direct, particular functions of X. Thereby the genitive indicates that Y is not only a physical but also a functional part of X. Turning to the structure of the basic meaning of word (Prototype → Function, cf. chap. 2, § 1, section 1.5; § 2, section 1.1), we formulate the following:

(1)   *Y X*-Gen (basic meaning) = Prototype: "A non-composite object, X, has an inalienable physical part, Y" → Function 'The function of Y is part of the general function of X, i.e. it contributes to this general function'.

Consider the following example. The general function of *vešalka* '(clothes) hanger' is 'to provide for the possibility to store clothes in a hanging position'. Imagine a hanger in the form of a board with hooks that has been nailed to the wall. Here every single hook adds up to the hanger's function, but the nails don't. The nails have a different function—to keep the hanger from falling; therefore, the expression *krjučok vešalki* 'the hook of the hanger' is correct, while the expression **gvozd' vešalki* 'the nail of the hanger' is not. Now imagine that the outermost left and right hooks broke and were replaced by nails hammered into the board, on which the clothes are now hung. In this case, the expression *levyj gvozd' vešalki* 'the left nail of the hanger' will be quite correct, because this nail contributes to the general function of the hanger.

As soon as physical connection between X and Y is lost, the genitive construction becomes incorrect. If the spout of a teapot broke and was lying on the floor, it would be incorrect to say **nosik čajnika* 'the spout of the teapot'; the correct phrase would be *nosik ot čajnika* 'the spout from the teapot'. If we see a wheel lying by a car, we say *koleso ot mašiny* 'the wheel from the car', not **koleso mašiny* 'the wheel of the car'.

4. The derivative meanings of the nominal genitive

Similarly to words, which may have extended meanings, the nominal genitive construction also has extended (metaphoric) meanings derived from the basic meaning, as shown in (1):

a) 'Y is a portion of substance X': *stakan moloka* 'a glass of milk', *kilogramm mjasa* 'a kilogram of meat';

b) 'Y belongs to X', if Y and X are autonomous objects: *kniga Ivana* 'Ivan's book', *mašina načal'nika* 'the boss's car';

c) 'Y 'belongs' to X': *aktër kino* 'the actor of the movies', and the like.

For a more detailed discussion of the different meanings of the nominal genitive see Shakhmatov (2001: 314–318).

5. Objects with a multilevel partitive structure

Let us consider a bicycle. As a first approximation, its function may be formulated as follows:

(2)   Bicycle (function) = 'a wheeled means of transport allowing a person to move while sitting on it; the person turns its wheels by pushing on the pedals with his feet and steers it by turning the handlebars to the left or to the right'

The main parts of a bicycle are the frame, handlebars, saddle, wheels, and pedals (hence the correctness of the phrases *rama/rul'/siden'e/kolësa/pedali velosipeda* 'the frame/handlebars/saddle/wheels/pedals of the bicycle'), but not the spokes, pump, bell, lamp, chain, brake, tires, etc. (hence the incorrectness of the phrases **spicy/nasos/zvonok/fonar'/cep'/tormoz velosipeda* 'the spokes/pump/bell/lamp/chain/brake of the bicycle'). Meanwhile it is quite correct to say *tormoz perednego kolesa* 'the brake of the front wheel', *šina zadnego kolesa* 'the tire of the rear wheel', *velosipednye spicy* 'bicycle-Adj spokes' or *velosipednyj fonar'* 'bicycle-Adj lamp'.

The hierarchical structure of the bicycle

The main parts of the bicycle (wheels, saddle, handlebars, etc.) form the first level of functional hierarchy; parts of these parts (the spokes and tire of each wheel, saddle springs, etc.) form the second level, and parts of these (spoke nuts, tire valves) the third level. As mentioned earlier, the incorrect use of the construction *Y X*-Gen can entail one of two things: either the given part belongs to a lower level of X's partitive hierarchy, or Y is functionally independent of X altogether, although it is connected with it physically, cf.: *nasos velosipeda 'the pump of the bicycle' or *fonar'rulja 'the lamp of the handlebars'.

It may be assumed that a native speaker of Russian can decide whether the expressions given above and many other similar expressions are correct just because, on the one hand, he is familiar with the general function of the bicycle as defined in (2) and with how it works in principle and, on the other hand, he hears such expressions from the people around him. Thanks to this knowledge, he intuitively builds ("computes") the hierarchical structure of the bicycle and its functional parts as described above.

An objection could be raised that the described partitive structure is too complicated for the average native speaker, and that he is unlikely to know and use it. However, were this the case the speaker would most probably not be capable of judging the correctness or incorrectness of many expressions of the kind given above.

6. The partitive structure of plants

It may be assumed that the native speaker's knowledge of the functions of objects is subconscious. Definition (1) allows us to use the genitive construction Y X-Gen to explicate the partitive structure of various objects and their general functions. So far we have discussed the genitive construction only with regard to the non-organic objects that this construction describes. Let us now consider cases where X is a living organism. Take a tree, for example. A native speaker of Russian subconsciously interprets its functional structure as substantially different from the structure of an inanimate object. He assumes that practically all physical parts of the tree—not just the roots, trunk, and branches, but also the leaves, buds, and bark—belong to the tree as a whole. In other words, the tree has a single-level partitive structure. This is demonstrated by the correctness of the expressions vetvi/korni/stvol dereva 'the branches/roots/trunk of the tree' and list'ja/počki dereva 'the leaves/buds of the tree'. It seems that the leaves and buds should be a second level in the hierarchy, as they physically belong to the branches; however, the incorrectness of the expressions *list'ja/počki vetok 'the leaves/buds of the branches' shows that there is no second level in the hierarchy. This is also true with regard to the roots, which are part of the tree and not of the trunk, cf.: *korni stvola 'the roots of the trunk'. Neither can one say *sučok stvola 'the twig of the trunk' or *sučok vetki 'the twig of the branch'.

This observation is of a general character: any single part (that is, a part with a function) of a living organism is an immediate functional constituent of the organism as a whole. This claim will be shown to be true with regard to humans as well (see section 7).

Note that the functional subordination of some parts of the tree is twofold: *kora stvola* 'the bark of the trunk' and *kora dereva* 'the bark of the tree', *serdcevina stvola* 'the heartwood of the trunk' and *serdcevina dereva* 'the heartwood of the tree'. However, this does not contradict the general conclusion made above: the bark, being subordinate to the tree, is also in local functional subordination.

An interesting, but quite explainable, exception to this general rule should be mentioned: at a certain moment in time the speaker begins to view the fruit of the tree as functionally autonomous "alien" parts of the tree. Thus, the phrase *Zavjazi ètoj jabloni xorošo vzjalis'* 'The ovaries of this apple-tree have taken on well' is correct, while **Jabloki ètoj jabloni uže sozreli* 'The apples of this apple-tree have already ripened' is not. Meanwhile the phrase *Jabloki ètoj jabloni uže v korzinax (prodany)* 'The apples of this apple-tree are already in the baskets (sold)' is quite correct. The genitive construction here has the metaphoric meaning 'the relationship of belonging', because the apples are interpreted as autonomous objects separated from the apple-tree—compare with a similar expression *synov'ja materi* 'the sons of the mother'.

This interpretation sometimes escapes the attention of researchers. Thus, Liashevskaia (2004) observes: "The secret of countability of nuts, berries and beans lies in the fact that they designate these fruit as **parts** of the plant, cf.: *jagody eževiki* 'the berries of the blackberry bush', *boby kanavalii* 'the beans of Canavalia [a kind of legume]'..." (p. 237; original emphasis). In view of what has been said above, these phrases do not express a 'part-whole' relationship between the berries and the blackberry bush or between the beans and the legume because the fruit has already been picked and **separated** from the plants. If, however, the fruit is still attached to the plant and ripening, thus remaining, physically, part of the plant, such expressions are incorrect.

Any alien entity physically connected with a tree (a bird's nest, a starling-house or a basket ring nailed to the tree, a rope-swing tied to the tree branch, etc.) is interpreted by the speaker as functionally autonomous, hence incorrectness of the expressions **gnezdo/skvorečnik **dereva*** 'the nest/starling-house of the tree' or **kačeli **dereva*** 'the swing of the tree'.

Now, is a tree growing from the ground and physically connected with it an independent, functionally autonomous object (organism), or is it part (Y) of the ground (X)? Incorrectness of the expressions **derevo zemli/xolma/veršiny* *utësa* 'the tree of the ground/hill/top of the cliff' shows that the speaker views the tree as an autonomous organism.

To conclude this section, let us take a quick look at the partitive structure of an apple. The following main functional parts of an apple can be singled out: the skin, the flesh, the pips (seeds), and the pedicel (or fruit stalk[2]) on which it is suspended while growing and ripening. This is confirmed by correctness of the expressions *kožura*/*mjakot'*/*zërnyški*/*plodonožka jabloka* 'the skin/flesh/pips/pedicel of the apple'. This set of parts is not accidental; it stems from the speaker's intuitive understanding of the general function of the

Fig. 1

apple: 'to ensure the ripening and subsequent germination of the pips—the apple seeds'. Each part from the set contributes to the realization of this function. The skin serves a protective function, the flesh provides nourishment for the germinating seeds, and the pedicel supplies nourishment necessary for the growth and development of seeds and the apple as a whole. As an illustration, consider the apple in Fig. 1. It is quite correct to say *plodonožka jabloka* 'the pedicel of the apple', but incorrect to say **listik jabloka* 'the leaf of the apple' or **listik plodonožki* 'the leaf of the pedicel'.

The explanation is simple: the speaker, guided by the function of the apple and its parts, understands at once that, by contrast to the pedicel itself, a leaf that grows from it does not contribute either to the general function of the apple or to the particular function of the pedicel.

7. The partitive structure of animals and humans

We will now consider the functional structure of humans and the human body. It will be shown that in terms of the part-whole relationship this structure is similar to the structure of a tree.

Rakhilina (2000) gives a detailed analysis of the uses of the genitive construction *Y X*-Gen with reference to parts of the human body. Briefly, her approach is as follows. Expressions such as *pal'cy levoj ruki* 'the fingers of the left hand', *pjatka pravoj nogi* 'the heel of the right foot' are correct because there is another, alternative whole X to which Y belongs (the left hand for the fingers, the left foot for the heel). If, however, there isn't such an alternative for Y, the use of the genitive becomes incorrect, cf.: **ruki tela* 'the arms of the

---

[2] *Plodonožka* ['pedicel']—"part of the stalk that connects the fruit with the plant" (Ushakov, III: col. 302).

body', *pjatki nog 'the heels of the feet', *pupok života 'the navel of the belly';
"[...] one cannot say *uxo golovy ['the ear of the head'] since the ear is not
a part of something else, just as the navel is found only on the belly, heels on
the feet, and so on" (Rakhilina 2000: 39–40).

This interpretation is true about most of the uses of the genitive with reference to body parts. Yet it fails to cover a number of uses. For example, the
expression *nogti ruk 'the nails of the hands' is incorrect although there is an
alternative—nails on the toes. Similarly, the expression *volosy golovy 'the
hair of the head' is incorrect despite the existence of alternatives—hair on the
chest or legs.

Discussing such uses in detail, Raxilina also considers some exceptions to
the rule she herself formulates, such as the correctness of the expression kisti
ruk 'the wrists of the arms' (although only arms have wrists), the incorrectness
of the expression *pal'cy pravoj stupni 'the toes of the right foot' (although
there are toes on the left foot as well), the acceptability of the expression koža
ruk 'the skin of the hands' (while *koža pravogo boka 'the skin of the right
side' is unacceptable), etc.; in each such case she offers a particular interpretation of the exception.

In contrast, the basic meaning formulated in (1) seems to provide a uniform
interpretation to these and other similar cases. In fact, the expression *nogti
ruk 'the nails of the hands' is incorrect because nails do not add up to the function of hands; they contribute to the function of fingers (cf. nogti pal'cev 'the
nails of the fingers'). On the other hand, the claws of an eagle or tiger add up
to the direct function of the eagle's feet or tiger's paws; therefore, the expressions kogti orlinyx/tigrinyx lap 'the claws of the eagle's feet / tiger's paws' are
correct. Compare the correct phrases Kogti lap podrezany 'The claws of the
paws have been clipped' and Tak inogda lukavyj kot [...] Razinet kogti xitryx
lap 'Thus would sometimes a playful cat [...] Display the claws of its sly
paws' [Pushkin. Count Nulin], and the incorrect phrase *Nogti ruk podstriženy
'The nails of the hands have been trimmed'. Wrists, on the contrary, add up to
the function of the arms, therefore the expression kisti ruk 'the wrists of the
arms' is correct.

In a similar way, the unacceptability (or questionability) of the expression
*pal'cy pravoj stupni 'the toes of the right foot' is due to the fact that, unlike,
for example, the fingers of the right hand, which are controlled by the hand
and contribute to its function (pal'cy pravoj kisti 'the fingers of the right
hand'), the toes are weakly controlled by the foot and do not contribute to its
function (*pal'cy pravoj stupni 'the toes of the right foot'). They contribute to
the jogging function of the foot, which explains the correctness of the expres-

sion *pal'cy nogi* 'the toes of the foot'.[3] The sole and heel, by contrast, contribute to the function of the foot, making expressions such as *pjatka/podošva stupni* 'the heel/sole of the foot' quite acceptable. It is possible to say *koža ruk* 'the skin of the hands' only on condition that the skin performs some specific function of the hands, for example to show how well the hands of a woman are taken care of, cf.: *šelkovistaja koža eë ruk* 'the silky skin of her hands'. If, however, a farmer or a worker is described, the state of his skin will be characterized in a different way, for example, *ogrubevšaja koža na ego rukax* 'the callous skin on his hands' (compare with the questionable expression ?*ogrubevšaja koža ego ruk* 'the callous skin of his hands').

In addition, some extrinsic formations may appear on a human body which have nothing to do with the functions of the body itself, cf.: **mozol'pjatki* 'the corn of the heel', **mozol' čeloveka* 'the callousness of the man', *borodavka nosa 'the wart of the nose' (the correct expression would be *borodavka na nosu* 'the wart on the nose').

Thus, similarly to a tree, almost all parts of the human body are functionally subordinate to the person and not to his body, cf.: *telo/golova/ruki/nogi/ glaza/uši/bok/koža čeloveka* 'the body/head/hands/feet/eyes/ears/side/skin of a person'. Sometimes such functional subordination is twofold: *kisti čeloveka* 'the wrists of the person' and *kisti ego ruk* 'the wrists of his arms', *nogti čeloveka* 'the nails of a person' and *nogti ego pal'cev* 'the nails of his fingers', etc.

Just as in the case of the fruit of plants, a human fetus is not viewed as a functional part of the female that bears it; the expression *plod ženščiny 'the fetus of the female' is incorrect, and the acceptable expressions are *plod* 'the fetus' or *materinskij plod* 'the mother's fetus'. The situation here is even more obvious. While ovaries are, up to a certain moment, viewed as functional parts of a tree—cf. the acceptable expression *zavjazi jabloni* 'the ovaries of the apple-tree'—a human fetus is viewed as functionally autonomous from the start; hence incorrectness of the expression *zarodyš materi 'the embryo of the mother' (one should say *materinskij zarodyš* 'the mother's embryo' or simply *zarodyš* 'the embryo'). It is possible to say *rebënok materi* 'the baby of the mother' only about a baby that has been born and physically separated from the mother. This expression would become anomalous if used to refer to a baby still in the womb.

---

[3] In Russian, *noga* may refer both to the entire lower limb (leg) and to the foot, while *stupnja* (also *stopa*, from the verb *stupat'* 'step') refers only to the foot. This creates certain difficulties in translating expressions such as *pal'cy stupni/nogi.—Translator's note.*

§ 2. On structural and genetic similarity of lexical and grammatical categories. The meaning of transitivity

Chapter 2 was devoted to an analysis of lexical meanings of sensory words (nouns and verbs), that is, words (such as *stol* 'table', *derevo* 'tree', *bežit* 'is running', *udaril* 'hit', etc.) whose typical referents (objects and actions) are quite explicit: they are identified by their appearance, without the help of any context. We can always distinguish between a typical table and a typical chair, or between a typical running event and a typical walking event, and so forth.[4] As a result of such an analysis, we identified two general structures bearing on the semantics of sensory words.

1. The structure of basic meaning

In §§ 1–4, the following structure of the basic meaning of a word was identified:

(1) Basic meaning = visual Prototype → Function.

Here the Prototype defines the typical visual (or perceptual, in a broad sense) feature of word referents, and the Function defines the functional (causal, intentional) feature characteristic not only of typical but of all referents. This structure is a first step towards developing a cognitive language of thought. The components of the structure—the prototype, the function, and the relationship of interpretation—are of a purely cognitive, non-verbal nature. Concrete and motor concepts made up of these components are basic units of this special language, the language of thought.

2. The structure of polysemy

In chapter 2, § 5, it was shown with a number of examples that lexical polysemy has, approximately, the following structure. A sensory word, typically, has one basic meaning (it is more concrete and obvious, and is given first in explanatory dictionaries) and a range of derivative meanings that are metaphoric and metonymic extensions from the basic meaning. In other words, the following claim seems justified:

---

[4] It should be noted that not all concrete nouns are sensory in this sense. For example, certain parts of objects such as the leg of a sofa/chair, the shaft of an umbrella or the base of a standard lamp, in order to be recognized, require context—that is, the object, of which they are parts (for more details see § 1).

(2) The structure of meanings of a sensory word is as follows: basic
     meaning—a variety of meanings derived from the basic meaning (meta-
     phors and metonymies).

The structure given in (2) allows us to explain the mechanisms for the
emergence of new word meanings and occasional uses. As has been mentioned
in § 5, the most important feature of human language is the ability to use its
lexical and grammatical items in an occasional way, that is, in novel senses
that have not been encountered before. Thereby the already existing linguistic
means are used to describe novel real world phenomena. Thus, explaining the
mechanisms of occasional word uses is one of the central problems in the
theory of cognitive semantics. One possible solution of this problem is provided by the structure in (2).

In what follows it will be shown that a great number of grammatical items
also include sensory units, and their meanings are structurally and genetically
similar to lexical meanings. In particular, the basic meaning of a sensory
grammatical unit has the structure shown in (1), while its polysemy is structured as shown in (2). In other words, the lexical and grammatical meanings
of sensory linguistic units are structurally and genetically indistinguishable.
The validity of this hypothesis for verb transitivity will be shown in the next
section, and for voice, in § 3.

3. The meaning of transitivity

There is a long-standing tradition to give a semantic interpretation of the syntactic feature of transitivity—the ability of a verb to take a direct object in the
accusative (cf. relevant references in Letuchii 2014). Here we will touch upon
the direction of research that aims to define the prototypical transitive event,
or the transitive scenario, and is represented in the works of Slobin (1982),
Givón (1990: 565), and Wierzbicka (1996). For example, siding with Givón,
Wierzbicka writes:

> In my terms, the prototypical transitive scenario can be represented as follows:
>
> (61) at some time, someone was doing (did) something to something
>   because of this,
>   something happened to this something at the same time
>   this person wanted this (to happen)
>
> Of course "transitive sentences" don't have to meet all the aspects of
> this scenario, but a departure from any of them is likely to lead to a de-

crease in syntactic transitivity (manifested in case assignment, passivizabil-
ity, and so on) (Wierzbicka 1996: 420).

Upon closer scrutiny this otherwise clear formulation gives rise to a number
of questions. For example, what is the meaning of the words "something happened"? If someone hit a ball with his foot (*udaril po mjaču nogoj*), did
"something happen" to the ball or did it not? If something did happen, why is
the verb *udaril* 'hit' used intransitively? Or, when a boy is reading a book
(*mal'čik čitaet knigu*), does something happen to the book or not? If nothing
happens, why is a transitive verb used?

In our definition of transitivity two notions are introduced: Prototype—
visual (objective) changes in the object caused by the Agent's contact with the
object—and Function (interpretation); they indicate that the changes in the
object, both observable and unobservable, are caused by the Agent, are relevant to the Agent, and are the Agent's goal. For example, if a farmer measures
the field (*izmerjaet pole*), it changes, from his point of view, as it acquires a new
important property—the square area. Therefore, the use of a transitive verb is
appropriate here, although the field doesn't undergo any visible changes.

Thus, our definition of semantic transitivity includes the following: **prototype**, which is similar to Wierzbicka's interpretation and describes typical
cases (scenarios) of transitivity, and **function**, which describes the interpretation of the actions by the Agent. This interpretation covers **all** (not just typical)
cases of transitivity.

(T) Verb transitivity (basic meaning) =
> Prototype: The Agent performs an observable CONTACT action with
> the direct object (Patient) which simultaneously undergoes visible
> changes →
> Function: The Agent performs an action THEREFORE the direct object
> simultaneously undergoes changes that are relevant to the Agent and
> are the Agent's goal.

By this definition, verb transitivity is included in the category of sensory units.
It should be noted that there are certain ties between the properties of the
prototype and the function. Firstly, the relation 'Agent in CONTACT with
direct object' is a manifestation of the causal relation 'Agent performs an action THEREFORE the direct object undergoes changes'. If we recall the experiments conducted by Leslie (see chap. 2, § 7, section 2), they have shown
that at 7 months infants interpret the collision (contact) of a moving ball with
a stationary ball as the cause of the subsequent motion of the latter (cf. also
Pinker 2007: 67). Secondly, the visible change in the direct object is a mani-

festation of objective relevance of its change, not just from the point of view of the Agent. These two properties are typical of verbs that designate actions of Agent coming into physical contact with objects, these actions causing visible changes in the objects: *gruzit'* 'load', *myt'* 'wash', *krasit'* 'paint', *rubit'* 'chop' and so forth. Cf.:

> [...] In the three object syntagms given above (*vzjal topor* 'took an ax', *srubil derevo* 'felled a tree', and *postroil dom* 'built a house') the roles of arguments [...] differ on many features (and this difference may be linguistically substantial), but from the point of view of the Russian language they display more common features than differences: all three roles correspond to the "object" (or "patient") which is the final point of application of energy on the part of a conscious doer ("agent") and which, as a result, suffers observable physical changes (Plungian 2011: 114).

Some changes in the object (its destruction, change of shape or location, etc.) are objectively relevant to human ethnic communities; therefore, verbs from respective classes (*razdavit'* 'crush/squash', *ubit'* 'kill', etc.) are transitive in many languages (Letuchii 2014). In this respect, the Russian verb *udarit'* 'hit-PF' is of special interest. In the Russian lingua-culture the shaking of an object, caused by something or someone hitting this object, is not interpreted as a relevant change in the object; therefore, in phrases such as *Ivan udaril po mjaču nogoj / po zaboru palkoj* 'Ivan hit the ball with his foot / the fence with a stick' the verb *udarit'* is used intransitively. However, when it is a human or an animal that is hit, the verb is used transitively, cf.: *Ivan udaril Petra/sobaku* 'Ivan hit Peter / the dog'. In this case, the changes in the Patient (the suffering of pain) are interpreted as relevant.

In some cases, the relevance of changes in the object, caused by the Agent, are of a subjective character. If the speaker interprets such changes as substantial, he uses a transitive verb, whereas if he interprets them as unsubstantial, he uses an intransitive verb. For example, a girl complains about her brother to her mother: *On menja **obryzgal** vodoj* 'He spattered me with water' (a transitive verb is used because the changes are relevant to the sister). Her brother doesn't see the changes as relevant, and his response is: *Da ja **bryznul** na neë vsego paru raz*, lit. 'Well, I spattered [water] on her just a couple of times' (an intransitive verb is used; see an exhaustive analysis in Pinker 2007: 42–51).

A whole range of transitive verbs designate changes in the object that are subjective by their very nature and are not universally relevant. For example, in the clause *Ivan osveščaet dorogu fonarikom*, lit. 'Ivan lights the road with a flashlight', the observed action ('lights') of the Agent does not, strictly speaking, change the road. To Ivan, however, the road changes in an obvious way; therefore, this use satisfies the function from definition (T). Transitivity of the phrase *Mal'čik čitaet knigu* 'The boy is reading a book' is explained in a similar way. The changes that occur here are relevant only to the boy reading the book: to him, the part of the book that has been read differs from the unread part of the same book. Compare also the following uses: *Ivan smotrit na knigu* 'Ivan is looking at the book' (the direction of his gaze is fixed, the book does not undergo any changes) and *Ivan smotrit knigu*, lit. 'Ivan is looking [through] the book' (is leafing through the book to learn what it is about—to him, the book undergoes changes). The clauses *Vrač smotrit na pacienta* 'The doctor is looking at the patient' and *Vrač smotrit pacienta*, lit. 'The doctor is looking [= examining] the patient' are another example of similar uses. The transitive expression *razgljadyvat' kartinu*, lit. 'to scrutinize the picture', means to shift one's gaze, to look at it from different angles and learn something new about it that changes the picture in the eyes of the beholder; the same is true about the transitive expression *analizirovat' kartinu* 'to analyze the picture'. By contrast, the intransitive expression *vsmatrivat'sja v kartinu* 'to peer at the picture' indicates that the subject is looking intently at the picture; whether he learns something new about it or not remains unspecified.

Heretofore we have considered examples of transitive verbs used in their basic meaning; the situations they designated satisfied the function from definition (T). Let us now look at the metaphoric and metonymic uses of transitive verbs.

Consider transitive verbs designating states, taking, as an example, the sentence *Maša požalela bezdomnogo* 'Masha took pity on the homeless man'. This sentence is an example of **metaphoric** use of transitivity which does not satisfy the function from (T). The referent of the verb in this case is not the action performed by Masha, but the change of her state. Moreover, the semantic roles of the predicate arguments have changed: Masha is not the Agent, she is the Experiencer (she perceives visual and acoustic data), and the homeless man is not the Patient but the Stimulus (the source of data for Masha). At the same time, the homeless man has changed from Masha's point of view—now he makes her pity him. The metaphor created from the basic meaning is founded just on this similarity. As can be seen, metaphoric use of transitivity results in a loss of important features of the basic meaning.[5]

---

[5] This is typical of metaphors. In the metaphoric phrase *Ivan bežit na meste* 'Ivan is running on the spot' the crucial features of running are absent—Ivan's motion and his goal to reach a certain point in space. The metaphoric use of *bežit* 'is running' is motivated solely by the apparent similarity between running on the spot and just running. This ex-

This begs the question: how can transitivity of the verb of state in the sentence *Maša žaleet bezdomnogo* 'Masha pities the homeless man' be explained if no changes occur whatsoever? The answer is rather simple: this is transitivity in a **metonymic** sense (Reformatskii 1996: 47). The verb *žaleet* 'pities' designates the resultant state of the process "požalel" ('took pity'), i.e. transition from one state to another. (Cf.: *Voda napolnjaet vannu* 'The water is filling the bathtub' (a process) and *voda napolnjaet vannu* 'the water fills the bathtub' (a resultant state: the tub is full)—a metonymy.) Nothing changes in the state of the homeless person; therefore, this transitive use is extremely far from the basic meaning (T). However, the metonymic mechanism frees the speaker from the necessity to invent new linguistic items for designating Masha's final state, allowing him to use the means that are already available, namely, verb transitivity and the mechanism of metonymy.

§3. The basic and derivative meanings of voice. The active, passive, and reflexive meanings

1. A cognitive approach to the analysis of voice meanings

As has already been noted, the so-called "listing" approach to defining linguistic meanings comes short of explaining the mechanisms involved in the formation of new meanings and occasional uses of polysemous linguistic items. Nevertheless, it is precisely this approach that reigns in the description of grammatical forms—particularly voice forms, which are almost invariably identified as a list of 20 to 30 meanings usually unrelated to one another (Kniazev 2007: 262–263). As has been shown by Koshelev (2016), this array of meanings may be represented as a ramified chain whose links are connected by metaphoric and metonymic transfers. This claim will be briefly illustrated

---

ample is a good illustration of the opportunities, provided by language to the speaker, to use familiar linguistic forms to express new content: the apparent similarity of the observed action to the known referent of the verb provides motivation for designating the action "to quickly shift one's feet on the spot" (which has little to do with running) by the verb *bežit* 'is running' (with an addition of context that elucidates the designated referent: *bežit na meste* 'is running on the spot'). The aforesaid, however, does not mean that there are no limits to metaphorization. Not any goal-object similar to the source-object can be metaphorically designated by the name of the source. For example, a lion or a tiger can be called a cat, but a wolf cannot be called a dog, a spoon cannot be called a fork, and so forth (cf. Koshelev 2015b: 291, 318–323). The formation of metonymies is also subject to strict rules (see Note in §3, section 3).

in the rest of this paragraph, where the meaning of the reflexive voice will be shown to be a metonymy from the active voice, and the meaning of the passive voice a metaphor from the reflexive voice.

There is a lot of literature on the meanings of voice (for bibliographic reviews see: Testelets 2001: 435–436; Plungian 2011: 223–227; for a brief case history see: Kulikov 2011: 368–369). Traditionally, voice is defined as the relationship between the structure of semantic roles of verb arguments (Agent, Patient, etc.) and the structure of their syntactic roles (subject, direct object, etc.). For example, in the active voice of a transitive verb Agent is expressed by the subject and Patient by the direct object in the accusative (*Maša*-Nom *pričësyvaet kuklu*-Acc 'Masha is combing the doll['s hair]'). In the passive voice the same semantic roles are designated differently—Patient by the subject and Agent by the indirect object (*Kukla*-Nom *pričësyvaetsja Mašej*-Ins). Finally, in the reflexive voice both semantic roles are combined and are designated by the subject (*Maša pričësyvaetsja* 'Masha is combing [her hair]'). A different approach uses the concept of 'communicative rank' of the verb argument (cf., e.g., Plungian 2011: 187–188).

The approach discussed below is, essentially, as follows. Among many real world phenomena relevant for the vital functions of human beings, changes that occur in the world are, perhaps, the most important. Therefore, in human adaptive interactions with the world, perception and categorization of the observed changes in living beings, objects, dry substances, liquids, scenery, and so forth play a crucial role. We believe that the meanings of the active, passive, and reflexive voice reflect three most general types of change undergone by the Agent. The active voice reflects **independent** changes in the Agent (*Mal'čik moet mašinu* 'The boy is washing the car'), the passive reflects **dependent** changes (*Mašina moetsja* 'The car is being washed'), and the reflexive both **independent** and **dependent** simultaneous changes (*Mal'čik moetsja* 'The boy is washing himself').

Let us assume that the dichotomy **independent** vs. **dependent** changes in the object is intrinsically primary for humans. We believe that a human individual perceiving a change occurring in an object instantly identifies it, categorizing it either as an independent change (for example, a person is running/falling/waving a hand) or a dependent change (e.g., a stone is getting warm: the sunrays light the stone THEREFORE it gets warm; a boat is sailing: the wind fills the sail THEREFORE the boat sails). It is likely that the human ability to distinguish between independent and dependent changes is species-specific and does not depend on language. This ability becomes manifested in children during the first 12 months and from then on it keeps improving.

Acquisition of the laws of nature by children and the causal relationships that exist in the world are discussed in more detail in chap. 2, § 7.

The formation of the dichotomy "independent vs. dependent changes" is based on the ability of humans to distinguish pairs of observable changes that are linked by a causal relationship: Change 2 occurs BECAUSE Change 1 occurs (e.g. a stationary ball, 1, began to move BECAUSE a rolling ball, 2, collided with it). Change 2 is a dependent change. If, at the same time, there isn't Change 0 such that it directly causes Change 1, the latter is an independent change. An independent change may be both single (when it doesn't cause another, dependent change) and dual, causing another, dependent change. In language, single changes are described by intransitive verbs (*čelovek bežit/ padaet* 'a person is running/falling', *veter duet* 'the wind is blowing'), and dual changes by transitive verbs (*čelovek režet xleb / vzjal knigu / uronil nož* 'the person is cutting the bread / took the book / dropped the knife'). This claim needs clarification.

Consider an action such as "Ivan režet xleb nožom" ["Ivan is cutting/slicing the bread with a knife"]. It consists of two separate actions linked by a causal relationship:

(C) *Ivan režet xleb nožom* 'Ivan is cutting/slicing the bread with a knife' = Bringing the knife into contact with the loaf of bread, Ivan is moving the blade of the knife across the loaf (independent action) THEREFORE the loaf is divided in two parts at the point of contact (dependent action).

As can be seen, this isn't a single action; there are two causally linked actions. However, just as in the case of a single action, they are designated by a single verb. This may account for the false impression the speaker gets that (C) is also a single action performed by Ivan, and this action "passes over" onto the loaf.

According to the contemporary view, a verbal predicate is the main part of the clause that defines the referent situation. Keeping to an earlier tradition (Testelets 2001: 88–89), we believe that a clause designates a situation that is defined by the predicative nucleus of the clause—a nominal subject and a verbal predicate. In such a case, the **voice meaning of the verb indicates the kind of change in the agent**, the referent of the clause subject. The phrase *Ivan ubiraet urožaj* 'Ivan is harvesting the crops-Acc' describes an **independent** action of Ivan (the active voice), while the phrase *Urožaj ubiraetsja Ivanom* 'The crops-Nom are harvested by Ivan-Ins' describes a **dependent** action (the passive voice).

There is one more category of changes that refer mostly to humans—self-induced changes: a person performs an independent action, directing it at himself and causing dependent changes in himself (e.g. a boy runs a knife across his finger THEREFORE his finger starts bleeding). Such changes in the subject are expressed by the verb predicate in the reflexive voice: *Mal'čik porezalsja nožom* 'The boy cut himself with a knife'.

Thereby the reflexive meaning defines one more type of change in the subject of the predicate (the participant of higher communicative rank, in another terminology). Thus, there are three types of voice meaning that correspond to the three categories of change introduced above:

1) in the active voice the subject undergoes independent changes: *Ivan bežit* 'Ivan is running', *Reka tečët* 'The river flows', *Maša pričësyvaet kuklu* 'Masha is combing the doll['s hair])', *Veter sorval kryšu* 'The wind blew off the roof', *Kloun razmaxivaet kartonnym mečom* 'The clown is wielding a cardboard sword';

2) in the passive voice the subject undergoes dependent changes: *Kukla pričësyvaetsja Mašej* 'The doll['s hair] is combed-Refl by Masha', *Dom razrušaetsja*, lit. 'The house is destroying-Refl' ('The house is going to ruin'), *Voriška nakazyvaetsja plet'mi* 'The pilferer is punished-Refl with a lashing';

3) in the reflexive voice the subject simultaneously undergoes two types of changes—an independent change and a dependent change caused by the subject; in other words, the subject changes himself or itself: *Maša pričësyvaetsja* 'Masha is combing [her hair]'.

The semantic interpretations of voice offered above possess a universal, non-linguistic status as they make use of strictly cognitive concepts—the types of changes in the subject. Because of this, a single semantic basis can be used for cross-linguistic comparisons of voice meanings. It may also be claimed that the active, the passive, and the reflexive voice are all sensory units.

Our next goal is to analyze two meanings of the postfix -*s'/sja*: the reflexive meaning (*mal'čik moetsja*, lit. 'the boy is washing-Refl', *čelovek breetsja*, lit. 'a person is shaving-Refl') and the passive meaning (*dom stroitsja*, lit. 'the house is building-Refl', *bel'ë sušitsja*, lit. 'the linen is drying-Refl'), and to demonstrate that they are derivative from the active voice (*mal'čik moet mašinu* 'the boy is washing the car'). More specifically, one could speak of the following sequence: the active voice—the reflexive voice (a metonymy derived from the active voice)—the passive voice (a metaphor derived from the reflexive voice).

2. The active voice

A discussion of the meanings of the postfix *-s'/sja* should start with a definition of basic meaning of a transitive verb, as it is the source of all other meanings. We will give a simplified concrete definition, in which the second interpretation (after the equation symbol "=") plays a crucial role: it provides an
explicit definition of the expression "the Agent's action passes onto the Patient".

(1) *Mal'čik moet mašinu* 'The boy is washing the car' (active voice) = a tran-
     sitive verb in the active voice designates a situation in which
     the subject in the role of Agent performs an **independent** and purpose-
     ful action; the action passes onto the direct object in the role of Patient
     and changes it =
     the subject in the role of Agent performs an independent and purposeful
     action; THEREFORE the direct object in the role of Patient simulta-
     neously undergoes important **dependent** changes.

3. The reflexive voice: *myt'sja* 'wash-Refl', *kutat'sja* 'muffle-Refl up [in something]', *brit'sja* 'shave-Refl'

Most researchers view reflexivity as the expression "of a special type of co-
reference, namely, a full or partial coincidence of the object (or some other
participant) and the subject of an action" (Geniushene and Nedialkov 1991:
246; see also Faltz 1985; Givón 1990). Wierzbicka (1996: 420) gives the following definition of prototypical reflexive meaning:

> I hypothesize that the prototypical meaning which, on a subconscious level,
> guides linguists in their actual use of the term "reflexive" can be repre-
> sented as follows:

> (R) at some time, someone did something
>   because of this,
>   something happened to the same person at the same time.

Our definition, given in (2) below, is similar to the definition in (R).
However, the important distinction is that the meaning of the reflexive voice is
interpreted as metonymically derived from the meaning of the active voice, (1).

(2) *Mal'čik moetsja* (reflexive voice—metonymic transfer from the active
     voice) = a verb with the postfix *-s'/sja* designates a situation in which
     the subject in the role of Agent performs an independent and purposeful
     action,
     which passes onto the subject playing the role of Patient and changes it =

the subject in the role of Agent performs an independent and purposeful action;

THEREFORE the same subject, which also plays the role of Patient, simultaneously undergoes **dependent** changes.

Let us ask ourselves: why do we easily understand that the subject in this case refers not only to the doer (Agent), as in (1), but also to the direct object? The answer "because they are physically combined in one person" is not good enough. In the clause *Mal'čik moet sebja* 'The boy is washing himself' they are also combined, yet we understand the clause in a customary way: the subject (*mal'čik*) and the direct object (*sebja*) are independent, separate, and designated by the subject and direct object, respectively. This fact indicates that the difference in participant roles prevails over physical combination. It may be assumed that our understanding of the clause *Mal'čik moetsja* 'The boy is washing-Refl' is based in a universal mechanism of metonymic transfer. The subject in this clause metonymically designates two participants which have different roles but closely interact with one another as they are physically combined. It is similar to the case described by the clause *Ivan celuju tarelku s"el*, lit. 'Ivan ate a whole plate[ful]', where the form *tarelku* 'plate-Acc' is used metonymically and also refers to two different but closely interacting (because of physical contact) objects—a plate and its content.

> **Note.** Metonymy is usually described as the transfer of a name motivated by spatial or temporal contiguity (Reformatskii 1996: 47). This condition, however, is not sufficient. It is necessary that there be, between the source object and the contiguous object, a generally relevant functional interaction that links both objects. For example, one can use the word *tarelka* 'plate' metonymically in *Ja s"el tarelku syra* 'I ate a plate[ful] of cheese' only in the case when the plate is filled with cheese cut into little pieces that fill the plate repeating its shape. If the very same cheese lies on the plate in one or two large chunks, such a metonymic use becomes incorrect. Small pieces of cheese are in a functional interaction with the plate, while a single large piece is not.

Another peculiarity of a clause with a reflexive verb is that with the loss of direct object it loses the means to indicate what part of the Agent-Patient is involved in the action. Therefore, understanding the reflexive meaning of a verb depends on the knowledge of the **typical** part of the Agent involved in the Agent's interaction with self. If there are several such parts, the priority is given to the largest part by default. The clause *Mal'čik moetsja* 'The boy is washing-Refl' indicates, by default, that the 'entire body' is being washed, without any explicit clarification or special support from the context. Therefore, the clause *Mal'čik moet ruki* 'The boy is washing [his] hands' does not have a reflexive meaning. Similarly, the clause *Mužčina breetsja* 'The man is shaving' (in a referential use) means, by default, that the man is shaving his face. If the man is bald but growing a beard, periodically shaving only his neck, he can say *Ja brejus'* 'I'm shaving-Refl' (= 'I'm shaving my neck'), but only to those close to him, accustomed to such shaving. That being said, it becomes clear why the utterances such as ⁷*Ženščina breetsja* 'The woman is shaving-Refl' or ⁷*Ivan čistitsja* 'Ivan is cleaning-Refl' are questionable: it remains unspecified to what part of the agent the action is applied. For example, Ivan may be cleaning either his shoes, his suit, or his teeth. The clause *Ivan krasitsja*, lit 'Ivan paints-Refl', is less opaque: most likely, it means that Ivan dyes his hair.

4. The passive voice: *mašina moetsja* 'the car is washing-Refl', *bel'ë sušitsja* 'the linen is drying-Refl', *dom stroitsja plotnikom* 'the house is building-Refl by the carpenter'

Let us first consider the function of the passive voice compared with the active voice. Comparing the following sentences:

(a) *Bol'šinstvo teoretikov otverglo ètot argument.*
     'The majority of theoreticians have rejected this argument'
(b) *Ètot argument byl otvergnut bol'šinstvom teoretikov.*
     'This argument has been rejected by the majority of theoreticians'

Plungian (2011) argues that the difference between them "consists in the fact that in (a) the speaker, most likely, wants to make some assertion *about the theoreticians*, while in (b) an assertion is made *about the argument*. […] This pragmatic distinction has a formal correlate: clauses (a) and (b) have different subjects" (pp. 183, 187).

While concurring with this argument, we would like to point out the following. The passive voice is intended to ascertain the state of the Patient (either intermediate or final), namely, that "the Patient is in a **state of change** caused by the action of some Agent (usually unknown or absent at the moment of observation)". Let us clarify our claim. Imagine that a person has noticed that a car that was dirty not long ago is now clean. Clearly, the car must have been washed, but the person doesn't know who did it. The passive voice allows the speaker to report only the observed result (final state of the car): *Mašina vymyta* 'The car [has been] washed', without any indication as to who the doer of the action was. One can also say *Mašinu vymyli*, lit. 'The car [they] washed', but in this case it is not the state ('clean car') that is reported, but a transition to this state. Consider another example: if we notice that the construction of the house has moved on (and neither the architect nor construction workers can be seen or are known to us), this intermediate result can be ascertained by the utterance *Dom stroitsja* 'The house is building-Refl'.

What has been said above can be illustrated by the use of verbs in their real-time meanings.[6] Here, the difference between the active voice used to refer to an observed **action** performed by the agent (the said action causing changes in the patient) and the passive voice used to refer to the observed **state** of change of the patient comes to the fore. Consider the questionability of the clause *?Mašina (sejčas) moetsja mal'čikom* 'The car is (being) washed-Refl by the boy', when the Agent and the action performed by the Agent can be directly observed and identified; this interferes with interpreting the washing of the car as a state of the car. At the same time, the phrase *Mašina moetsja* 'The car is being washed-Refl' in the same situation is quite correct. However, it describes the **state** of the car ("to be in a car-wash") and not any current changes caused by the action "to wash".

Similarly, the clause *Dom stroitsja rabočimi* 'The house is built-Refl by construction workers' is correct just because the verb *stroit'* 'build' is used in its actual, not real-time meaning; we cannot ascertain at once that the observed changes with the house caused by the workers are the signs of ongoing construction and not, for example, of renovation. To make sure which is the case, we need to observe the state of the house over a number of discontinuous time intervals. However, as soon as we imagine a situation in which the action "build" is identified and, respectively, the given verb used in real time—*Mal'čik stroit dom (iz kubikov)* 'The boy is building a house (with building blocks)'—the clause *?Dom stroitsja mal'čikom* 'The house is being built by the boy' becomes questionable.

We take the meaning of the passive voice to be a metaphoric extension of the reflexive on the following grounds: in either case the Patient is the subject of the verbal predicate (sentential subject) and undergoes dependent changes.

(3)   *Mašina moetsja* 'The car is [being] washed-Refl'; *Dom stroitsja plotnikom* 'The house is [being] built-Refl by the carpenter' (the passive is a

---

[6] It seems reasonable to assume that it is precisely the real-time uses of verbs referring to the unfolding "events" directly observed "here-and-now" that represent the source, or basic, meanings on which other aspectual meanings of verbs are founded (topical or background meanings, as in *stroit' dom* 'build a house', *pisat' roman* 'write a novel' and the like (for a discussion, see Koshelev 2015b: 308–309). It is worthy of notice that, similarly, Givón (2001: 73) draws on real-time uses of verbs to define the prototype event for transitivity.

metaphoric extension of the reflexive) = 'The subject of the predicate, which plays the role of Patient, is in a state of dependent change caused by an independent action of another participant—Agent or Cause[7]' =

The subject of the predicate, which plays the role of Patient, is in a state of **dependent** change BECAUSE **another** participant (Agent or Cause) performs an independent action.

Shakhmatov (2006: 95–96) pointed out a group of verbs that have a passive meaning when used with an animate subject: *obvinjaetsja* '[is] accused-Refl', *štrafuetsja* '[is] fined-Refl', *nakazyvaetsja* '[is] punished-Refl', *obličaetsja* '[is] denounced-Refl', *vyzyvaetsja* '[is] summoned-Refl' and so forth; apparently, these are the verbs that have an unspecified collective as the doer of the action, with regard to which a single individual may become an object. Definition (3) still holds for them; it is just that the doer of the action here is a third force—neither Agent nor Cause, but Collective, to which the subject is in some social relationship.

---

[7] Here, Cause is "a participant (typically, inanimate or acting unconsciously) that is the cause of the situation (*dožd' zatopil posevy* ['the rains flooded the crops']; *strax gnal ego v put'* ['fear drove him on']" (Plungian 2011: 116; original emphasis).

Chapter 5

On the single structure of lexical meanings of nouns and verbs

§ 1. Object and the system of its parts (the partitive concept)

1. Object and its parts

As has been noted previously, a native speaker does not experience any difficulty in subdividing objects into parts and naming these distinct parts. The
explanation of this human ability is far from trivial.[1] In this paragraph I will
reiterate some of the conclusions from chap. 4, § 1 in order to include them in
a different system of reasoning. In that paragraph and elsewhere (Koshelev
2006; 2008: 35–38; 2011a: 23–24, 28; 2015a: 25–113) it has been demonstrated, using several examples, that the objects around us, both artifacts (such
as chairs, bicycles, etc.) and natural objects (such as lakes, rivers, bananas,
trees, etc.) possess specific functions that reflect the human interpretation of
the essence of these objects, that is, how such objects "work": a chair allows a
person to rest in a sitting posture, a tree grows and bears fruit, etc. Because of
this, the object concept that defines the mental image of an object has a dual
structure: "Prototype → Function". Parts of objects possess similar structures,
"Prototypical Physical Part → its particular Function". It has also been shown

---

[1] It appears that a detailed discussion of the range of issues pertaining to this problem
was attempted for the first time in Ivan Sechenov's seminal work *The Elements of Thought*,
first edition of which was published in 1878 in St. Petersburg in the journal *Vestnik Evropy*
'The European Bulletin'; herein it is cited from a later edition (Sechenov 1952). The current approaches to the problem are discussed in a review article by Tversky et al. (2008).
For a comparison of my view with the approach of Tversky and co-authors see the end of
section 8.

that objects (concepts) are mentally represented as sets of object parts, that is, in a partitive hierarchy.

Consider the following example:

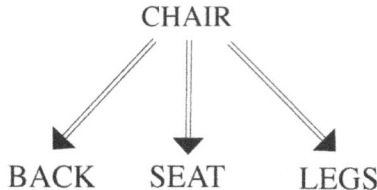

Here, the object concept CHAIR is constituted by the pair "Prototypical Chair → its Function": 'allows an individual to take a sitting posture'; and the parts BACK, SEAT, and LEGS are constituted by similar pairs: "Prototypical Part → the Part's Function".

In what follows, an abridged notation for the partitive hierarchy will be used: CHAIR ⇒ (BACK, SEAT, LEGS). The arrow ⇒ (or ⇓) indicates the "Whole ⇒ Parts" relationship. Here are some examples:

LAKE ⇒ (BOTTOM, WATER, SHORE)
BANANA ⇒ (SKIN, FLESH, FRUIT STEM)
KNIFE ⇒ (HANDLE, BLADE)
NUT ⇒ (SHELL, KERNEL)
BICYCLE ⇒ (WHEELS, FRAME, HANDLEBARS, SADDLE, PEDALS)
RIVER ⇒ (BANKS, WATER FLOW, RIVERBED, MOUTH, SOURCE)
TREE ⇒ (ROOTS, TRUNK, BRANCHES)

2. The function of an object as the sum of the functions of its parts

It was also shown in chap. 4, § 1, that an object is subdivided into parts according to the object's general function. The division of an object into functional parts marks the next, and much deeper, level of comprehension of the object. We intuitively understand the role of a separate part of an object and its contribution to the general function of the object. This general function, therefore, appears to be the sum of the particular functions performed by separate parts of an object. For example, the seat of a chair has one particular function (it 'serves as a support for the buttocks of a sitting person'), the back another (it 'serves as a support for the back of a sitting person'), and the legs a third (they 'support the seat of the chair—and, therefore, the sitting person—at a required level above the ground'). Thus, we have three functional parts of a chair, the seat, the back, and the legs. **Their particular functions collectively constitute the general function of a chair.**

Similarly, the general function of a lake ('a continuously sustained large mass of still fresh water covering an area of ground, directly available for human perception and use') consists of three functional parts: 'a large mass of still fresh water', 'the shores within which the water is held', and 'the bottom that prevents the water from draining'. Similarly, the general function of a banana ('a ripe fruit of a banana tree used as food') allows for its division into three functional parts: 'the flesh of a banana, consumed as food', 'the banana skin that protects the flesh from birds and insects', and 'the fruit stem through which the flesh receives nourishment'.

Soon after the age of 24 months, children learn the nominal genitive Y + X-Gen constructions of the type *stvol dereva* 'the trunk of the tree', *dver' komnaty* 'the door of the room', etc. This type of construction expresses the relationship 'Y is a functional part of X'; as is observed by Tseitlin (2000: 135), "at the age of 24 to 36 months, children learn […] constructions with the meaning 'part—whole'." However, as has been shown in chap. 4, § 1, the noun, Y, in these constructions refers not to just any part, but only to a functionally relevant part of the object, X; this functionally relevant part contributes directly to the general function of the object. For example, in Russian the expression *ručka dveri* 'handle door-Gen' ('the handle of the door') is quite correct as the handle performs a specific function attributed to the door—it is used to open or shut the door. By contrast, the expressions **glazok dveri* 'the peephole of the door' and **krjučok dveri* 'the hook of the door' (about a hook nailed to the door) are incorrect. One should say *dvernoj glazok* 'the door peephole' / *dvernoj krjučok* 'the door hook', because the peephole and the hook possess their own separate functions not related to the function of the door. Similarly, the expression *stvol dereva* 'the trunk of the tree' is correct, while **gnezdo dereva* 'the nest of the tree' (about a nest made in the tree) is not; the nest does not take part in the vital functions of the tree.

It would appear, then, that the nominal genitive cannot be learned without an understanding of the partitive structure of an object (a door, tree, etc.). Thus, it may be assumed that children understand the functions of objects around them, and the functions of object parts, early on.

3. The role-based hierarchy of object parts

Let us now try to answer the following question: is the composition of an object's functional parts something unique? May there be two or more alternatives to how an object is subdivided? I believe that the composition of an object's parts is unique and forms a **role-based hierarchy** according to the following rule. First, that part is singled out from the physical parts of an object which is dominant in the realization of the general function of the object; it becomes the **main** functional part. Then other physical parts are distinguished which, not unlike a king's entourage, perform functions that are **supplementary to the main part**. These particular functions supplement the main function; thus, together they constitute the function of an object as a whole. In what follows these parts are referred to as **supplementary** to the main function, and the relationships between the main and supplementary functions will be referred to as **role relationships**.

We will highlight the name of an object's main part in bold type to designate twin-argument role relationships between the main part, which is always at the center, and supplementary parts that surround it and are in contact with it. For example, the main part of a chair is **SEAT**; it is dominant for the general function of a chair, while BACK and LEGS are supplementary parts. for a banana, the main part is **FLESH**, and the supplementary parts SKIN and FRUIT STEM. the main part of a lake is MASS OF WATER, and the supplementary parts SHORE and BOTTOM.

The partitive and role-based hierarchies complement each other. The former only shows the composition of the functional parts of an object, while the latter ties these parts into a system as a single whole. It is not enough to know that a chair consists of three parts, a seat, back, and legs. It is important to know how they are connected and how their functions add up to yield the general function of a chair. The general rule for an object "assembly" is as follows: **each supplementary part is joined to the main part**. Such joining is determined by the role relationship. For example, the main part of a chair is **SEAT**; therefore, BACK and LEGS are joined to the seat, each part in its specific manner. as for the other points of juncture, be it between the back and the rear legs or just between the legs, they are irrelevant for the general function of the chair.

Thus, the role relationship shows (a) the position in space of a supplementary part in regard to the main part (prototype), due to which position (b) the function of the supplementary part is added to the function of the main part (function of the object). Role relationships will be designated by numbered arrows, as in the following examples:

(1)   a. **THE SEAT OF A CHAIR** −1−> THE BACK OF A CHAIR =
        Prototype: "The part BACK is positioned relative to the part **SEAT** as

follows: (picture: the lower part of the back is in contact with the rear side of the seat)" → Function: 'BACK serves as a support for the back of a sitting person'.

   b. **THE SEAT OF A CHAIR** −2−> THE LEGS OF A CHAIR = Prototype: "The part LEGS is positioned relative to the part **seat** as follows (picture)" → function: 'LEGS support the seat above the ground'.

(2) **THE FLESH OF A BANANA** −3−> THE SKIN OF A BANANA = Prototype: "The part SKIN is positioned relative to the part **FLESH** as follows (picture: the skin covers the flesh)" → function: 'SKIN PROTECTS **FLESH**'.

As may be seen, a role relationship with specific arguments is not just an abstract notion; it is a visible conceptual unit with the same dual structure as an object concept, "Prototype → Function". It is constituted by the relationship between the prototypical parts and the relationship between their functions.

4. The developed concept

By combining the partitive hierarchy "Whole ⇒ Part" with the role-based hierarchy "**Main part** −N−> Supplementary part", we get a system of the parts of an object concept. We call such a system a **partitive concept**, or a **partitive extension** of a basic-level concept. The basic-level concept itself along with its partitive concept, we will call a **developed concept**.

Consider (3) as an example of a developed concept. The following is an abridged designation for the developed concept:

(3) Developed concept CHAIR =
   a. Basic-level concept   CHAIR
      The relationship of development   ◊
   b. Partitive concept   BACK <−1− **SEAT** −2−> LEGS

The relationship (the sign, ◊) that connects the basic concept with the partitive concept we call the **relationship of development**.

Here the main part **SEAT** is highlighted in bold type and the numbered arrows designate role relationships. In accordance with the general theory of development (see chap. 1, § 9, section 2), a partitive concept, as in (3b), is a developed state of the whole concept.

Presented explicitly, the developed concept (3) may be visualized as follows:

(4)

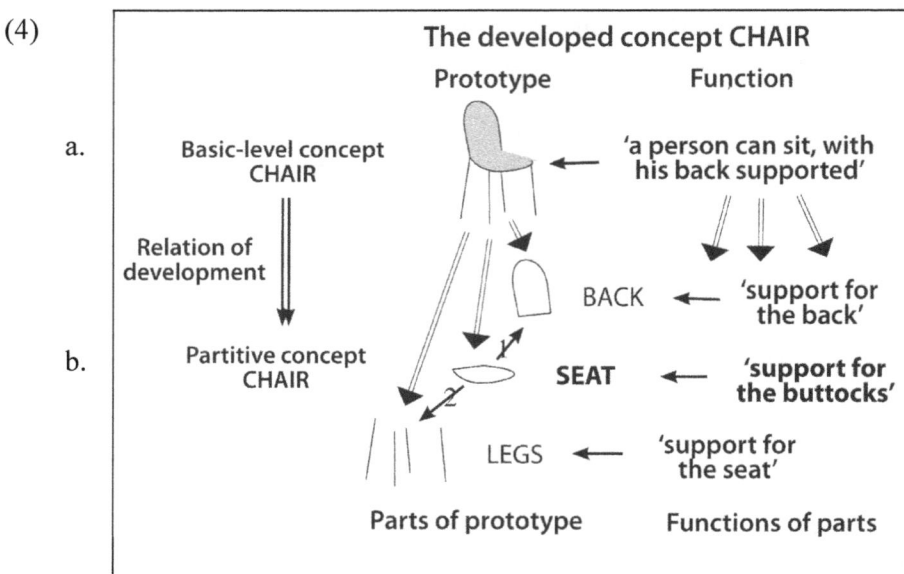

The developed concept CHAIR

Prototype   Function

a.   Basic-level concept   'a person can sit, with
          CHAIR   his back supported'

Relation of
development

b.   Partitive concept   BACK ← 'support for
          CHAIR   the back'

                                              SEAT ← 'support for
                                                          the buttocks'

                                              LEGS ← 'support for
                                                          the seat'

Parts of prototype   Functions of parts

The validity of the name 'Relationship of development' may be illustrated by the structure of a flower, which is isomorphic to the partitive concept shown in (3b)–(4b). Indeed, the pistil (1) and the petals (2–5) are parts of the bud. Additionally, the pistil—the main and central part—is connected with the petals by the role relationship −1−>: the petals are specifically located around the pistil and are physically connected to it, just like parts of an armchair—the back, armrests, and legs that are located around and have contact with the seat; because of this, their functions supplement the function of the seat.

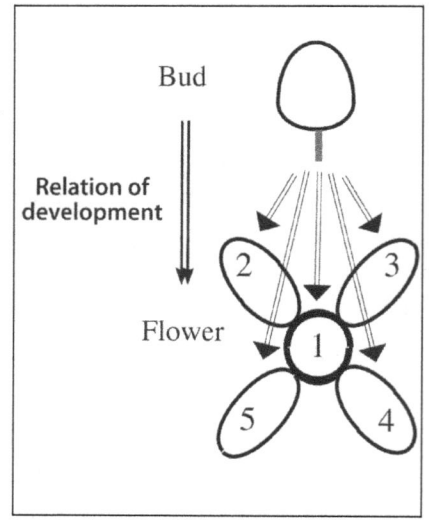

Consider some examples. Let the following be an even shorter designation of a partitive concept of the type (3b), in the form of a list (**SEAT**, BACK, LEGS).

(5)   Developed concept BANANA =
      a. Basic-level concept: BANANA
                                          ◊
      b. Partitive concept: (SKIN, **FLESH**, FRUIT STEM)

Presented explicitly, the developed concept (5) may be seen as similar to the developed concept (4a)–(4b) CHAIR:

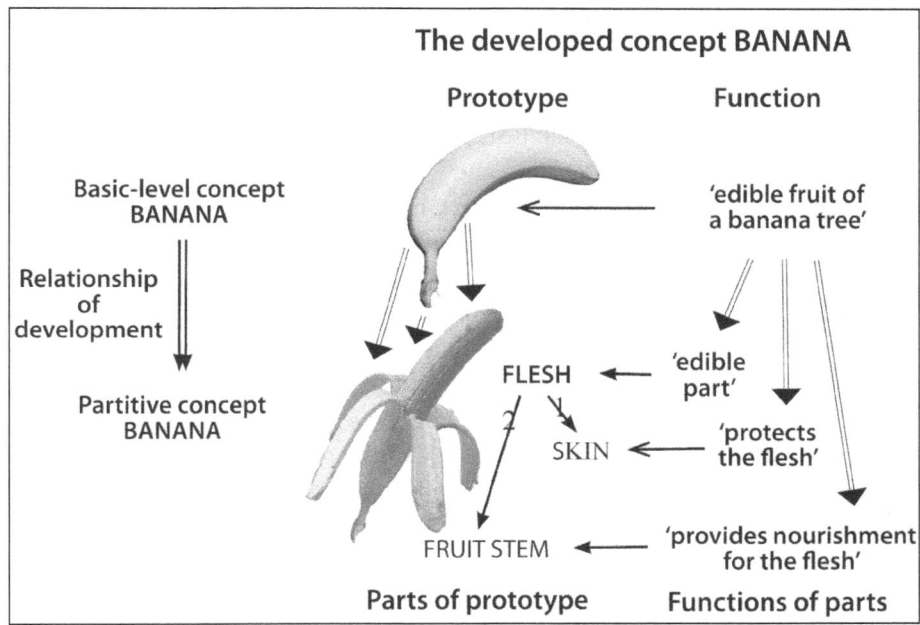

The developed concept BANANA

Prototype   Function

Basic-level concept
BANANA

'edible fruit of
a banana tree'

Relationship
of
development

'edible
FLESH   part'

Partitive concept
BANANA

SKIN   'protects
the flesh'

FRUIT STEM   'provides nourishment
for the flesh'

Parts of prototype   Functions of parts

(6) Developed concept LAKE =
   a. Basic-level concept: LAKE
                                          ◊
   b. Partitive concept: (SHORE, **WATER**, BOTTOM)

   From now on, the following abridged designation will also be used:

LAKE ◇ (SHORE, **WATER**, BOTTOM)

where the sign ◇ stands for the relationship of development.

Let us continue the analysis of our examples. Clearly, the main functional part of a knife is the **BLADE**, of a nut the **KERNEL**, of a bicycle the **FRAME** (it connects all the other parts), of a river the **WATER FLOW**, of a tree the **TRUNK** (it supports the branches and supplies nourishment from the roots), and so forth. Thus, we get the following developed concepts:

KNIFE◇(**BLADE,** HANDLE);
NUT◇(**KERNEL,** SHELL);
RIVER◇(SHORES, RIVERBED, **WATER FLOW**, MOUTH, SOURCE);
TREE◇(ROOTS, **TRUNK**, BRANCHES WITH LEAVES);
BICYCLE◇(HANDLEBARS, SADDLE, **FRAME**, PEDALS, WHEELS).

5. How is the main part of an object determined?

Sometimes the question of which functional part of an object is the main part cannot be easily answered. For example, it could be argued that the roots of a tree are more important than the trunk or the seeds of an apple more important than its flesh. There is a simple naming method to determine the main part of an object: only the main part can be referred to by the name of the object while any other part cannot. For example, the word *nut* can be used to refer either to a whole nut or its kernel (the main part), but not to the nutshell. The blade of a knife without a handle can be called a knife, but a handle without a blade cannot. The roots of a tree cannot be called a tree, but a trunk without roots and branches can. The flesh of an apple can be called "apple", but its seeds or skin cannot. We can imagine something fantastic, such as a wide horizontal water flow sustained in midair by an invisible gravitational channel; in such a case, we can call this water flow a river even though we cannot see its bottom or bed.

It may be presumed that the credibility of the results obtained is increased by the mutual support of these methods from two separate knowledge areas: cognitive rules for singling out the main part of an object and linguistic rules for its denotation.

6. The functional and physical parts of an object

The functional parts of an object should be strictly differentiated from its physical parts that are visually distinguished due to their specific shape. For example, a pump which has been attached to the frame of a bicycle, while being physically attached to the bicycle, is not a functional part (it is not directly involved in the process of cycling). A bird's nest is not a functional part of the tree in which the nest has been made (it does not play any role in the vital functions of the tree). A fish is not a functional part of the lake in which it swims (the fish does not affect preservation of water in the lake).

The Russian nominal genitive, discussed above, helps to determine whether a given physical part of an object (a part that is in contact with the object) is a functional part of that object. When it is not, as in the case of the bicycle pump, bird's nest, fish in a lake, etc., the nominal genitive construction becomes incorrect, cf.: *nasos velosipeda* pump bicycle-Gen 'the pump of the bicycle', *gnezdo dereva* nest tree-Gen 'the nest of the tree', *ryba ozera* fish lake-Gen 'the fish of the lake', etc.

Some clarification should be made here. The relationship "Whole → functional Part" is not a transitive one. If Y is a functional part of X and Z a functional part of Y, then Z is not a functional part of X because its function is attributed to Y and does not exist outside of Y. In such cases the nominal genitive is incorrect. One cannot say *spicy velosipeda* spokes bicycle-Gen 'the spokes of the bicycle' (the correct phrase is *spicy kolesa velosipeda* spokes wheel-Gen bicycle-Gen 'the spokes of the bicycle wheel'), because the spokes are a functional part of the wheel. Therefore, the partitive structure of a functional part of an object is independent; it does not depend on the partitive structure of the object as a whole (for more details, see chap. 4, § 1).

7. On the radial position of the parts of an object

The layout of the spatial positions of the functional parts of an object (in the case of a simple artifact or natural object) has one noteworthy property. This layout is similar to that of a flower: the main functional part is always at the center, like a pistil, and the supplementary parts surround it and are physically connected to it, like the petals. For example, the water in a lake takes the central position while the bottom and shores surround it, the flesh of a banana is contained within while the skin and fruit stem surround it, and so forth.

This radial contact positioning of supplementary parts has a simple explanation. The function of every supplementary part must be added to the function of the main part. And this happens only when there is direct physical contact between the supplementary parts and the main part (on account of the property of intransitivity of the parts' functions, as discussed above). Other physical parts may have contact with the main part even though their functions do not contribute to the main function (for example, a bicycle pump attached to the frame of a bicycle does not contribute to the function of the frame, neither does a tool bag attached to the saddle). However, if the function of a certain part contributes to the function of the main part of the object, this specific part must have physical contact with the main part.

In view of the aforesaid, the spatial positioning of the parts of a partitive concept may be described as follows: "**main** (central) **part** –N–> supplementary (contact) parts", where –N–> stands for the role relationships. Based on this characteristic, a developed object concept has the following structure:

(7)   Developed concrete CONCEPT =
       a. Basic-level concept: OBJECT
                                                      ◊
       b. Partitive concept: (**Main part** (in the center) –N–> Supplementary parts
                               (around and in contact with the main part))

8. A developed concept represented as a circle

The radial structure of functional parts described above may be easily visualized. To achieve such a visualization, the well-known recursive structure "circles in a circle" (Gelernter 2016) must be interpreted as follows: the large outer circle represents the basic-level concept and the inner circles represent parts of the basic-level concept, the concentric circle for the main part and the smaller contact circles for the supplementary parts.

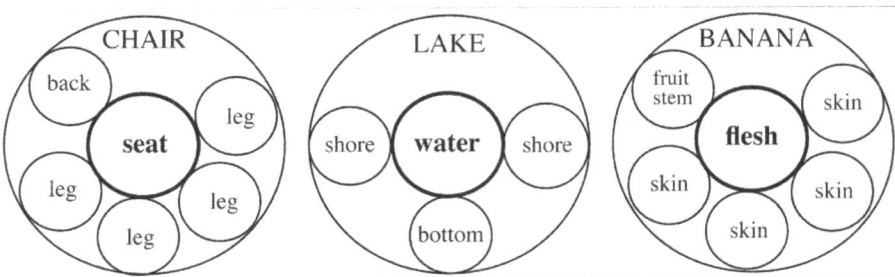

This diagram is a clear representation of a partitive concept derived from a basic-level concept. It embodies both hierarchies of a partitive concept: (1) 'whole—functional parts', and (2) the role relationships '**main part** (inner concentric circle)—supplementary parts (the circles around it)'; their contact with the central circle shows that the supplementary parts are in physical contact with the main part, and this physical contact determines the addition of the functions of the supplementary parts to the function of the main part.

The diagram "circles in a circle" may be treated as a universal pattern for the human cognition of the world. In particular, it explains the development of human ideas about the visible world—objects, properties, actions, situations, etc.

> **Note**. Tversky et al. (2008: 439, 444–445) also observe that both objects and parts of objects have functions. Our approach differs by the following three propositions: 1) not only do artifacts have functions, but natural objects do as well; 2) the functions of an object's parts contribute to the general function of the object; 3) among the parts of an object there is a main part, which carries the main share of the general function of the object, and supplementary parts positioned around the main part and having points of contact with it. These propositions lead to a number of corollaries discussed above: (a) the main factor in subdividing an object is the division of its general function into particular functions; (b) the subdivision of an object into parts is unambiguous; (c) an object should be viewed as constituted by functional and non-functional parts (parts whose functions do not contribute to the general function of the object), etc.

9. The recursiveness of a partitive concept

Since every functional part of an object has its own particular function, it may itself be subdivided into functional parts. Moreover, these parts are not necessarily characterized by a distinctive shape. For example, the leg of a chair may be subdivided into three functional parts, the upper, middle, and lower part; the main part is the middle part because it carries the primary share of the function of the leg (to support the seat at a required level). Let us consider another example, the wheel.

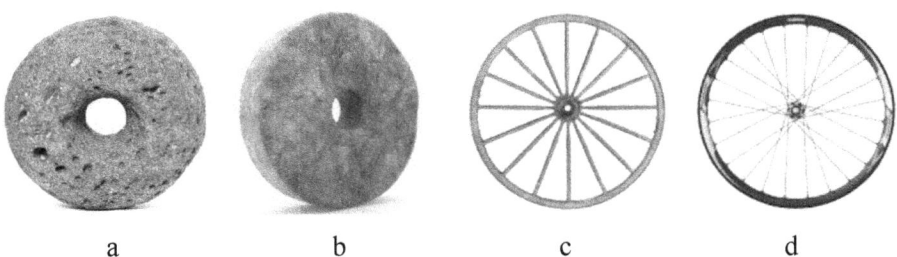

a   b   c   d

Fig. 1. The evolution of the wheel and the differentiation of its parts:
a, b—ancient stone wheels with undifferentiated parts (inner, interior, outer),
c, d—modern gig and bicycle wheels with differentiated parts (rim, spokes, hub)

The functional parts of an ancient stone wheel (Fig. 1a, b)—the inner part (which has contact with the axle), outer part (which has contact with the road), and intermediate part—are syncretic: they are not differentiated by any peculiarity in shape. However, in the wheels of modern design these parts are physically differentiated. Each part has its own shape and name. It is clear that the main part is the interior, that is, the spokes. Thus, we get the developed concept WHEEL ◇ (**SPOKES**, HUB, RIM). But a spoke also consists of three parts: the rod (middle part), flange (hooked tip holding the spoke in the hub), and nipple (which fixes the thread tip to the rim). Therefore, the developed concept (8) BICYCLE acquires the following structure:

(8) Developed concept BICYCLE =
  a.   BICYCLE
          ◇
  b. (HANDLEBARS, **FRAME**, SADDLE, PEDALS, WHEELS)
          ◇
      (RIM, **SPOKES**, HUB)
         ◇
   (FLANGE, **ROD**, THREAD TIP (NIPPLE).

In a similar way, we can get the structure of the developed concept APRICOT:

APRICOT
◊
(FRUIT STEM, **FLESH**, OUTER SKIN, STONE)
◊
(**SEED**, SHELL)
◊
(**KERNEL**, SKIN).

The recursiveness characteristic of these structures may also be represented by a sequence of "circles in a circle" diagrams:

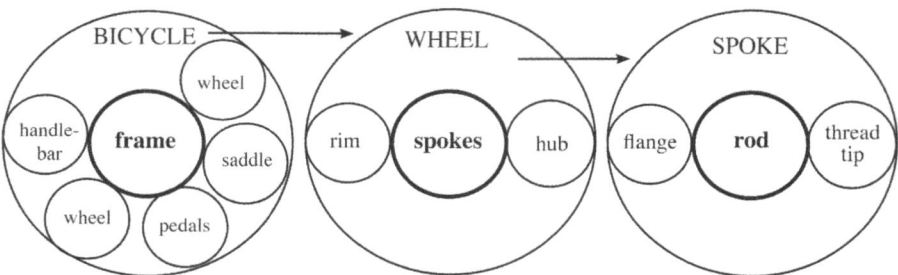

Fig. 2. The developed concept BICYCLE represented as circles

10. A vocabulary of elementary cognitive units

According to some experimental data, children begin to subdivide objects into parts around the age of 24 months. As experimental data show, this is the time when infants begin to mentally single out separate parts in the objects around them (though they single out body parts in humans and animals earlier). Cf.:

> At the end of the second and the beginning of the third year, children begin to single out separate components and details in objects. For example, children at the age of 22 to 24 months may try to pick a flower by grasping its stem; they take the lid of a sugar bowl by the knob rather than the lid as a whole, and so forth (Kol'tsova 1980: 37).

> During this period children already ask for the names of objects and their parts. Zhenja I. (aged 2) claps her hand on the seat of a toy-tractor, looks at her mother, produces vocalizations, and does not stop until her mother gives the names for the tractor parts (steering wheel, seat, etc.) (Isenina 1986: 54).

By extension, before the age of 24 months the minimal units of the physical world construed by children are whole objects and the relationships between them (the properties of objects will be discussed below). After the age of 24 months, a child's toolbox of cognitive units features new, finer units—parts of objects. Let us discuss their structure and the process of formation in more detail.

It is known that children are strongly guided by shape when naming objects (see § 2, section 2.3 below). However, unlike the shape of a whole object, the shape of the parts of an object may differ considerably from object to object. The leg of a chair and the leg of a couch are quite different in shape, as are the functionally similar parts of a flower, mushroom, standard lamp, pair of compasses, wine glass, umbrella, and so forth. Yet Russian children hear all these parts called *nožka* 'leg-dimin.'. Due to the parallel process of subdividing objects and distinguishing the specific functions of object parts, children quickly begin to understand the principle: all such parts perform the same specific function. In the mind of a child the idea is formed of the **common part** *nožka* 'leg-dimin.'—a part of various objects that does not have a single prototype but has a common function: 'resting on the ground, to keep the rest of the object from falling down'. Consider another example. At a certain point, children begin to differentiate their back as a separate part of their body. When this happens, the specific function of the back of an object (*spinka* 'back-dimin.'), 'provides support for the back', also becomes separate. Hereafter the word *spinka* unites differently shaped backs of various objects (the back of a chair, couch, etc.) into a single common part.[2]

It must be emphasized that what is at issue is not just artifacts and their parts, but also natural and living objects. For example, the outer layer of an apple, banana, or orange is a common part of these fruits and has the same name in Russian, *kožura* 'skin', though these parts are outwardly far from being identical. What matters is that they are nearly all inedible and carry a protective function in regard to the edible part of the fruit, the flesh. Similarly, children gradually come to realize that both trees and flowers receive their nourishment from the ground. At the same time children differentiate the underground part of a tree or flower, because they hear their caregivers call this part by the same word, *root*. Thus, children form an idea of a common part, ROOT, which has its own specific function and name.

---

[2] Cf. the dictionary definition of the word *spinka*: "Support for the back provided by an armchair, couch, chair, bench" (Ushakov, IV: col. 435).

Thus, the common function and common name serve for children as a basis for conceptualizing a common object part; that is, the same functional parts of different objects are united into a single class of referents. Therefore, the store of elementary cognitive units used by children to construe the visible world—a set of basic-level concepts ("Prototype → Function" pairs)—is enlarged by a set of finer cognitive units, common parts of objects, defined by the pair "Name—Specific Function": "*spinka* ['back-dimin.']—'provides support for the back'", etc.

At the same time, the common part has not just one prototype, as in the case of an object, but several prototypes (the back of a chair, bench, etc.), i.e. it is a general concept of the type "Set of object part prototypes → Function of object part". As children continue to develop, each common part is differentiated into concrete parts: back (*spinka*) into the back of a chair, couch, etc., skin into the skin of an apple, banana, etc. These concrete parts receive names in the form of two-word genitive constructions such as *spinka stula* 'the back of a chair', *kožura banana* 'the skin of a banana', and so forth. Now the concrete part has a single prototype, that is, it becomes a concept: "Object part prototype → Function of object part". Many concrete parts are quickly committed to a child's memory and enlarge the store of elementary cognitive units.

Let us use, as in the case of concepts, capital letters to designate concrete parts and initial capitals to designate common parts. The connection of a common part with its different realizations, the concrete parts, shall be described as a genus-species relationship and marked with the sign $\triangleright$:

(9)   Back $\triangleright$ BACK OF A CHAIR; Back $\triangleright$ BACK OF A COUCH.

The first argument (the genus) is a common part, and the second (the species) a concrete part, or realization of the common part. In the case of object parts with which we are quite familiar, the genus-species relationship shown in (9) is reduced, because after the concrete parts have been memorized we use only these parts. But a concrete part of a new object is formed as a species realization of the common (genus) part.

Therefore, in an explicit representation, the partitive concept is supplemented by a genus-species relationship:

(10) a. Basic concept: CHAIR
                                            ◇

   b. Partitive concept: (Back   <–1–   **Seat**   –2–>   Legs)
                              ▽   ▽   ▽
                            BACK   **SEAT**   LEGS
                        OF A CHAIR   **OF A CHAIR**   OF A CHAIR

When concrete parts come into play, the generalized parts are at once reduced and replaced by the concrete parts, as in (10c).

c. Partitive concept: (BACK   <–1–   **SEAT**   –2–>   LEGS
                        OF A CHAIR   **OF A CHAIR**   OF A CHAIR)

11. On distinguishing physically connected objects

Mental representations of the objects around us in the form of partitive concepts allow us to see the world of objects in more detail; particularly, they enable us to distinguish physically connected objects from objects and their parts. For example, a lamp attached to a desk by screws is not a part of the desk; it is incorrect to say *lampa stola* 'the lamp of the desk'. However, parts of the desk, such as a desk cabinet door or drawer, can be quite correctly identified as *dverca stola* 'the door of the desk' and *jaŝik stola* 'the drawer of the desk'.

Let us consider another example. Looking at the door of an apartment from the outside we can see a handle, a peephole, a metal number plate and the head of the screw that secures it on the door. Aware of the function of the door handle, we understand that it is a part of the door and not a separate object (although it may be made of metal and attached to a wooden door). However, the peephole and the number plate attached to the very same door with screws are not parts of the door, because they have quite different functions not related to the function of the door—'to shut and open an opening for entry and exit', cf. Pinker (1997: 259–260).

§ 2. An object and the system of its properties (the attributive concept). The basic meaning of a concrete noun

1. An object and its properties

The formation of a system for the sensory properties of an object is a somewhat different process, because, unlike object parts, these properties do not occupy any volume in space; they are all localized within the space occupied by the object. Let us distinguish between a common property of an object, such as Shape, Color, Size, Weight, Material, etc., and a concrete property, a variant kind of a common property, such as GREEN, RED, etc.; LARGE, SMALL; HEAVY, LIGHT; WOODEN, STONE, etc. (as before, common properties will be designated by capitalized words and concrete properties by words in capital letters).

Shape might be defined as a two-dimensional shell, a spatial border that separates the object from the surrounding space. However, in such a case the object could not be viewed as the sum of its properties because none of the object properties are characterized by three-dimensionality, the constitutive feature of an object. We will follow another, more widely accepted approach in which shape is seen as a three-dimensional property of an object (for a description of perception of three-dimensional shapes by infants, see Pereira and Smith (2009)). In such an approach, **Shape** becomes the main property that characterizes a three-dimensional object (highlighted in bold type, like the main part of an object), and the other properties become supplementary because they are located on or in it and supplement it, completing the object as a whole (their contribution is much smaller than that of shape). Therefore, the properties of an object display similar role relationships: **Shape** −1−> Color; **Shape** −2−> Size, and so forth. Each relationship shows (1) the type of property, and (2) its position with regard to the shape, that it is located on or in it (this also applies to supplementary properties). In addition, the properties of an object enter into an attributive relationship, "Whole (Object) ⇒ its Common properties", which is similar to the partitive relationship "Whole (Object) ⇒ its Parts".

Common properties, just like common parts, are used to define a genus-species relationship: Color ▷ GREEN, Weight ▷ HEAVY, and so forth. Thus, the same three relationships are defined for object properties as for object parts.

Consider an example. The developed concept CHAIR, (1), consists of a basic-level concept, (1a), and a system of its properties, (1b).

(1)   Developed concept CHAIR =
       a. Basic-level concept: CHAIR
                                               ◊
       b. Attributive concept: Size   <−1− **Shape** −2−>   Weight
                                    ▽   ▽   ▽
                         LARGE   **CONCRETE SHAPE**   LIGHT

Here, the main property, **Shape**, is highlighted in bold type, and numbered arrows indicate the role relationships. The concept, (1a), shall be called "basic-level concept", and the system of its properties, (1b), "attributive concept", or "attributive extension of basic-level concept".

As may be seen, the structure of object properties is the same as the structure of object parts; the attributive concept is isomorphic to the partitive concept (cf. (3a)–(3b) and (10a)–(10b) in §1). Thus, parallel to the partitive branch, an attributive branch emerges—another line of development of the concrete concept.

Clearly, not only basic-level concepts but also their parts have attributive concepts. The conventional notation is shown in (1) and (2):

(2)   CHAIR ⬦ (Size ▷ LARGE, **Shape ▷ CONCRETE SHAPE,**
            Weight ▷ LIGHT),
        BANANA⬦ (Color ▷YELLOW, **Shape ▷ CONCRETE SHAPE,**
            Taste ▷ SWEET).

The sign ◊ (or ⬦), as before, stands for the **relationship of development**.

After the concrete (species kind) properties have emerged, the common (genus kind) properties are instantly reduced and replaced by their species kind realizations, cf.: CHAIR ⬦ (LARGE, **CONCRETE SHAPE**, LIGHT), BANANA ⬦ (YELLOW, **CONCRETE SHAPE**, SWEET).

In a more general case, the following developed attributive concept, (3), is derived:

(3)   a. Basic-level concept: OBJECT
                                          ◊
       b. Attributive concept: (Size ▷..., **Shape** ▷..., Color ▷..., ...)

As in the case of object parts, the main property, Shape, may be referred to by the name of the object while other properties may not. The shape of a chair may be called "chair", but not its material, weight, or size. The same is true of the shape of a banana or any other object.

Because all other properties of an object are located in its shape, we can consider this as a particular (degenerate) case of the radial structure of an object's parts, where supplementary parts are positioned around and in contact with the main part but occupy separate places in space.

2. Conceptualization of concrete properties

2.1. Conceptualization of color properties by infants. As has been shown by some studies (Sechenov 1952: 272–426; Bower 1974: chap. 5), as children continue to develop, their syncretic ideas of objects undergo differentiation and sensory properties are distinguished: the shape of an object, its color, size, etc. At 18 months, children differentiate the shape and weight of an object, and these acquire the status of separate properties. Concrete (sensory) color properties are among the latest to be differentiated as separate, roughly between 2.5 and 3 years of age. Let us discuss this in more detail.

There is a revealing paradox about how children acquire adjectives. Unlike nouns and verbs, which children learn to use semantically correctly almost at once,[3] the ability to correctly use adjectives as names for visible colors of objects develops significantly later (Gasser and Smith 1998; Tseitlin 2009: 167 and 2000: 125; Blackwell 2005). While adjectives become part of a child's active vocabulary at the age of about 18 months, their use is not initially based on their meaning and is simply an imitation of the ambient speech. Let us take, as an example, the use of the color naming adjectives *red*, *green*, etc., the so-called "basic color terms", according to Berlin and Kay (1969). Children are known to begin distinguishing the colors of objects (such as toys) not later than the age of 18 months (see, for example, the experimental studies by Rozengart-Pupko (1948 and 1963) and the discussion of their results in (Voeikova 2011: 114)). Nevertheless, it takes almost another 18 months for children to learn to use color-naming adjectives semantically correctly. This fact has been noted by many researchers (see, for example, Andrick and Tager-Flusberg 1986; Tseitlin 1996: 5–7). Voeikova (2011: 217–218) draws special attention to this phenomenon:

> Long ago, observing the linguistic development of his children, Charles Darwin noticed that their first use of color adjectives was so inadequate as to make him think, for some time, that they we color-blind (see Bornstein 1985: 387–388). [...] The necessity of a detailed study of early adjectives is determined by the fact that they constitute a whole group of words used by children not just the wrong way, but inexplicably, without any connection with the real properties of objects. [...] Children reveal the following characteristic feature: understanding, early on, to what semantic classes adjectives belong, they do not distinguish the meanings of adjectives in these classes [...] Children rarely say *bad* instead of *green*, but they can confuse *bad* and *good*, or *green* and *red*. [...] The said phenomena are typical at least for some Indo-European languages; it may be assumed that such phenomena should be observed in most languages that feature a developed system of adjectives, see (Dixon 1982; 2004).

This is an obvious paradox; on the one hand, children at the age of 18 months distinguish the concrete colors of objects, yet, on the other hand, over the next 12 or even 18 months they seem to be incapable of naming the colors using the

---

[3] As some data suggest (Xu and Carey 1996; Xu 2007; Waxman 2008), children begin to learn the categories and names of objects at the age of 12 months, and the categories and names of actions 2–3 months later.

appropriate adjectives, despite the fact that children hear color-naming adjectives used correctly all the time.

I believe this paradox has the following explanation. Children discern the concrete color of an object as a syncretic visual image; for a while, this color is not distinguished as a separate property. Therefore, there is not anything to which children could correlate the adjectives they hear. When shown a display of a red apple, yellow banana, red plum, and yellow lemon, and asked to group these fruits by their color, children solve the task easily (this task is a variation on the theme of Rozengart-Pupko's experiments). However, for the adjective *red* to refer to a red apple it is necessary that a child's idea of an apple not be syncretic (when the color red does not have an independent status among the other concrete properties) but systemic, taking the form of a set of separate common properties (Color, Size, etc.) attributed to the apple, that is, its three-dimensional volume in space. Moreover, it is also necessary that concrete sensory color images be differentiated within the common property Color: red, green, etc. Then the adjective *red* can acquire its meaning-concept, a separate sensory feature 'red' in the mental representation of an apple, and the use of this adjective becomes semantically justified.

> **Note.** This proposition can be clarified with the help of a concrete example. Imagine a person having sweet tea for the first time and experiencing its taste holistically, not knowing that the taste is the result of the combination of the taste of water, tea brew, and sugar dissolved in water. No matter how many times he heard the phrases *židkij/krepkij čaj* 'weak/strong tea' or *nesladkij/sladkij čaj* 'unsweetened/sweet tea' he would not be able to understand the meaning of the adjectives because the designated gustatory properties have not been singled out in his conception of the taste of tea as separate concept-features. At the same time, he would, most likely, distinguish between sweet tea and less sweet tea. However, he could characterize this distinction only with the help of the general adjective *vkusnyj/nevkusnyj* 'tasty/untasty' or a descriptive phrase *like honey*. Only after he began to make tea himself—steeping tea in boiling hot water, pouring the brew in a cup, adding boiling water and sugar—or to observe others do it, would he learn about the aforementioned properties as separate components of the taste of sweet tea, properties that may be strengthened or weakened. Only then would his gustatory percept of sweet tea transform from syncretic to systemic, and he would be able to begin to adequately relate the corresponding adjectives to these components of the taste of tea, thereby learning the meanings of these adjectives.

It may be assumed that children complete the differentiation of concrete colors (red, green, etc.) by the age of 36 months, because by this time semantic mistakes in the use of color adjectives disappear from their speech. More on the development of the notion of object properties and, particularly, on the differentiation of a concrete color into hues may be found in Koshelev 2011a: 225–228 and Koshelev 2017: 453–455.

2.2. Differentiation of concrete properties. All that has been said above of the property Color holds true for the property Size. Particularly, when learning the words *large* and *small*, children confuse them just the same way as in the case of color adjectives (cf. Voeikova 2011: 218). It is noteworthy that abnormalities in the prefrontal cortex may lead to a regression, in which previously distinguished conceptual characteristics of size are lost. However, the ability to use more archaic syncretic correlates of such characteristic features is preserved. For example, a patient diagnosed for such an abnormality can successfully score a shot at any of three baskets positioned at different distances from the patient while being unable to tell which of the baskets is the nearest and which the farthest. The separate concrete properties FARTHER/NEARER have been lost by the patient, but his perception of the distance to the basket, as a syncretic component of his holistic percept of the basket, is preserved. Another patient with similar damage to the prefrontal cortex could grasp objects of various sizes without making mistakes but could not indicate with thumb and index finger the size of the objects grasped (cf. Chuprikova 2015: 430–431).

The specific nature of mistakes made by infants in the use of adjectives suggests that the process of differentiating concrete properties follows the general trend of consecutive differentiation and integration of sensory modalities (cf. Bower 1974: chap. 5) and goes through two stages. First, common properties are differentiated—the color of an object, its size, weight, etc.— which are, basically, types of sensory modalities. From this moment on children do not confuse the adjectives that name common properties; they do not say *large* instead of *green*, though they may confuse *green* and *red* or *large* and *small*. Second, concrete properties are conceptualized within each common property (concrete sensory images of each modality), and children begin to use color, size, and other adjectives semantically correctly.[4]

---

[4] The two-stage process of differentiation of real world phenomena revealed by children often comes to the fore in situations where a certain general property may have alternative meanings. Similar to the examples of confusion given above, children confuse the lexical indicators of time *yesterday* and *tomorrow*: *We went to the wood **tomorrow*** (Nastia, 2 years 4 months); *I'll go to the granny's **yesterday*** (Voeikova 2011: 115–116, 173). Such mis-

Notice here the absolute similarity to the two-stage process of developing the concrete parts of objects: first, a common part is developed, for example, Nožka 'leg-dimin.', and only then its concrete types, NOŽKA STULA / DIVANA 'LEG CHAIR-Gen./COUCH-Gen', etc. (see § 1 section 10).

2.3. Conceptualization of concrete shape. Given the above, it may be assumed that children first distinguish a common property (sensory modality), e.g. Shape, and then concrete properties (sensory percepts), e.g. *kruglyj—krug* 'circular—circle', *šarovidnyj—šar* 'spherical—sphere' and other more complex properties.

> **Note.** As some experimental data show, the speech-thought development of children displays a novelty around the age of 18 months: children begin to use the shape of an object as its main characteristic feature. This tendency has been named the "shape bias" (Landau et al. 1988). In various experiments, children were shown a new object of a peculiar shape and given its name, which they did not know, for example, *This is a dax!* Then children were shown a number of different objects laid out before them, among which was an object with a similar shape, and asked which of the objects had the same name. After the age of 18 months children repeatedly pointed at the new object of the same shape, while over the age period of 18 to 30 months attention to the shape kept growing. At the same time, children between the ages of 12 to 18 months did not pay regular attention to the shape of objects in such naming tasks (cf. Pereira and Smith 2009: 67). As observed by Markson et al. (2008: 204): "when children learn a new object name, they tend to generalize that name to other objects similar in shape... This has been dubbed "the shape bias" [...] The shape bias emerges once the child makes the second-order generalization that words in contexts such as 'This is a __' are generalized on the basis of shape".

2.4. Why are general properties subdivided? Let us ask the question: on what grounds are object properties differentiated? Unlike the parts into which objects are subdivided as a result of their particular functions being singled

---

takes, made by children, have a similar explanation. After the age of 24 months, children divide their holistic idea of time into "present time" and "non-present time". However, the latter has not yet been divided into "past-yesterday" and "future-tomorrow"; therefore, children do not have semantic grounds for the use of the words *yesterday* and *tomorrow* and so confuse them.

out from the general function of a given object, general properties do not have similar functions. The question was answered by Sechenov (1952) more than a hundred years ago:

> We perceive an orange as a round or spherical object of characteristic color that has a specific scent and taste. In this complex percept, the object's contour and color are given to us by the eye; the spherical shape—largely by the hand with its muscular structure (but also by the eye), and the latter two qualities by the olfactory and gustatory systems [...]. The outcome is an associated sensory group whose parts are given by the separate reactions of the visual, tactile, olfactory, and gustatory apparatus. [...]
>
> It is clear, furthermore, that the combination of all of the sensorily accessible properties or characteristics determines the actual sensory image of any object. [...]
>
> To put it plainly: any and all sensorily accessible features or properties of objects are products of separate physiological reactions of perception, and the number of the former is strictly determined by the number of the latter (p. 354).

According to Sechenov, general properties (sensory modalities) become separate because they rely on separate perception mechanisms ("are products of separate physiological perception reactions"). As these mechanisms in children develop, they are differentiated out from the syncretic perception mechanism, cf.:

> There are seven different reactions characteristic of the eye and as many feature categories (color, flat shape, size, remoteness, direction, corporeality, and motion). For the sense of touch, because of the muscular sensation of the hand and of the entire body, the number of reactions is at least nine, and to these correspond: warmth, two-dimensional shape, size, distance, direction, corporeality, compressibility, weight, and motion. For the ear, the number of basic reactions and features does not exceed three (duration in time, pitch, and timbre). Finally, there are single forms of reaction for the senses of smell and taste. Therefore, the maximum number of sensory features of an object cannot exceed 21. But it should be borne in mind that these categories allow for a multitude of variations within the limit of 21 (p. 355).

It is these separate perception mechanisms that play the same role as the functions of the parts of objects. Sechenov's proposition is corroborated by the cases of prefrontal cortex abnormalities mentioned above, when patients lose mental representations of separate conceptual features of size in spite of the fact that their ability to use the syncretic correlates of these features is preserved.

It is noteworthy that only common properties are subdivided based on physiological mechanisms of perception ("physiological reaction"). As has been shown elsewhere (Koshelev 2016: 344–346 and 2017: 454), concrete properties, such as a color palette, are formed under the influence of functional motivations.

2.5. The level of attributive cognitive units. Differentiation of an object's properties accounts for further extension of a child's vocabulary of elementary cognitive units when common properties are added to the store: Color, Weight, etc. (sensory modalities), concrete properties: GREEN, HEAVY, SOLID, etc. (sensory percepts), and also three relationships: (1) "Object $\Rightarrow$ its properties: SHAPE, Color, Weight, etc.", (2) "**Shape** (main property) $-N\rightarrow$ Supplementary common properties", and (3) the genus-species relationship "Common property $\triangleright$ Concrete properties" (Color $\triangleright$ (GREEN, RED, etc.)).

3. The partitive-attributive extension of a concrete concept and the basic meaning of a concrete noun

3.1. The partitive-attributive extension of an object (basic-level concept). As children continue to develop cognitively, basic-level concepts—the ideas of holistic objects which children have—are supplemented by two systems: of parts and properties (cf. partitive concept (10b), § 1, section 10, and attributive concept (3b)). These concepts represent two separate lines of development for a basic-level concept as the dual structure "Prototype $\rightarrow$ Function". The partitive concept expresses the development of a basic concept into a system of parts, while the attributive concept expresses the development of a basic concept into a system of properties. In other words, a developed object concept stored in the memory of a three-year old child[5] is represented by a two-level

---

[5] Vygotsky (1998) writes: "It is only by the age of 3 that a child's perception becomes maximally close to the perception of an adult person" (p. 158). Lakoff (1987) also observes that three-year-olds "have mastered *basic-level* categorization perfectly" (p. 49). Having mastered an object's partitive structure, children have a much clearer idea of the category 'object' (cf. Koshelev 2013b: 752–754). A two-year-old without such a partitive system has a more vague idea of the object category. Based on the results obtained by Mervis (1987), Lakoff (1987) emphasizes that "two-year-olds have mastered basic-level categorization, but have come up with different categories than adults" (p. 49; also, cf. Rakison 2000: 80–81).

development tree with a top (basic concept) and two extensions (partitive and attributive) which are connected to the top by a relationship of development ($\Diamond$). For example, the developed concepts CHAIR and BANANA are represented as follows:

(4) a. Basic-level concept: CHAIR
               Partitive concept $\Diamond$ $\Diamond$ Attributive concept
      b.   (BACK, **SEAT**, LEGS) (Size $\triangleright$..., **Shape** $\triangleright$..., Weight $\triangleright$...)

(5) a. Basic-level concept: BANANA
               Partitive concept $\Diamond$ $\Diamond$ Attributive concept
      b. (SKIN, **FLESH**, FRUIT STEM) (Color $\triangleright$..., **Shape** $\triangleright$..., Taste $\triangleright$...)

Remarkably, much of what has been discussed in paragraphs 1 and 2 was long ago analyzed by Sechenov. Cf.:

> Mental abstraction of parts and properties from an object as a single whole is based on the separateness and difference of the physiological reactions of perception; the first general effect of an external stimulus corresponds to the object, and the particular reaction of seeing the object in detail corresponds to its feature (Sechenov 1952: 360).

> Another line [of mental development] is defined by subdividing [sensory] concretes into parts or by mentally isolating parts from a whole. Every isolated part is individuated, obtains the right to exist separately, and is given a certain designator (Ibid: 280).

Concretes, according to Sechenov, were perceptually accessible components of the world (objects, properties, etc.)—similar to what we call sensory cognitive units.

3.2. The basic meaning of a concrete noun. As has been shown in chap. 2, § 1, section 1.5, the basic meaning of a concrete noun is a basic-level concept, that is, a dual structure:

(6) Basic meaning = basic-level concept = Prototype $\rightarrow$ Function

where Prototype reflects the typical (mostly visual) properties of noun referents and Function the characteristic feature of all its direct referents, both typical and non-typical. The arrow connecting these components ($\leftarrow$) stands for the relationship of interpretation.

The extensions of the basic-level concept thus obtained—the partitive and attributive concepts—are naturally included in the basic meaning, (7), turning it into a subdivided two-level development structure. In this structure the first level is occupied by the basic-level concept, shown in (4a)—(5a), and the second level by the systems of parts and attributes, shown in (4b)—(5b), that have developed from the basic-level concept.

As shown above, native speakers actively use these systems in their discourse. Thus, when using nominal genitive constructions, native speakers distinguish between the functional and non-functional parts of an object. If a native speaker talks about the parts of a multi-tool pocket knife that has non-functional parts, for example a fork and a corkscrew, he may say *lezvie noža* 'the blade of the knife' but not **vilka noža* 'the fork of the knife' or **štopor noža* 'the corkscrew of the knife'. He may also use the role-based hierarchy "Main Part—Supplementary Parts". For example, he may well call a blade with a missing handle a knife (the blade is the main part of the knife and carries its main function), but not a handle without a blade. The same hierarchy is used when objects are named. For example, in Russian such disparate parts of objects as the stem of a wine glass and the leg of a couch are referred to using the word *nožka* 'leg-dimin.' The grounds for calling such obviously different parts by one word, *nožka*, are twofold: firstly, its function—'to support the object above the ground', and secondly, its position (below the object) defined by the role-based hierarchy. Attributive concept structures are also actively used by native speakers. For example, Russian native speakers will not say about an overripe banana **staryj banan* 'old banana' because the property Age is not one of a banana's properties.

As may be seen from the discussion above, the basic meaning of the word *banan* 'banana' in the cognitive vocabulary is the developed concept shown in (5a)—(5b), in which all the components are filled in with concrete data. The prototype of the basic-level concept BANANA is filled in with a typical three-dimensional image of a ripe banana, and its function with the general function of bananas—'a ripe fruit of a banana tree used as food'. The partitive concept of a banana is filled in similarly: the prototypes of its parts are filled in with typical images of banana flesh (main part), skin, and fruit stem (supplementary parts), and their functions with concrete particular functions: 'the flesh of a banana consumed as food', 'the banana skin that protects the flesh from birds and insects', and 'the fruit stem through which the flesh receives nourishment'. The attributive concept of a banana is filled in similarly: its general properties—Shape, Size, Weight, Color, Ripeness, Taste, Smell—are filled in with concrete meanings associated with a typical ripe banana. Certainly, a complete dictionary entry should include a sequence of 'time samples' for the typical states of a banana, from the freshest to overripe and rotten banana.

Note. As we can see, the basic meaning of a concrete noun is a developed concept—a general cognitive structure independent of language and isomorphic to the structure of external reality (actual bananas). In other words, this meaning does not possess its own linguistic content. The same is true for the basic meaning of action verbs, see § 3 below.

§3. A motor concept and its two extensions: partitive and attributive. The basic meaning of an action verb

I will now show that a motor concept has a structure quite similar to the structure of a developed object concept. In fact, the basic meaning of an action verb is structurally similar to the basic meaning of a concrete noun.

1. The motor concept SXVATIT'[6] 'GRASP' (seize an object by the hand)

Consider how a single action which has its own general function develops into a system of its parts (particular actions). As an example, let us discuss, briefly, the development of a child's ability to perform the action GRASP. Newborn babies are known to be capable of reaching for toys and grasping them. To them, this is, undoubtedly, a single syncretic action. However, after the age of 26 weeks it is subdivided into two separate actions, REACH FOR (without grasping) and GRASP, according to Bower's (1974: chap. 5) analysis. We believe that the motivating factor in this case (just as in the case of subdividing an object into parts) is the subdivision of the general function of this action— 'to begin to hold an object with one's hand in order to be able to freely manipulate it'—into two particular functions, 'bring the hand near an object' and 'begin to hold an object'. At first, the function 'grasp an object' is singled out. The action **GRASP** becomes the main action, because it is this action that embodies the general purpose of the combined action. The action REACH FOR becomes supplementary. Both particular functions are connected by the role relationship, REACH FOR <−1− **GRASP**, which shows that the action REACH FOR is localized on the time axis immediately before the action **GRASP** and that its function is to prepare for the main action, namely, 'bring the hand close to the object'.

---

[6] *Sxvatit'* is a perfective verb, while its imperfective counterpart is *xvatat'*. In the context of this section, where an observable action, SXVATIT', is analyzed, GRASP should also be interpreted as an observable action.—*Translator's note.*

Thus, the general function of an action is the sum of the functions of the particular actions, and the function of the sum of consecutive particular actions is equal to the sum of the particular functions of these actions. For example, the function of the holistic action GRASP is equal to the sum of the functions of consecutive actions REACH FOR and **GRASP**. This gives us the following:

(1) Developed concept GRASP =
   a. Basic-level motor concept: GRASP
                                           ◊
   b. Partitive concept   REACH FOR <−1− **GRASP**.

As before, the sign ◊ (or <>) stands for the relationship of development.

As can be clearly seen, the developed motor concept in (1) is isomorphic to the developed concrete concept (3), CHAIR (see § 1 section 4).

Based on Bower's (1974) analysis mentioned above, the following claim can be made: the action GRASP is subdivided into two functional actions, TOUCH (feel) the toy (the initial phase of the action GRASP, when the child cautiously touches and feels the toy with his fingers) and SQUEEZE (the child grasps the toy with his fingers) (cf. Koshelev 2011a: 228–230). Clearly, the last action becomes the main one, accounting for the outcome. Thereby the single concept GRASP becomes, in its turn, a developed concept: GRASP <> (TOUCH <−2− **SQUEEZE**).

In the end, the developed motor concept, (1), acquires an additional level of partitive development:

(1) a.   GRASP
                                  ◊
     b.   REACH FOR <−1− **GRASP**
                                  ◊
     c.   TOUCH <−2− **SQUEEZE**

It is quite similar to the concrete concept (8), BICYCLE, described in § 1 section 9.

It is worthy of note that the action REACH FOR also consists of two functionally different actions, DRAWING NEAR (of the hand to the toy) and PARTING THE FINGERS (for subsequent grasping). They are not, however, subdivided into separate actions because the fingers begin to part not after the hand has drawn near the toy but prior to that, during the final stage of drawing near (cf. Koshelev 2011a: 229–233).

As with the main part of an object, the main particular action may be called by the name of the action as a whole, while the supplementary parts cannot. Thus, in a sequence of three actions (REACH FOR, TOUCH, **SQUEEZE**) the final action is the main one. It can be called by the name of the action as a whole, *grasp*, whereas none of the preceding actions may be.

2. The action BEŽAT'[7] 'RUN'

A similar interpretation is applicable to the concept X-BEŽIT ('X-IS-RUNNING'), where X is a bipedal animal (human, ostrich, goose, etc.). Below, the main variant of this concept is described, ČELOVEK-BEŽIT ('A PERSON-IS-RUNNING') (MAN / WOMAN / CHILD / OLD MAN IS RUNNING). The general purpose of the action here is 'to move quickly using one's legs to a set point in space, Z'. The motor concept ČELOVEK-BEŽIT ('MAN-IS-RUNNING') is a cyclic repetition of the action MOVE, which consists of three actions:

Motor concept: MOVE (in the direction of Z)
◊
Partitive concept: PUSH (with one leg), **FLY** (in the direction of Z), LAND (with the other leg).

Here, the flight of the runner, moving the runner forward, is the main particular action. Thus, the action MOVE appears to be a system of its particular actions. And the general function of the action RUN (move to point Z) is equal to the sum of the particular functions of a sequence of movements in the direction of Z. Thus, we get the following developed motor concept:

(2)   Developed motor concept ČELOVEK-BEŽIT ('MAN-IS-RUNNING') =
   a. Basic-level motor concept: ČELOVEK-BEŽIT ('MAN-IS-RUNNING')
◊
   b. Partitive concept: (MOVE, MOVE, … **MOVE TO Z**)

The last movement, whereby the agent reaches its spatial goal, Z, is the main movement in this sequence. All the other movements are subordinated to it by the role relationships.

---

[7] There are two imperfective verbs in Russian for the action RUN, *bežat'* and *begat'*; prototypically, *bežat'* is used in situations of immediate perception and furnishes the English concept 'BE-RUNNING'.—*Translator's note.*

3. The attributive motor concept

The attributive concept of an action is quite similar to the attributive concept of an object. It has a similar main property, the shape of an action. Shape is easily recognizable—this can be checked out by visiting the site of Thomas F. Shipley's lab in Philadelphia (https://astro.temple.edu/~tshipley/mocap/dot-Movie.html, access 05.04.2018). There, one can see three-second point-light animations of various human actions that are instantly recognizable, such as shot-putting, kicking a ball, etc.

The properties that supplement Shape are general properties: Speed ▷ (FAST, NOT FAST, SLOW), Duration ▷ (LONG, NOT LONG, BRIEF). They are attributed to the shape, that is, they are given a spatial locus in it; in this respect, they are supplementary to it. As a result, an attributive concept of the action ((3b)) emerges which is similar to the attributive concrete concept ((3b)) described in § 2 section 1:

(3) a. Basic-level motor concept: ČELOVEK-BEŽIT ('MAN-IS-RUNNING')

◊

b. Attributive concept: (Speed <–1– **Shape** –2–> Duration)

▽   ▽   ▽

FAST **CONCRETE SHAPE** LONG

Combining (2b) and (3b), we get a partitive-attributive extension (4b) of the motor concept ČELOVEK-BEŽIT ('MAN-IS-RUNNING') which is similar to the extension of the concrete concept CHAIR:

(4) a. Basic-level motor concept: ČELOVEK-BEŽIT ('MAN-IS-RUNNING')

◊   ◊

b.   Partitive concept (2b)   Attributive concept (3b)

4. The basic meaning of action verbs

It was shown in chap. 2, § 2, that the basic meaning of an action verb is a basic-level motor concept with the structure "Action Prototype → Its Function". The extensions (partitive and attributive) we have for a motor concept are also included in the basic meaning of the verb, turning it into a subdivided two-level development structure. In this structure, the first level is occupied by the basic-level concept and the second level by the systems of parts and attributes developed from the basic-level concept. For example, the basic meaning of the verb *grasp* in the cognitive dictionary is a developed concept ((1a), (1b) and (1c)) in which all of the components are filled in with concrete data. The prototype of the action GRASP is filled in with a typical image of a moving human hand reaching for and grasping an object, and its function is filled in with the concrete function of grasping—'to begin to hold an object with one's hand in order to be able to freely manipulate it'. The partitive and attributive concepts ((1b) and (1c)) are filled in similarly, with the prototypes and functions of the particular actions of reaching for and grasping and the attributive features of the action GRASP: QUICKLY, etc.

References

Akhutina, T. V. *Nejrolingvističeskij analiz leksiki, semantiki i pragmatiki* [Neuro-linguistic Analysis of Vocabulary, Grammar and Pragmatics]. Moscow: Jazyki slavjanskoj kul'tury, 2014.

Aktivnyj slovar' sovremennogo russkogo jazyka [An Active Dictionary of Modern Russian], edited by Iu. D. Apresian. Pervyj vypusk. Vol. 1, 2. Moscow: Jazyki slavjanskoj kul'tury, 2014.

Alexander, R. M. *The Human Machine*. N. Y.: Columbia University Press, 1992.

Alexiadou, A., Anagnostopoulou, E., and M. Everaert, eds. *The Unaccusativity Puzzle. Explorations of Syntax-lexicon Interface*. Oxford: Oxford University Press, 2004.

Alpatov, V. M. "Nekotorye zametki po istorii lingvistiki [Some notes on the history of linguistics]." In *Tipologija i teorija jazyka: ot opisanija k ob"jasneniju. K 60-letiju A. E. Kibrika*, edited by E. V. Rakhilina and Ia. G. Testelets. Moscow: Jazyki russkoj kul'tury, 1999.

Andrick, G. R. and H. Tager-Flusberg. "The acquisition of colour terms." *JCL* 13 (1986): 119–37.

Aoshuan, Tan'. *Kitajskaja kartina mira: jazyk, kul'tura, mental'nost'* [The Chinese World View: Language, culture, mentality]. Moscow: Jazyki slavjanskoj kul'tury, 2004/2012.

Apresian, Iu. D. *Leksičeskaja semantika: sinonimičeskie sredstva jazyka* [Lexical Semantics. The synonymical means of language]. Moscow: Nauka, 1974. 2nd ed., *Izbrannye trudy*. Vol. 1, *Leksičeskaja semantika: sinonimicheskie sredstva jazyka*. Moscow: Škola "Jazyki russkoj kul'tury", Izdatel'skaja firma "Vostočnaja literatura" RAN, 1995.

— —. "O moskovskoj semantičeskoj škole [On the Moscow semantic school]." *Voprosy jazykoznanija* 1 (2005): 3–30.

— —. *Issledovanija po semantike i leksikografii* [Explorations in Semantics and Lexicography]. Vol. 1, *Paradigmatika*. Moscow: Jazyki slavjanskix kul'tur, 2009.

— —. "Vvedenie [Introduction]." In *Prospekt aktivnogo slovarja russkogo jazyka* [A Project: An Active Dictionary of Russian Language], edited by Iu. D. Apresian, 17–54. Moscow: Jazyki slavjanskix kul'tur, 2010a.

— —. "Instrukcija po sostavleniju slovarnyx statej Aktivnogo slovarja (AS) russkogo jazyka [Instructions for compiling the Active Dictionary (AD) of Russian]." In *Prospekt aktivnogo slovarja russkogo jazyka* [A Project: An Active Dictionary of Russian Language], edited by Iu. D. Apresian, 55–152. Moscow: Jazyki slavjanskix kul'tur, 2010b.

— —. "Ob Aktivnom slovare russkogo jazyka." In *Aktivnyj slovar' sovremennogo russkogo jazyka.* [An Active Dictionary of Modern Russian], edited by Iu. D. Apresian. Vol. 1, 5–36. Moscow: Jazyki slavjanskoj kul'tury, 2014.

Arkad'ev, P. M. "Struktura sobytija i semantiko-sintaksičeskij interfejs. Obzor novejšix rabot [Event structure and the semantic-syntactic interface. Review of recent works]." *Voprosy jazykoznanija* 2 (2008): 107–36.

Austin, J. L. *Philosophical Papers.* Oxford: Clarendon Press, 1961.

Bahner, W. "'Paradigm' or 'current' in the theory of language." In *Proceedings of the XIIIth International Congress of Linguists. Proceedings Publishing Committee,* edited by S. Hattori and K. Inoue, 847–49. Tokyo: Proceedings Publishing Committee, 1983.

Baillargeon, R. "How do infants learn about the physical world?" *Current Directions* 3 (1994): 133–40.

— —. "Young infants' expectations about hidden objects: A reply to tree challenges." *Developmental Science* 2, no 2 (1999): 115–33.

— —. "The acquisition of physical knowledge in infancy: A summary in eight lessons." In *Blackwell Handbook of Childhood Cognitive Development,* edited by U. Goswami, 47–83. Oxford: Blackwell Publishing, 2002.

Bates, E. "Modularity, domain specificity and the development of language." *Discussions in Neuroscience* 10, no 12 (1994): 136–49.

Beaugrande, R. *Linguistic Theory: The Discourse of Fundamental Works.* L.: Longman, 1991.

Berlin, B. and P. Kay. *Basic Color Terms: Their Universality and Evolution.* Berkeley: University of California Press, 1969.

Bernshtein, N. A. *Biomexanika i fiziologija dviženij* [Biomechanics and Physiology of Movements]. Moscow: Medgiz, 1947. Reprint, Moscow; Voronež, 2008.

— —. *Fiziologija dviženij i aktivnost'* [Physiology of Movements and Activity]. Moscow: Medgiz, 1990.

Bernstein, N. A. *The Co-ordination and Regulation of Movements.* Oxford: Pergamon Press, 1967.

Bickerton, D. *Language and Species.* Chicago: University of Chicago Press, 1990.

— —. "Language evolution: A brief guide for linguists." *Lingua* 117 (2007): 510–26.

— —. *Adam's Tongue: How Humans Made Language, How Language Made Humans.* N. Y.: Hill and Wang, 2009.

— —. "On two incompatible theories of language evolution." In *The Evolution of Human Language: Biolinguistic Perspectives*, edited by R. K. Larson, V. M. Déprez, and H. Yamakido, 199–210. Cambridge: Cambridge University Press, 2010.

Bingham, G. P., Schmidt, R. C., and L. D. Rosenblum. "Dynamics and the orientation of kinematic forms in visual event recognition." *Journal of Experimental Psychology: Human Perception and Performance* 21, no. 6 (1995): 1473–93.

Bingham, G. P. and E. A. Wickelgren. "Events and actions as dynamically molded spatiotemporal objects: A critique of the motor theory of biological motion perception." In *Understanding Events: How Humans See, Represent, and Act on Events*, edited by T. F. Shipley and J. M. Zacks, 255–85. N. Y., NY: Oxford University Press, 2008.

Blackwell, A. A. "Acquiring the English adjective lexicon: Relationships with input properties and adjectival semantic typology." *Journal of Child Language* 32, iss. 3 (2005): 535–62.

Blake, R. and M. Shiffrar. "Perception of human motion." *Annual Review of Psychology* 58 (2007): 47–73.

Bloom, P. *How Children Learn the Meanings of Words*. Cambridge, MA; L.: MIT Press, 2000.

Bloomfield, L. *Language*. L.: George Allen & Unwin, 1973.

Boduen de Kurtene, I. A. "Nekotorye obščie zamečanija o jazykovedenii i jazyke [Some general remarks on linguistics and language]." In I. A. Boduen de Kurtene. *Izbrannye trudy po obščemu jazykoznaniju*. Vol. 1, 47–77. Moscow: Izd-vo AN SSSR, 1963.

Bol'shoj tolkovyj slovar' russkogo jazyka (BTS) [Great Explanatory Dictionary of Russian language], edited by S. A. Kuznecov. Saint Petersburg: Norint, 1998.

Bornstein, M. H. "Colour-name versus shape-name learning in young children." *JCL* 12 (1985): 387–93.

Bower, T. G. R. *Development in Infancy*. San Francisco, CA: W. H. Freeman, 1974.

Brown, R. *Social Psychology*. N. Y.: Free Press, 1965.

Brugman, C. and G. Lakoff. "Cognitive topology and lexical networks." In *Lexical Ambiguity Resolution: Perspectives from Psycholinguistics, Neuropsychology, and Artificial Intelligence*, edited by S. L. Small, G. W. Cottrell, and M. K. Tanenhaus, 477–508. San Mateo, CA: Morgan Kaufman, 1988.

Carey, S. *The Origin of Concepts*. N. Y.: Oxford University Press, 2009.

Carlson, N. R. *Physiology of Behavior*. Boston: Allyn and Bacon, 1998.

Chomsky, N. *Language and Mind*. N. Y.: Harcourt Brace & World, 1968. Reprint, Cambridge University Press, 2006.

— —. *Rules and Representations*. Columbia University Press, 1980.

— —. "Language and nature." *Mind* 104, no. 413 (1995): 161.

— —. *On Nature and Language*. Cambridge: Cambridge University Press, 2002.

— —. "Some simple evo-devo theses: How true might they be for language?" In *The Evolution of Human Language: Biolinguistic Perspectives*, edited by R. K. Larson, V. M. Déprez, and H. Yamakido, 45–62. Cambridge: Cambridge University Press, 2010.

Chuprikova, N. I. *Umstvennoe razvitie. Princip differenciacii* [Mental Development. The Principle of Differentiation]. St. Petersburg: Piter, 2007.

— —. *Psixika i psixičeskie processy: sistema ponjatij obščej psixologii* [Psychic and Mental Processes: General Psychology System of Concepts]. Moscow: Jazyki slavjanskoj kul'tury, 2015.

Chenki, A. (A. Chienki). "Sovremennye kognitivnye podxody k semantike: sxodstva i različija v teorijax i celjax [Contemporary cognitive approaches to semantics: Similarities and differences in theories and goals]." *Voprosy jazykoznanija*, 1 (1996): 68–78.

Collins, S. H., Adamczyk, P. G., and A. D. Kuo. "Dynamic arm swinging in human walking." *Proceedings of the Royal Society of London B* 276 (2009): 3679–88.

Csibra, G., Biro, S., Gergely, G., and O. Koós. "One-year-old infants use teleological representations of actions productively." *Cognitive Science* 27, no 1 (2003): 111–33.

Dal', V. *Tolkovyj slovar' živogo velikorusskogo jazyka* [Explanatory Dictionary of the Living Great Russian Language]. 4 vols. Moscow: Russkij jazyk, 1989.

Dem'iankov, V. Z. "Paradigma v lingvistike i teorii jazyka [Paradigms in linguistics and in language theory]." In *Gorizonty sovremennoj lingvistiki: Tradicii i novatorstvo: Sb. statej v čest'E. S. Kubrjakovoj*, 27–37. Moscow: Jazyki slavjanskix kul'tur, 2009.

Dixon, R. M. W. *Where Have all the Adjectives Gone? And Other Essays in Semantics and Syntax*. Berlin: Mouton, 1982.

— —. "Adjectives classes in typological perspective." In *Adjective Classes: A Cross-linguistic Typology*, edited by R. M. W. Dixon and A. Y. Aikhenvald, 1–49. Oxford: Oxford University Press, 2004.

Dobrushina, E. R. and D. Paiar. "Pristavočnaja paradigma russkogo glagola: semantičeskie mexanizmy [The prefix paradigm of the Russian verb: Semantic mechanisms]." *In Russkie pristavki: mnogoznačnost' i semantičeskoe edinstvo*, edited by E. R. Dobrushina, E. A. Mellina, and D. Paiar. Moscow: Russkie slovari, 2001.

Dobzhansky, T. "Biology, molecular and organismic." *American Zoologist* 4, no 4 (1964): 443–52.

Eliseeva, M. B. *Fonetičeskoe i leksičeskoe razvitie rebënka rannego vozrasta* [Phonetic and Lexical Development of Young Children]. Saint Petersburg: Izd-vo RGPU im. A. I. Gercena, 2008.

Erteschik-Shir, N. and T. Rapoport., ed. *The Syntax of Aspect. Deriving Thematic and Aspectual Interpretation*. Oxford: Oxford University Press, 2005.

Evans, V. *How Words Mean: Lexical Concepts, Cognitive Models, and Meaning Construction*. Oxford: Oxford University Press, 2009.

— —. "A unified account of polysemy within LCCM Theory." *Lingua* 157 (2015): 100–23.

Evans, N. and S. C. Levinson. "The myth of language universals: Language diversity and its importance for cognitive science." *Behavioral and Brain Sciences* 32, no 5 (2009): 429–92.

Falikman, M. V. *Obščaja psixologija* [General Psychology]. Vol. 4, *Vnimanie*. Moscow: Academia, 2010.

Faltz, L. M. *Reflexivization: A study in universal syntax*. N. Y.; L.: Garland, 1985.

Fillmore, Ch. J. "Frame semantics." In *Linguistics in the Morning Calm*, 111–37. Seoul: Hanshin Publishing Co, 1982.

— —, Kay, P., and M. C. O'Connor. "Regularity and idiomaticity in grammatical constructions: The case of 'let alone'." *Language* 64, no 3 (1988): 501–38.

Fitch, W. T. *The Evolution of Language*. N. Y.: Cambridge University Press, 2010.

— —, Hauser, M. D., and N. Chomsky. "The evolution of the language faculty: Clarifications and implications." *Cognition* 97 (2005): 179–210.

Fogassi, L. and P. F. Ferrari. "Mirror systems." *Wiley Interdisciplinary Reviews: Cognitive Science* 2 (2011): 22–38.

Gak, V. G. *Sopostavitel'naja leksikologija* [Comparative Lexicology]. Moscow: Meždunarodnye otnošenija, 1977.

Gallese, V. and G. Lakoff. "The brain's concepts: The role of the sensory-motor system in conceptual knowledge." *Cognitive Neuropsychology* 22, no 3/4 (2005): 455–79.

Gardner, H. *The Mind's New Science: A History of the Cognitive Revolution*. N. Y.: Basic Books, 1985.

Gasser, M. and L. Smith. "Learning nouns and adjectives: A connectionist account." *Language and Cognitive Processes* 13, no 2/3 (1998): 269–306.

Gelernter, D. "Recursive structure." Accessed December 3, 2016. https://www.edge.org/response-detail/10574

Geniushene, E. Sh. and V. P. Nedialkov. "Tipologija refleksivnyx konstrukcij [Typology of reflexive constructions]." In *TFG. Personal'nost'. Zalogovost'*, 241–76. Saint Peterburg: Nauka, 1991.

Gentner, D. "Why verbs are hard to learn." In *Action Meets Word: How Children Learn Verbs*, edited by K. Hirsh-Pasek and R. Golinkoff, 544–64. N. Y.: Oxford University Press, 2006.

Gergely, G., Nádasdy, Z., Csibra, G., and S. Bíró. "Taking the intentional stance at 12 months of age." *Cognition* 56, no 2 (1995): 165–93.

Givón, T. *Syntax: A Functional-typological Introduction.* Vol. 2. Amsterdam: John Benjamins, 1990.

Goldberg, A. T. *Constructions: A Construction Grammar Approach to Argument Structure.* Chicago: University of Chicago Press, 1995.

— —. *Constructions at Work: The Nature of Generalization in Language.* Oxford: Oxford University Press, 2006.

Golinkoff, R., Chung, H. L., Hirsh-Pasek, K., Liu, J., Bertenthal, B. I., Brand, R., Maguire, M. J., and E. Hennon. "Young children can extend motion verbs to point-light displays." *Developmental Psychology* 38, no 4 (2002): 604–14.

Granger, G.-G. *Pensée formelle et sciences de l'homme.* Paris: Aubier, 1960.

— —. *Langages et épistémologie.* Paris: Klinksieck, 1979.

Hauser, M. D., Chomsky, N., and W. T. Fitch. "The faculty of language: What is it, who has it, and how did it evolve?" *Science* 298 (2002): 1569–79.

Hewes, G. W. "Language origin theories." In *Language Learning by a Chimpanzee: The Lana Project*, edited by D. M. Rumbaugh. N. Y.: Academic Press, 1977.

Humboldt, W. von. *Über das vergleichende Sprachstudium in Beziehung auf die verschiedenen Epochen der Sprachentwicklung.* Berlin: G. Reimer, 1820.

Isenina, E. I. *Doslovnyj period razvitija reči u detej* [The Pre-lexical Period of Speech Development in Children]. Saratov: Izd-vo Saratovskogo universiteta, 1986.

Ivanchei, I. "Teorii implicitnogo naučenija: protivorečivye podxody k odnomu fenomenu ili neprotivorečivye opisanija raznyx? [Theories of implicit learning: Contradictory approaches to the same phenomenon or consistent descriptions of different types of learning?]" *Rossijskij žurnal kognitivnoj nauki* 1, no 4 (2014): 17–30.

Jackendoff, R. "Multiple subcategorization and the Theta-Criterion: The case of 'climb'." *Natural Language and Linguistic Theory* 3, no 3 (1985): 271–95.

— —. *Language, Consciousness, Culture: Essays on Mental Structure.* Cambridge, MA: MIT Press, 2007.

— —. "Your theory of language evolution depends on your theory of language." In *The Evolution of Human Language: Biolinguistic Perspectives*, edited by R. K. Larson, V. M. Déprez, and H. Yamakido. Cambridge: Cambridge University Press, 2010.

— — and S. Pinker. "The nature of the language faculty and its implications for evolution of language (Reply to Fitch, Hauser, and Chomsky)." *Cognition* 97 (2005): 211–25.

Jakobson, R. "Beitrag zur allgemeinen Kasuslehre (Gesamtbedeutungen der russischen Kasus)." *Travaux du Cercle linguistique de Prague* 6 (1936): 240–88.

———. *Selected Writings.* Vol. II, *Word and Language.* The Hague: Mouton, 1971.

Johansson, G. "Visual perception of biological motion and a model for its analysis." *Perception & Psychophysics* 14 (1973): 201–11.

———. "Spatio-temporal differentiation and integration in visual motion perception: An experimental and theoretical analysis of calculus-like functions in visual data processing." *Psychological Research* 38 (1976): 379–93.

Kasevich, V. B. "Ontolingvistika kak central'nyj razdel jazykoznanija [Ontolinguistics as the central section of linguistics]." In *Problemy ontolingvistiki — 2009. Materialy meždunarodnoj konferencii (17–19 ijunja 2009 g., Sankt-Peterburg),* 39–46. Saint Petersburg: Zlatoust, 2009.

———. "Javljaetsja li lingvistika naukoj? (Po povodu stat'i Žil'bera Lazara) [Is linguistics a science? (about Žil'ber Lazar's article)]." In *Kognitivnaja lingvistika v poiskax identičnosti,* 19–27. Moscow: Jazyki slavjanskoj kul'tury, 2013. Originally published in *Materialy XXIX mežvuz. nauč.-metodič. konf. prepodavatelej i aspirantov.* Vol. 14, *Sekcija obščego jazykoznanija.* P. 1, 16–22. Saint Petersburg: Zlatoust, 2000.

Kategorija posessivnosti v slavjanskix i balkanskix jazykax [The Possessive Category in Slavic and Balkan Languages], edited by Viach. Vs. Ivanov. Moscow: Nauka, 1989.

Kibrik, A. E. "Sovremennaja lingvistika: otkuda i kuda [Modern linguistics: From where to where]." *Vestnik MGU. Ser. Filologija* 5 (1995): 93–103.

———. *Konstanty i peremennye jazyka* [Constants and Variables in Language]. Saint Petersburg: Aletejja, 2003.

Kniazev, Iu. P. *Grammatičeskaja semantika: Russkij jazyk v tipologičeskoj perspective* [Grammatical Semantics: The Russian Language from a Typological Perspective]. Moscow: Jazyki slavjanskix kul'tur, 2007.

Kognitivnaja psixologija. Učebnik dlja vuzov [Cognitive Psychology. A Textbook for University Students], edited by V. N. Druzhinina and D. V. Ushakova. Moscow: PER SÈ, 2002.

Kol'tsova, M. M. *Razvitie signal'nyx sistem dejstvitel'nosti u detej* [Development of Reality Signal Systems in Children]. Leningrad: Nauka, 1980.

Koshelev, A. D. "Ob osnovanijax jazykovoj klassifikacii dviženij, zadavaemyx glagolami dviženija [On the bases of classification of movements designated by the verbs of motion]." In *Semiotika i informatika.* Vol. 29, 177–200. Moscow: VINITI, 1989.

———. "Klassifikacija aspektual'nyx značenij processnyx glagolov po referentno značimym priznakam [Classification of aspectual meanings of process verbs according to the referentially significant features]." In *Tožd estvo i podobie.*

240 References

Sravnenie i identifikacija. Logičeskij analiz jazyka, 218–26. Moscow: Nauka, 1990.

— —. "Referencial'nyj podxod k analizu jazykovyx značenij [A referential approach to the analysis of linguistic meanings]." In *Moskovskij lingvističeskij al'manax*. Vol. 1, 82–194. Moscow: Škola "Jazyki russkoj kul'tury", 1996.

— —. "O sxeme leksičeskogo značenija predmetnogo suščestvitel'nogo i eë funk-cionirovanii v akte kommunikacii [On the lexical meaning schema of a con-crete noun and its functioning in the act of communication]." In *Verenica liter: Sb. st. k 60-letiju V. M. Živova*, 516–70. Moscow: Jazyki slavjanskix kul'tur, 2006. https://independent.academia.edu/AlexeyKoshelev

— —. "Ob osnovnyx paradigmax izučenija estestvennogo jazyka v svete sovremen-nyx dannyx kognitivnoj psixologii [On the main paradigms in explorations of language in the light of the contemporary cognitive psychology data]." In *Voprosy jazykoznanija* 4 (2008): 15–40. https://independent.academia.edu/AlexeyKoshelev

— —. "V poiskax universal'noj sxemy razvitija [In search of a universal develop-ment schema]." In *Integracionno-differencionnaja teorija razvitija*, compiled by N. I. Chuprikova and A. D. Koshelev, 217–34. Moscow: Jazyki slavjanskix kul'tur, 2011a. https://independent.academia.edu/AlexeyKoshelev

— —. "Počemu polisemija javljaetsja jazykovoj universaliej? (Kognitivnaja priroda i jazykovaja funkcija mnogoznačnyx slov) [Why is polysemy a language uni-versal?]." In *Slovo i jazyk: Sb. statej v čest' 80-letija Iu. D. Apresiana*, 695–735. Moscow: Jazyki slavjanskix kul'tur, 2011b. http://www.ruslang.ru/doc/apres-jan_festschrift2011/Koshelev.pdf

— —. "Značenie slova kak generativnyj kompleks: kognitivnoe značenie (svjazan-naja so slovom struktura konceptov) → jazykovoe značenie (nabor uzual'nyx smyslov) [Word meaning as a generative complex: Cognitive meaning → lin-guistic meaning]." In *Smysly, teksty i drugie zaxvatyvajuščie sjužety: Sb. statej v čest' 80-letija I. A. Mel'čuka*, 301–29. Moscow: Jazyki slavjanskoj kul'tury, 2012. http://www.ruslang.ru/doc/melchuk_festschrift2012/Koshelev.pdf

— —. "Sovremennaja teoretičeskaja lingvistika kak Vavilonskaja bašnja [Modern theoretical linguistics as the Tower of Babel]." *Izvestija RAN. Ser. jazyka i literatury* 72, no 6 (2013a): 3–22. https://independent.academia.edu/AlexeyKoshelev

— —. "Kognitivistika pered vyborom: dal'nejšee uglublenie protivorečij ili postroe-nie edinoj meždisciplinarnoj paradigmy [Cognitivism facing a choice: Further deepening of contradictions or construction of a single interdisciplinary para-digm]." In U. T. Fitch. *Èvoljucija jazyka*, 680–767. Moscow: Jazyki slavjan-skoj kul'tury, 2013b. https://independent.academia.edu/AlexeyKoshelev

— —. *Kognitivnyj analiz obščečelovečeskix konceptov* [Cognitive Analysis of Universal Concepts]. Moscow: Rukopisnye pamjatniki Drevnej Rusi, 2015a. https://independent.academia.edu/AlexeyKoshelev

— —. "O referencial'nom podxode k leksičeskoj polisemii [On the referential approach to lexical polysemy]." In *Jazyk i mysl': sovremennaja kognitivnaja lingvistika*, edited by A. A. Kibrik, A. D. Koshelev, A. V. Kravchenko, Iu. V. Mazurova, and O. V. Fedorova, 287–349. Moscow: Jazyki slavjanskoj kul'tury, 2015b. https://independent.academia.edu/AlexeyKoshelev

— —. "O strukturnom i genetičeskom sxodstve leksičeskix i grammatičeskix značenij (kognitivnyj analiz glagol'noj perexodnosti i zaloga) [On the structural and genetic similarity of lexical and grammatical meanings]." In *Izv. RAN. Serija literatury i jazyka* 75, no 3 (2016): 19–39. https://independent.academia.edu/AlexeyKoshelev

— —. *Očerki èvoljucionno-sintetičeskoj teorii jazyka* [Essays on the Evolutionary-Synthetic Theory of Language]. Moscow: Izdatel'skij Dom JaSK, 2017. https://independent.academia.edu/AlexeyKoshelev

Kourtzi, Z. and N. Kanwisher. "Activation in human MT/MST by static images with implied motion." *Journal of Cognitive Neuroscience* 12, no 1 (2000): 48–55.

Kravchenko, A. V. "O predmetnoj oblasti jazykoznanija [On the subject domain of linguistics]." In *Jazyk i mysl': sovremennaja kognitivnaja lingvistika*, edited by A. A. Kibrik, A. D. Koshelev, A. V. Kravchenko, Iu. V. Mazurova, and O. V. Fedorova, 574–94. Moscow: Jazyki slavjanskoj kul'tury, 2015.

Krongauz, M. A. *Semantika* [Semantics]. Moscow: RGGU, 2001.

Kubriakova, E. S. "Èvoljucija lingvističeskix idej vo vtoroj polovine XX veka (opyt paradigmal'nogo analiza) [Evolution of linguistic ideas in the second half of the 20th century]." In *Jazyk i nauka konca 20 veka*, edited by Iu. S. Stepanov, 144–238. Moscow: RGGU, 1995.

Kuhn, T. S. *The Structure of Scientific Revolutions*. Chicago, L.: University of Chicago Press, 1962.

Kulikov, L. "Voice typology." In *The Oxford Handbook of Linguistic Typology*, edited by J. J. Song, 368–98. Oxford: Oxford University Press, 2011.

Kuryłowicz, J. *Études indo-européennes*. I. Kraków: Gebethner & Wolff, 1935.

— — (Kurilovich, E.). "Zametki o značenii slova [Notes on word meaning]." *Voprosy jazykoznanija* 3 (1955): 73–81.

Kustova, G. I. *Tipy proizvodnyx značenij i mexanizmy jazykovogo rasshirenija* [Types of Derived Meanings and Language Expansion Mechanisms]. Moscow: Jazyki slavjanskoj kul'tury, 2004.

Lakoff, G. "Classifiers as a reflection of mind." In *Noun Classes and Categorization*, edited by C. Craig, 13–51. Amsterdam: John Benjamins, 1986.

———. *Women, Fire, and Dangerous Things: What Categories Reveal about the Mind.* Chicago: University of Chicago Press, 1987.

Landau, B., Smith, L. B., and S. S. Jones. "The importance of shape in early lexical learning." *Cognitive Development* 3, no 3 (1988): 299–321.

Lazard, G. "La linguistique est-elle une science?" *Bulletin de la Société de la Linguistique de Paris* XCIV, fasc. 1 (1999).

Leshchëva, L. M. *Leksičeskaja polisemija v kognitivnom aspekte* [Lexical Polysemy from a Cognitive Perspective]. Moscow: Jazyki slavjanskoj kul'tury, 2014.

Leslie, A. M. "The perception of causality in infants." *Perception* 11 (1982): 173–86.

———. "Spatiotemporal continuity and the perception of causality in infants." *Perception* 13 (1984): 287–305.

Letuchii, A. B. "Perexodnost' [Transitivity]." In *Materialy dlja proekta korpusnogo opisanija russkoj grammatiki. Na pravax rukopisi.* Moscow, 2014. http://rusgram.ru

Lewin, K. "Regression, retrogression and development." In *Field Theory in Social Science: Selected Theoretical Papers*, edited by D. Cartwright, 87–129. L.: Tavistock, 1952.

Liashevskaia, O. N. *Semantika russkogo čisla* [Semantics of the Russian Category of Number]. Moscow: Jazyki slavjanskoj kul'tury, 2004.

Longman Dictionary of Contemporary English. Italy, 2009.

Lyons, J. *Introduction to Theoretical Linguistics.* L.: Cambridge University Press, 1968.

Manoonpong, P. and F. Woergoetter. "Efference copies in neural control of dynamic biped walking. Robotics and autonomous systems." *Elsevier Science* 57, no 11 (2009): 1140–53.

Markson, L., Diesendruck, G., and P. Bloom. "The shape of thought." *Developmental Science* 11, no 2 (2008): 204–8.

Maslov, Iu. S. *Vvedenie v jazykovedenie* [Introduction to Linguistics]. Moscow: Vysšaja škola, 1987.

Meillet, A. "Sur la terminologie de la morphologie générale." *Revue des études hongroises* 6 (1928).

Mel'čuk, I. A. *Opyt teorii lingvističeskix modelej "Smysl ↔ Tekst". Semantika, sintaksis* [An Outline of a Theory of Meaning-Text Linguistic Models. Semantics and Syntax]. Moscow: Nauka, 1974. Reprint, Moscow: Jazyki russkoj kul'tury, 1999.

———. "Zavisimosti-2011: Otnošenie zavisimosti v jazyke i v lingvistike [Dependency-2011: Dependency relationships in language and linguistics]." *Voprosy jazykoznanija* 1 (2012a): 3–26.

———. *Jazyk: ot smysla k tekstu* [Language: From Meaning to Text]. Moscow: Jazyki slavjanskoj kul'tury, 2012b.

Mervis, C. "Child-basic object categories and early lexical development." In *Concepts and Conceptual Development: Ecological and Intellectual Factors in Cate-*

gorization, edited by U. Neisser, 201–33. N. Y.: Cambridge University Press, 1987.

—— and E. Rosch. "Categorization of Natural Objects." *Annual Review of Psychology* 32 (1981): 89–115.

Michotte, A. *The Perception of Causality.* Andover, MA: Methuen, 1962.

Müller, F. M. *Lectures on the Science of Language.* Vol. 2. Longmans, Green, and Company, 1885.

Murphy, G. L. *The Big Book of Concepts.* Cambridge, MA: MIT Press, 2002.

——. "Review of *How words mean: Lexical concepts, cognitive models, and meaning construction*, by Vyvyan Evans. Oxford: Oxford University Press, 2009." *Language* 87, no. 2 (2011): 393–6.

Mustaioki, A. *Teorija funkcional'nogo sintaksisa. Ot semantičeskix struktur k jazykovym sredstvam* [Functional Syntax Theory]. Moscow: Jazyki slavjanskoj kul'tury, 2010.

Nelson, K. "Some evidence for the cognitive primacy of categorisation and its functional basis." *Merrill-Palmer Quarterly* 19 (1973): 21–39.

Newmeyer, F. J. *Language Form and Language Function.* Cambridge, MA: MIT Press, 1999.

Norvig, P. and G. Lakoff. "Taking: A study in lexical network theory." In *Proceedings of the 13th Berkeley Linguistics Society Annual Meeting*, 195–206. Berkeley: BLS, 1987.

Ozhegov, S. I. *Slovar' russkogo jazyka* [Dictionary of Russian]. Moscow: Sovetskaja Ènciklopedija, 1970

Palmer, D. and L. Palmer. *Èvoljucionnaja psixologija: Sekrety povedenija Homo sapiens* [Evolutionary Psychology: The Secret of Homo Sapiens Behavior]. Saint Petersburg: Prajm-EVROZNAK, 2003.

Panov, E. N. "Èmpiričeskij fakt i ego traktovki v ètologii [Empirical fact and its interpretation in ethology]." In E. N. Panov. *Izbrannye trudy po ètologii i èvoljucionnoj biologii*, 74–86. Moscow: Tovariščestvo naučnyx izdanij KMK, 2012.

——. "Posleslovie naučnogo redaktora [Editor's afterword]." In U. T. Fitch. *Èvoljucija jazyka*, 657–74. Moscow: Jazyki slavjanskoj kul'tury, 2013.

Pascal, B. *Thoughts, Letters, and Minor Works.* N. Y.: Cosimo, Inc., 2007.

Paul, H. *Prinzipien der Sprachgeschichte.* Studienausgabe der 8. Aufl. Tübingen: Max Niemeyer Verlag, 1970.

Pereira, A. F. and L. B. Smith. "Developmental changes in visual object recognition between 18 and 24 months of age." *Developmental Science.* 12 (2009): 67–80.

Pinker, S.. *The Language Instinct: The New Science of Language and Mind.* L.: The Penguin Press, 1994.

——. *How the Mind Works.* N. Y.: W. W. Norton & Company, 1997.

244 References

——. *The Stuff of Thought: Language as a Window Into Human Nature.* N. Y.: Viking, 2007.

—— and R. Jackendoff. "The faculty of language: What's special about it?" *Cognition* 97 (2005): 201–36.

Plungian, V. A. "Počemu sovremennaja lingvistika dolžna byt' lingvistikoj korpusov [Why modern linguistics should be the linguistics of corpora]." http://polit.ru/article/2009/10/23/corpus/

——. *Vvedenie v grammatičeskuju semantiku: grammatičeskie značenija i grammatičeskie sistemy mira* [Introduction to Grammatical Semantics: Grammatical Meanings and Grammatical Systems of the World]. Moscow: RGGU, 2011

Potebnia, A. A. *Èstetika i poètika* [Aesthetics and Poetics]. Moscow: Iskusstvo, 1976.

Pruden, S. M., Hirsh-Pasek, K., and R. M. Golinkoff. "Current events: How infants parse the world and events for language." In *Understanding Events: How Humans See, Represent, and Act on Events,* edited by T. F. Shipley and J. M. Zacks, 160–92. N. Y.: Oxford University Press, 2008.

Raibert, M. H. *Legged Robots that Balance.* Cambridge, MA: MIT Press, 1986.

Rakhilina, E. V. *Kognitivnyj analiz predmetnyx imen: semantika i sočetaemost'* [Cognitive Analysis of Concrete Names: Semantics and Combinability]. Moscow: Russkie slovari, 2000.

Rakison, D. H. "When a rose is just a rose: The illusion of taxonomies in infant categorization." *Infancy* 1, no 1 (2000): 77–90.

Reformatskii, A. A. *Vvedenie v jazykoznanie* [Introduction to Linguistics]. Moscow: Aspekt press, 1996.

Rizzolatti, G. and M. Fabbri-Destro. "The mirror system and its role in social cognition." *Current Opinions in Neurobiology* 18 (2008): 179–84.

Rizzolatti, G. and C. Sinigaglia. *Mirrors in the Brain: How Our Minds Share Actions, Emotions, and Experience.* N. Y.: Oxford University Press, 2008.

Rosch, E., Mervis, C. B., Gray, W. D., Johnson, D. M., and P. Boyes-Braem. "Basic objects in natural categories." *Cognitive Psychology* 8, no 3 (1976): 382–439.

Rozengart-Pupko, G. L. *Reč' i razvitie vosprijatija v rannem vozraste* [Speech and Development of Perception in Young Children]. Moscow: Učpedgiz, 1948.

——. *Formirovanie reči u detej rannego vozrasta* [Formation of speech in young children]. Moscow: Učpedgiz, 1963.

Rozina, R. I. "Dinamičeskaja model' semantiki glagola vzjat' [A dynamic model of the semantics of *take*]." In *Russkij jazyk segodnja.* Vol. 2, 227–46. Moscow: Institut russkogo jazyka im. V. V. Vinogradova RAN, 2003.

Runeson, S. "On the visual perception of dynamic events." In *Acta Universitatis Upsaliensis: Studia Psychologica Upsaliensia 9.* Stockholm: Almqvist & Wicksell, 1977.

—— and G. Frykholm. "Kinematic specification of dynamics as an informational basis for person-and-action perception: Expectation, gender recognition, and deceptive intention." *Journal of Experimental Psychology: General* 112 (1983): 585–615.

Sannikov, A. V. "Slovarnye stat'i polej 'pozor', 'mebel'" i 'pevčeskie golosa' [Dictionary entries for the fields 'shame', 'furniture', and 'singing voices']." In *Prospekt aktivnogo slovarja russkogo jazyka*, edited by Iu. D. Apresian, 661–76. Moscow: Jazyki slavjanskix kul'tur, 2010.

Saussure, F. de. *Course in General Linguistics*, edited by Ch. Bally and A. Sechehaye, in collaboration with A. Riedlinger. Translated, with an introd. and notes by W. Baskin. N. Y.: McGraw-Hill, 1966.

Schultz, D. P. and S. E. Schultz. *Modern Psychology: A History.* 10th edition. Wadsworth Cengage Learning, 2012.

Sechenov, I. M. *Izbrannye proizvedenija* [Selected Works]. Vol. 1, *Fiziologija i psixologija* [Physiology and Psychology], edited by and foreword by Kh. S. Koshtoiants. Moscow: Akad. nauk SSSR, 1952.

Seliverstova, O. N. "Glagol vzjat' (brat') [The verb to take-PF/IMP]." In O. N. Seliverstova. *Trudy po semantike*, 265–304. Moscow: Jazyki slavjanskoj kul'tury, 2004.

Sergienko, E. A. *Rannee kognitivnoe razvitie: Novyj vzgljad* [Early Cognitive Development: A New Perspective]. Moscow: Institut psixologii RAN, 2006.

Serio, P. "V poiskax četvĕrtoj paradigmy [In search of the fourth paradigm]." In *Filosofija jazyka: v granicax i vne granic.* Vol. 1, 37–52. Xar'kov: Oko, 1993.

Shaikevich, A. Ia. *Vvedenie v lingvistiku. Učebnoe posobie* [Introduction to Linguistics. A Tutorial]. Moscow: Akademija, 2005.

Shakhmatov, A. A. *Sintaksis russkogo jazyka* [Russian Syntax]. Moscow: Èditorial URSS, 2001.

——. *Učenie o častjax reči* [The Parts of Speech Teaching]. Moscow: Kom-Kniga, 2006.

Shapir, M. I. "'Tebe čisla i mery net': O vozmožnostjax i granicax 'točnyx metodov' v gumanitarnyx naukax ['You can't be counted, nor measured': On the potential and limits of exact methods in the humanities]." *Voprosy jazykoznanija* 1 (2005): 43–62.

Shipley, T. F. "The effect of object and event orientation on perception of biological motion." In *Psychological Science* 14 (2003): 377–80.

Shishkov, A. S. *Rassuždenie o starom i novom sloge rossijskogo jazyka* [A Discourse on the Old and New Style of the Russian Language]. Saint Petersburg, 1803. 2nd ed., Moscow: Librokom, 2010.

Shmelĕv, D. N. *Sovremennyj russkij jazyk: Leksika* [Modern Russian: The Lexicon]. Moscow: Prosveščenie, 1977.

Shor, P. O. "Krizis sovremennoj lingvistiki [The crisis in modern linguistics]." In *Jafetičeskij Sbornik*. Vol. 5, 32–71. Leningrad: Jafetičeskij institut RAN, 1926.

Skrebtsova, T. G. *Kognitivnaja lingvistika: klassičeskie teorii i novye podxody* [Cognitive Linguistics: Classical Theories and New Approaches]. Moscow: JaSK. 2018.

Slobin, D. I. "The origin of grammatical encoding of events." In *Studies in Transitivity*, edited by P. Hopper and S. Thompson, 409–22. N. Y.: Academic Press, 1982.

Slovar' Akademii Rossijskoj [The Russian Academy Dictionary]. 6 vols. Saint Peterburg: Imperatorskaja Akademija Nauk, 1789–94.

Slovar' russkogo jazyka v chetyrëx tomax (MAS) [The Russian Language Dictionary in Four Volumes], edited by A. P. Evgen'eva. 4 vols. Moscow: Russkij jazyk, 1985–88.

Spelke, E. S., Breinlinger, K., Macomber, J., and K. Jacobson. "Origins of knowledge." *Psychological Review* 99, no 4 (1992): 605–32.

— —, Philips, A., and A. L. Woodward. "Infants' knowledge of object motion and human action." In *Causal Cognition: A Multidisciplinary Debate*, edited by D. Sperber, D. Premack, and A. Premack, 44–78. Oxford: Clarendon Press, 1995.

Stachowiak, F.-J. "Metaphor production and comprehension." In *Aphasia In The Ubiquity of Metaphor: Metaphor in Language and Thought*, edited by W. Paprotte and R. Dirven, 559–99. Amsterdam: John Benjamins, 1985.

Subbotskii, E. V. *Strojaščeesja soznanie* [Consciousness Constructed]. Moscow: Smysl, 2007.

Talmy, L. "Semantics and syntax of motion." In *Syntax and Semantics 4*, edited by J. P. Kimball, 181–238. N. Y.: Academic Press, 1975.

— —. "Lexicalization patterns: Semantic structure in lexical forms." In *Language Typology and Syntactic Description*. Vol. III, *Grammatical Categories and the Lexicon*, edited by T. Shopen, 57–149. N. Y.: Cambridge University Press, 1985.

Testelets, Ia. G. *Vvedenie v obščij sintaksis* [Introduction to general syntax]. Moscow: RGGU, 2001.

Troje, N. F. "Decomposing biological motion: A framework for analysis and synthesis of human gait patterns." *Journal of Vision* 2, no 5 (2002): 371–87.

— —. "Biological motion perception." In *The Senses: A Comprehensive References*, edited by A. Basbaum et al., 231–38. Oxford: Elsevier, 2008.

Tseitlin, S. N. *Jazyk i rebënok: Lingvistika detskoj reči* [Language and Child: The Linguistics of Child Speech]. Moscow: Vlados, 2000.

— —. *Očerki po slovoobrazovaniju i formoobrazovaniju v detskoj reči* [Essays on Word Formation and Form Building in Child Speech]. Moscow: Znak, 2009.

Tsien, J. Z. "Neural coding of episodic memory." In *Handbook of Episodic Memory*, edited by E. Dere, A. Easton, L. Nadel, and J. P. Huston, 399–416. Amsterdam etc.: Elsevier, 2008.

— — et al. "On initial brain activity mapping of episodic and semantic memory code in the hippocampus." *Neurobiology of Learning and Memory* 105 (2013): 200–10.

Tsin', D. (J. Tsien). "Kod pamjati." In *V mire nauki* 11 (2007): 18–25.

Tversky, B., Zacks, J. M., and B. M. Hard. "The structure of experience." In *Understanding Events*, edited by Th. F. Shipley and J. M. Zacks, 436–64. Oxford: Oxford University Press, 2008.

Urgesi, C., Moro, V., Candidi, M., and S. Aglioti. "Mapping implied body actions in the human motor system." *The Journal of Neuroscience* 26, no 30 (2006): 7942–49.

Ushakov, D. N., ed. *Tolkovyj slovar' russkogo jazyka* [An Explanatory Dictionary of Russian]. 4 vols. Moscow: Gosudarstvennyj institut "Sovetskaja ènciklopedija", 1934–40.

Vinogradov, V. V. "Osnovnye tipy leksičeskix značenij slova [The main types of word's lexical meanings]." In V. V. Vinogradov. *Izbrannye trudy: Leksikologija i leksikografija*, 162–89. Moscow: Nauka, 1977.

Voeikova, M. D. *Rannie ètapy usvoenija det'mi imennoj morfologii russkogo jazyka* [Early Stages in Acquisition of Nominal Morphology of the Russian Language by Children]. Moscow: Znak, 2011.

— —, Kazakovskaia, V. V., and D. N. Satiukova. "Semantika prilagatel'nyx v reči vzroslyx i detej [Semantics of adjectives in adult and child speech]." In *Jazyk i mysl': sovremennaja kognitivnaja lingvistika*, edited by A. A. Kibrik, A. D. Koshelev, A. V. Kravchenko, Iu. V. Mazurova, and O. V. Fëdorova, 488–540. Moscow: Jazyki slavjanskoj kul'tury, 2015.

Vygotsky, L. S. *Thought and Language*, newly revised, translated, and edited by Alex Kozulin. Cambridge, MA: MIT Press, 1986.

— —. *The Collected Works*. Vol. 5, *Child Psychology*, edited by R. W. Rieber, translated by M. J. Hall. N. Y.: Plenum, 1998.

Waxman, S. R. "All in good time: How do infants discover distinct types of words and map them to distinct kinds of meaning?" In *Infant Pathways to Language: Methods, Models, and Research Directions*, edited by J. Colombo, P. McCardle and L. Freund, 99–118. Mahwah, NJ: Lawrence Erlbaum Associates, 2008.

Werner, H. *Comparative Psychology of Mental Development* (with a new prologue by Margery B. Franklin). Clinton Corners, NY: Percheron Press, 2004.

Whorf, B. L. "Science and linguistics." *Technol. Rev.* 42, no 6 (1940): 229–31, 247–48. http://web.mit.edu/allanmc/OldFiles/www/whorf.scienceandlinguistics.pdf

Wierzbicka, A. 1990. "Prototypes save: On the uses and abuses of the notion of 'prototype' in linguistics and related fields [Semantic universals and description of languages]." In *Meaning and Prototypes: Studies in Linguistic Categorization*, edited by S. L. Tsohatsidis, 347–367. L., N. Y.: Routledge, 1990.

— —. *Semantics: Primes and Universals.* Oxford: Oxford University Press, 1996.

— — (Vezhbitskaia, A.). *Semantičeskie universalii i opisanie jazykov* [Semantic Universals and Description of Languages]. Moscow: Jazyki russkoj kul'tury, 1999.

Wittgenstein, L. *Philosophical Investigations*, trans. by G. E. M. Anscombe. N. Y.: The Macmillan Company, 1953.

Xu, F. "Sortal concepts, object individuation, and language." *Trends in Cognitive Sciences* 11 (2007): 400–6.

— — and S. Carey. "Infants' metaphysics: The case of numerical identity." *Cognitive Psychology* 30 (1996): 111–53.

Zubkova, L. G. *Èvoljucija predstavlenij o jazyke* [Evolution of Ideas about Language]. Moscow: Jazyki slavjanskoj kul'tury, 2015.

— —. *Teorija jazyka v eë razvitii: ot naturocentrizma k logocentrizmu čerez sintez k lingvocentrizmu i k novomu sintezu* [Linguistic Theory and its Development]. Moscow: Izdatel'skij dom JaSK, 2017.

Index

Lightning Source UK Ltd.
Milton Keynes UK
UKHW011451010219
336593UK00003B/56/P